Mastering Angular Components
Second Edition

Build component-based user interfaces using Angular

Gion Kunz

BIRMINGHAM - MUMBAI

Mastering Angular Components
Second Edition

Acquisition Editor: Reshma Raman
Content Development Editor: Flavian Vaz
Technical Editor: Akhil Nair
Copy Editor: Safis Editing
Project Coordinator: Devanshi Doshi
Proofreader: Safis Editing
Indexer: Tejal Daruwale Soni
Graphics: Jason Monteiro
Production Coordinator: Nilesh Mohite

First published: June 2016
Second edition: July 2018

Production reference: 1170718

Published by Packt Publishing Ltd.
Livery Place
35 Livery Street
Birmingham
B3 2PB, UK.

ISBN 978-1-78829-353-2

www.packtpub.com

To our baby daughter, Zoé. The day of your birth in March 2018 was the most exciting day of my life. Looking into your eyes and seeing you smile makes my heart jump. I love you.

– Gion Kunz

`mapt.io`

Mapt is an online digital library that gives you full access to over 5,000 books and videos, as well as industry leading tools to help you plan your personal development and advance your career. For more information, please visit our website.

Why subscribe?

- Spend less time learning and more time coding with practical eBooks and Videos from over 4,000 industry professionals

- Improve your learning with Skill Plans built especially for you

- Get a free eBook or video every month

- Mapt is fully searchable

- Copy and paste, print, and bookmark content

PacktPub.com

Did you know that Packt offers eBook versions of every book published, with PDF and ePub files available? You can upgrade to the eBook version at `www.PacktPub.com` and as a print book customer, you are entitled to a discount on the eBook copy. Get in touch with us at `service@packtpub.com` for more details.

At `www.PacktPub.com`, you can also read a collection of free technical articles, sign up for a range of free newsletters, and receive exclusive discounts and offers on Packt books and eBooks.

Contributors

About the author

Gion Kunz has over 12 years of experience in writing interactive user interfaces using JavaScript. He's worked with AngularJS since 2012, is an early adopter of Angular 2 and loves to speak about Angular at conferences.

In 2018 he founded his own company Syncrea, where he helps customers create websites and applications using frontend web technologies. Besides working for his clients, Gion is a tutor at the SAE Institute in Zurich and loves to get his students enthusiastic about the web.

I'd like to thank my family, friends and everyone who supports me in my life. Especially, I'd like to thank you, my love, for all the support, patience and energy you've invested to help me complete this book.

About the reviewer

Phodal Huang is a developer, creator, and author. He works in ThoughtWorks as a Senior Consultant, and focuses on IoT and frontend. He is the author of Design IoT System and Growth: Thinking in Full Stack in Chinese.

He is an open source enthusiast, and has created a series of projects in GitHub. After daily work, he likes to reinvent some wheels for fun. He created the micro-frontend framework Mooa for Angular. You can find out more wheels on his GitHub page, @phodal.

He loves designing, writing, hacking, traveling, you can also find out more about him on his personal website at phodal(dot)com.

Packt is searching for authors like you

Table of Contents

Preface

Web components have long been touted as the next great leap forward in web development. With the new version of the Angular framework, we're closer than ever. Over the past couple of years, there's been a lot of buzz around web components in the web development community. New component-style directives in Angular will change developers' workflows and their thinking about shared and reusable blocks of custom HTML in the shadow DOM. By building a whole application from scratch, this book is a practical way to learn, giving readers the chance to build components of their own. With *Mastering Angular Components*, learners will get ahead of the curve in a new wave of web development by focusing on an area that's the key to unlocking the powers of Angular development.

Mastering Angular Components teaches readers to think in a component-based way when developing user interfaces. This rich guide to the new component-centric way of doing things in Angular teaches readers how to invent, build, and manage shared and reusable components for their web projects. This book will change how developers think about how to accomplish things in Angular, and the reader will work on useful and fun example components throughout.

Who this book is for

This book is for frontend and full-stack developers who already have a good understanding of basic frontend web technologies, such as JavaScript, HTML, and CSS. You will learn about the new component-based architecture in Angular and how to use it to build modern, clean user interfaces.

What this book covers

Chapter 1, *Component-Based User Interfaces*, looks at a bit of the history of UI development and provides a brief introduction to component-based user interfaces in general. We will see how Angular 2 handles this concept.

Chapter 2, *Ready, Set, Go!*, gets the reader started on their journey toward building an Angular 2 component-based application. It covers the basic elements of structuring an application with components.

Chapter 3, *Dealing with Data and State*, focuses on how to build a clean data and state architecture into our application. We'll learn about reactive programming using RxJS, the pure component, the container component, and many more concepts, and tools that can be used to combat application state mess.

Chapter 4, *Thinking in Projects*, focuses on the structure of the user interface and its basic components. Readers will compose an application by organizing an application layout into components, establishing the composition of components, and creating a reusable tab component to structure the application interface. Readers will also build a re-usable editor component and a commenting system.

Chapter 5, *Component-Based Routing*, explains how components react to routing and enables readers to add simple routing to existing components in the task management application. Readers will also work on the login process and gain an understanding of how to protect components using the router.

Chapter 6, *Keeping Up with Activities*, covers the creation of components that will visualize activity streams on both the project and task levels.

Chapter 7, *Components for User Experience*, guides readers on creating many small reusable components that will have a great effect on the overall user experience of the task management application. Benefits include the in-place editing of text fields, infinite scrolling, popup notifications, and drag-and-drop support.

Chapter 8, *Time Will Tell*, focuses on creating time-tracking components that help estimate time on a project and task level, but also for users to log the time they spend on tasks.

Chapter 9, *Spaceship Dashboard*, focuses on creating components to visualize data in the task management application using the third-party library Chartist.

Chapter 10, *Putting Things to the Test*, covers some basic approaches to testing Angular components. We will look at the options for mocking/overriding specific parts of a component for testing.

To get the most out of this book

This book will need a basic installation of Node.js on your Windows, Mac, or Linux machine. Since this book relies on Angular CLI 6.0.8, at least Node.js 8.9.0 is required.

Download the example code files

You can download the example code files for this book from your account at
www.packtpub.com. If you purchased this book elsewhere, you can visit
www.packtpub.com/support and register to have the files emailed directly to you.

You can download the code files by following these steps:

1. Log in or register at www.packtpub.com.
2. Select the **SUPPORT** tab.
3. Click on **Code Downloads & Errata**.
4. Enter the name of the book in the **Search** box and follow the onscreen instructions.

Once the file is downloaded, please make sure that you unzip or extract the folder using the latest version of:

- WinRAR/7-Zip for Windows
- Zipeg/iZip/UnRarX for Mac
- 7-Zip/PeaZip for Linux

The code bundle for the book is also hosted on GitHub at
https://github.com/PacktPublishing/Mastering-Angular-Components-Second-Edition. In case there's an update to the code, it will be updated on the existing GitHub repository.

We also have other code bundles from our rich catalog of books and videos available at https://github.com/PacktPublishing/. Check them out!

Conventions used

There are a number of text conventions used throughout this book.

CodeInText: Indicates code words in text, database table names, folder names, filenames, file extensions, pathnames, dummy URLs, user input, and Twitter handles. Here is an example: "Let's change the view encapsulation of our main component to use the ViewEncapsulation.None mode."

A block of code is set as follows:

```
import {Component, ViewEncapsulation} from '@angular/core';

@Component({
  selector: 'mac-root',
  templateUrl: './app.component.html',
  encapsulation: ViewEncapsulation.None
})
export class AppComponent {
  title = 'mac';
}
```

When we wish to draw your attention to a particular part of a code block, the relevant lines or items are set in bold:

```
...
import {TaskService} from './tasks/task.service';
...
@NgModule({
...
 providers: [TaskService],
  ...
})
export class AppModule {
}
```

Sometimes, on large code excerpts that require you to implement code changes in existing code files, we use the following format:

- New or replaced code parts are marked in bold
- Already existing and irrelevant code parts are hidden using an ellipsis character

Any command-line input or output is written as follows:

```
ng new mastering-angular-components --prefix=mac
```

Bold: Indicates a new term, an important word, or words that you see onscreen. For example, words in menus or dialog boxes appear in the text like this. Here is an example: "You should be able to see the generated application app with a welcome message saying **Welcome to mac!**"

 Warnings or important notes appear like this.

 Tips and tricks appear like this.

Get in touch

Feedback from our readers is always welcome.

General feedback: Email feedback@packtpub.com and mention the book title in the subject of your message. If you have questions about any aspect of this book, please email us at questions@packtpub.com.

Errata: Although we have taken every care to ensure the accuracy of our content, mistakes do happen. If you have found a mistake in this book, we would be grateful if you would report this to us. Please visit www.packtpub.com/submit-errata, selecting your book, clicking on the Errata Submission Form link, and entering the details.

Piracy: If you come across any illegal copies of our works in any form on the Internet, we would be grateful if you would provide us with the location address or website name. Please contact us at copyright@packtpub.com with a link to the material.

If you are interested in becoming an author: If there is a topic that you have expertise in and you are interested in either writing or contributing to a book, please visit authors.packtpub.com.

Reviews

Please leave a review. Once you have read and used this book, why not leave a review on the site that you purchased it from? Potential readers can then see and use your unbiased opinion to make purchase decisions, we at Packt can understand what you think about our products, and our authors can see your feedback on their book. Thank you!

For more information about Packt, please visit packtpub.com.

Component-Based User Interfaces

1

Although we'll cover a lot of Angular-related topics in this book, the focus will be mainly on creating component-based user interfaces. It's one thing to understand a framework like Angular, but it's a whole different thing to establish an effective workflow using a component-based architecture. In this book, I'll try to explain the core concepts behind Angular components and how we can leverage this architecture to create modern, efficient, and maintainable user interfaces.

Besides learning all the necessary concepts behind Angular, together, we will create a task-management application from scratch. This will allow us to explore different approaches to solve common UI problems using the component system that is provided by Angular.

In this chapter, we will take a look at how component-based user interfaces help us build greater applications. Over the course of this book, we will build an Angular application together, where we will use the component-based approach to its full potential. This chapter will also introduce you to the technologies that are used in this book.

The topics that we will cover in this chapter are as follows:

- An introduction to component-based user interfaces
- Encapsulation and composition using component-based user interfaces
- Evolution of UI frameworks
- The standard web components
- An introduction to the Angular component system
- Writing your first Angular component
- Basics of `NgModule`
- An overview and history of ECMAScript and TypeScript
- ECMAScript 7 decorators as meta annotations
- An introduction to Node.js-based tooling using Angular CLI

Thinking in components

Today's user interfaces do not consist of just a bunch of form elements that are cobbled together onto a screen. Modern users experience designing innovative visual presentations of interactive content challenges technology more than ever.

Sadly, we almost always tend to think in pages when we flesh out concepts for web applications, such as the pages within a printed book. Thinking about a book, this is probably the most efficient way to convey information for this kind of content and medium. You can skim through the pages one by one without any real physical effort, read paragraph by paragraph, and just scan through the chapters that you don't find interesting.

The problem with thinking in pages too much is that this concept, which is borrowed from books, does not really translate well to how things work in the real world. The world is created from components that form a system of components together.

Take our bodies as an example. We mostly consist of independent organs that interact with each other using electrical and chemical signals. Organs themselves consist of proteins that, on their own work, like machines to form a system. Down to the molecules, atoms, protons, and quarks, we can't really tell where one starts and where it ends. What we can tell for sure is that it's all about systems of components with inter-dependencies, and it is not about pages.

Modern user interfaces are very much like the real world consisting of systems of components. If, where, and how they are distributed to pages is subordinate while designing them. Also, they should work independently, and they should interact with each other on an interdependent level.

Components – the organs of user interfaces

"We're not designing pages, we're designing systems of components."
- Stephen Hay

This quote by Stephen Hay from BDConf in Orlando 2012 brings it to the point. Interface design is really not about pages. To create efficient user interfaces for not only the users but also the developers who maintain them, we need to think in systems of components. Components are independent, but they can interact with each other and create larger components when they are arranged together. We need to look at user interfaces holistically, and using components enables us to do this.

In the following topics, we're going to explore a few fundamental aspects of components. Some of these are already known from other concepts, such as **object-oriented programming** (**OOP**), but they appear in a slightly different light when thinking about components.

Encapsulation

Encapsulation is a very important factor when thinking about maintenance in a system. Having a classical OOP background, I've learned that encapsulation means bundling logic and data together into an isolated container. This way, we can operate on the container from the outside and treat it like a closed system.

There are many positive aspects of this approach when it comes to maintainability and accessibility. Dealing with closed systems is important for the organization of our code. However, this is even more important because we can organize ourselves while working with code:

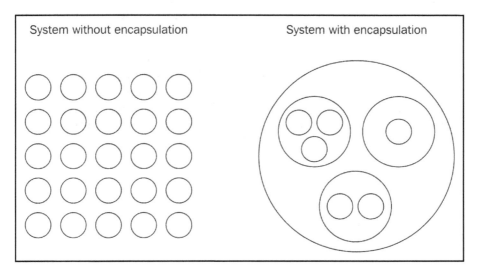

Organizing a system in encapsulated components allows us to reason about it much more easily

I have a pretty bad memory, and it's very important for me to find the right focus level when working on code. Immediate memory research has tells us that the human brain can remember about seven items at once on average. Therefore, it's crucial for us to write code in such a way that it allows us to focus on fewer and smaller pieces at once.

A clear encapsulation helps us in organizing our code. We can perhaps forget all the internals of the closed system and about the kind of logic and data that we've put into it. We should focus only on its surface, which allows us to work on a higher-abstraction level. Similar to the previous diagram, without using a hierarchy of encapsulated components, we'd have all our code cobbled together on the same level.

Encapsulation encourages us to isolate small and concise components and build a system of components. During development, we can focus on the internals of one component and only deal with the interface of other components.

Sometimes, we forget that all the organization of the coding we actually perform is for ourselves and not for the computer that runs this code. If this was for the computer, then we would probably all start writing in machine language again. A strong encapsulation helps us access specific code easily, focus on one layer of the code, and trust the underlying implementations within capsules.

The following TypeScript example shows you how to use encapsulation to write maintainable applications. Let's assume that we are in a T-shirt factory, and we need some code to produce T-shirts with a background and foreground color. This example uses some language features of TypeScript. If you're not familiar with the language features of TypeScript, don't worry too much at this point. We will learn about these later in this chapter:

```typescript
// This class implements data and logic to represent a color
// which establishes clean encapsulation.
class Color {
  constructor(private red: number, private green: number, private blue:
number) {}
  // Using this function we can convert the internal color values
  // to a hex color string like #ff0000 (red).
  getHex(): string {
    return '#' + Color.getHexValue(this.red) +
Color.getHexValue(this.green) +
      Color.getHexValue(this.blue);
  }
  // Static function on Color class to convert a number from
  // 0 to 255 to a hexadecimal representation 00 to ff
  static getHexValue(number): string {
    const hex = number.toString(16);
    return hex.length === 2 ? hex : '0' + hex;
```

```
    }
  }

  // Our TShirt class expects two colors to be passed during
  // construction that will be used to render some HTML
  class TShirt {
    constructor(private backgroundColor: Color, private foregroundColor:
  Color) {}
    // Function that returns some markup which represents our T-Shirts
    getHtml(): string {
      return `
        <t-shirt style="background-color: ${this.backgroundColor.getHex()}">
          <t-shirt-text style="color: ${this.foregroundColor.getHex()}">
            Awesome Shirt!
          </t-shirt-text>
        </t-shirt>
      `;
    }
  }

  // Instantiate a blue colour
  const blue: Color = new Color(0, 0, 255);
  // Instantiate a red color
  const red: Color = new Color(255, 0, 0);
  // Create a new shirt using the above colours
  const awesomeShirt: TShirt = new TShirt(blue, red);
  // Adding the generated markup of our shirt to our document
  document.body.innerHTML = awesomeShirt.getHtml();
```

Using a clean encapsulation, we can now work with the abstraction of color in our T-shirt. We don't need to worry about how to calculate the hexadecimal representation of colors at the T-shirt level because this is already done by the `Color` class. This makes your application maintainable and keeps it very open for change.

I strongly recommend that you read about the SOLID principles if you haven't done so already. As the name already suggests, this assembly of principles is a solid power tool that can change the way you organize code tremendously. You can learn more about the SOLID principles in the book *Agile Principles, Patterns, and Practices,* by Robert C. Martin.

Composability

Composition is a special kind of reusability. You don't extend an existing component, but you create a new, larger component by composing many smaller components together into a system of components.

In OOP languages, composition is often used to get around the multiple inheritance issues that most OOP languages have. Subclass polymorphism is always great until you reach the point where your design does not match the latest requirements in your project. Let's look at a simple example that illustrates this problem.

You have a `Fisher` class and a `Developer` class, both of which hold specific behaviors. Now, you'd want to create a `FishingDeveloper` class that inherits from both `Fisher` and `Developer`. Unless you're using a language that supports multiple inheritance (such as C++, which does this to a certain extent), you will not be able to reuse this functionality using inheritance. There is no way to tell the language that your new class should inherit from both superclasses. Using composition, you can easily solve this problem. Instead of using inheritance, you're composing a new `FishingDeveloper` class that delegates all behavior to an internal `Developer` and `Fisher` instance:

```
interface IDeveloper {
  code(): void;
}

interface IFisher {
  fish(): void;
}

class Developer implements IDeveloper {
 constructor(private name: string) {}

 code(): void {
   console.log(`${this.name} writes some code!`);
 }
}

class Fisher implements IFisher {
 constructor(private name: string) {}

 fish(): void {
   console.log(`${this.name} catches a big fish!`);
 }
}

class FishingDeveloper implements IFisher, IDeveloper {
```

```
constructor(private name: string) {
  this.name = name;
  this.developerStuff = new Developer(name);
  this.fisherStuff = new Fisher(name);
}

code(): void {
  this.developerStuff.code();
}

fish(): void {
  this.fisherStuff.fish();
 }
}

var bob: FishingDeveloper = new FishingDeveloper('Bob');
bob.code();
bob.fish();
```

Experience has taught us that composition is probably the most efficient way to reuse code. In contrast to inheritance, decoration, and other approaches to gain reusability, composition is probably the least intrusive and the most flexible.

Recent versions of some languages also support a pattern called traits, that is, `mixins`. Traits allow you to reuse certain functionality and attributes from other classes in a way that is similar to multiple inheritance.

If we think about the concept of composition, it's nothing more than designing organisms. We have the two `Developer` and `Fisher` organisms, and we unify their behaviors into a single `FishingDeveloper` organism.

Components, invented by nature

Components, embracing encapsulation, and composition are an effective way to build maintainable applications. Composed from components, applications are very resistant to the negative implications of change, and change is a necessary thing that will happen to every application. It's only a matter of time until your design will be challenged by the effects of change; therefore, it's very important to write code that can handle change as smoothly as possible.

Nature is the best teacher. Almost all the achievements in technological developments have their origin in observations of how nature solves problems. If we look at evolution, it's an ongoing redesign of matter by adapting to outer forces and constraints. Nature solves this by constant change using mutation and natural selection.

If we project the concept of evolution onto developing an application, we can say that nature does actually refactor its code in every single moment. This is actually the dream of every product manager—an application that can undergo constant change but does not lose any of its efficiency.

I believe that there are two key concepts that play a major role in nature that allows it to apply constant change in its design without losing much efficiency. This uses encapsulation and composition. Coming back to the example of our bodies, we can actually tell that our organs use a very clear encapsulation. They use membranes to create isolation, veins to transport nutrition, and synapses to send messages. Also, they have interdependencies, and they communicate using electrical and chemical messages. Most obviously, they form larger systems, which is the core concept of composition.

Of course, there are many other factors, and I'm not a professor in biology. However, I think it's a fascinating thing to see that we have learned to organize our code very similarly to how nature organizes matter.

The idea of creating reusable UI components is quite old, and it was implemented in various languages and frameworks. One of the earliest systems that used UI components was probably the Xerox Alto system back in the 1970s. It used reusable UI components that allowed developers to create an application by composing them on a screen where users could interact with them:

```
┌─────────────────────────────────────────────────────────────────────────┐
│ ┌───────────┐  Ready:                                      ┌───────────┐ │
│ ▓         ▓   Select file names with the mouse             │   Quit    │ │
│ ▓  Start  ▓   Red-Copy, Yel-Copy/Rename, Blue-Delete       ├───────────┤ │
│ ▓         ▓   Click 'Start' to execute file name commands  │   Clear   │ │
│ └───────────┘                                              ├───────────┤ │
│                                                            │   Type    │ │
│                  --                                        └───────────┘ │
└─────────────────────────────────────────────────────────────────────────┘
```

Pages: 832 ┌─────┐	Pages: 0 ┌─────┐
Files listed: 60 │ Log │	Files listed: 0 │ Log │
Files selected: 0 Delete: 0	Files selected: 0 Delete: 0
Copy/Rename: 0 Copy: 0	Copy/Rename: 0 Copy: 0

DP0: ⟨SysDir.⟩ *.*   No Disk: ⟨SysDir.⟩ *.*

```
~~ BEGINNING ~~
1012-AstroRoids.Boot.
Anonymous.1.
BattleShip.er.
BattleShip.RUN.
BlackJack.RUN.
BuildKal.cm.
CalcSources.dm.
Calculator.RUN.
Chess.log.
Chess.run.
Com.Cm.
CompileKal.cm.
CRTTEST.RUN.
DMT.boot.
EdsBuild.run.
empress.run.
Executive.Run.
Fly.run.
galaxian.boot.
Garbage.$.
Go9.run.
GoFont.AL.
Invaders.Run.
junk.
junk.press.
Kal.bcpl.
Kal.cm.
KalA.asm.
KalMc.mu.
Kinetic4.RUN.
LoadKal.cm.
MasterMind.RUN.
maze.run.
Mesa.Typescript.
Missile.run.
NEPTUNE.RUN.
othello.run.
Pinball-easy.run.
POLYGONS.RUN.
```

The user interface of file manager on the Xerox Alto system from the 1970s

Early frontend UI frameworks, such as DHTMLX, Ext JS, or jQuery UI implemented components in a more limited fashion that didn't provide great flexibility or extensibility. Most of these frameworks just provided widget libraries. The problem with UI widgets is that they mostly don't embrace the pattern of composition enough. You can arrange widgets on a page and they provide encapsulation, but with most toolkits, you can't create larger components by nesting them inside each other. Some toolkits solve this by providing a special kind of widget which was mostly called a container. However, this is not the same as a full-fledged component tree that allows you to create systems within systems. Containers were actually meant to provide a visual layout container rather than a composite container to form a larger system.

Usually, when working with widgets on a page of our application, we'd have a large controller that controls all these widgets, user input, and states. However, we are left with two levels of composition, and there's no way that we can structure our code more granularly. There is the page and there are the widgets. Having a bunch of UI widgets is simply not enough, and we are almost back to the state where we create pages plastered with form elements.

I've been a user of JavaServer Faces for years, and besides all its problems, the concept of having reusable custom elements was groundbreaking. Using XHTML, one could write so-called composite components that consisted of other composite components or native HTML elements. A developer could gain a fantastic level of reusability using composition. In my view, the big issue with this technology was that it did not address the concerns in the frontend enough to become really usable for complex user interactions. In fact, a framework like this should live completely within the frontend.

My UI framework wishlist

Usually, when UI frameworks get compared, they get measured against each other based on metrics, such as widget count, theming capabilities, and asynchronous data retrieval features. Each framework has its strengths and weaknesses, but leaving all the extra features aside and reducing it to the core concerns of a UI framework, I only have a few metrics left that I'd like to be assessed. These metrics are, of course, not the only ones that are important in today's UI development, but they also are the main factors toward building a clean architecture that supports the principle of change:

- I can create encapsulated components with clear interfaces
- I can create larger components by using composition
- I can make components interact with each other within their hierarchy

If you're looking for a framework which enables you to take full advantage of component-based UI development, you should look for these three key measures.

First of all, I think it's very important to understand the main purpose of the web and how it evolved. If we think of the web in its early days in the 1990s, it was probably only about hypertext. There were very basic semantics that could be used to structure information and display them to a user. HTML was created to hold structure and information. The need for custom visual presentation of information led to the development of CSS right after HTML started being widely used.

It was in the mid 1990s when Brendan Eich invented JavaScript, and it was first implemented in Netscape Navigator. By providing a way to implement behavior and state, JavaScript was the last missing piece for a full web customization:

Technology	Concern
HTML	Structure and information
CSS	Presentation
JavaScript	Behavior and state

We have learned to keep these concerns as separate as possible in order to maintain a clean architecture. Although there are different opinions on this and some recent technologies also move away from this principle, I believe that a clean separation of these concerns is very important to create a maintainable application.

Leaving this view aside, the standard definition of encapsulation from OOP is just concerned about coupling and isolation of logic and data. This probably applies well to classic software components. However, as soon as we consider a user interface as part of an architecture, there is a new dimension that is added.

Classical MVC frameworks are view centric, and developers organize their code based on pages. You'll probably go ahead and create a new view that represents a page. Of course, your view needs a controller and model, so you'll also create them. The problem with organization by pages is that there's little to no gain of reusability. Once you've created a page and you'd like to reuse only some parts of the page, you will need a way to encapsulate only a specific part of this model—the view and the controller.

UI components solve this problem nicely. I like to see them as a modular approach to MVC. Although they still embrace the MVC pattern, they also establish encapsulation and composability. This way, a view is a component itself, but it also consists of components. By composing views of components, one can gain a maximum amount of reusability:

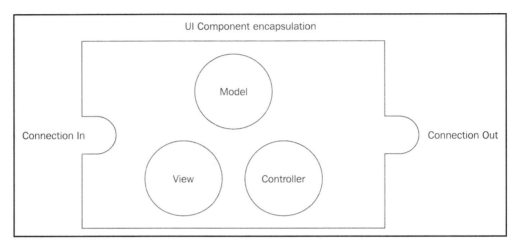

UI components embrace MVC, but they also support encapsulation and composition on a much lower level

Technically, there are some challenges when implementing components with web technologies. JavaScript was always flexible enough to implement different patterns and paradigms. Working with encapsulation and composition isn't an issue at all, and the controlling part and the model of components can easily be implemented. Approaches, such as the revealing module pattern, namespaces, prototypes, or the recent ECMAScript 6 modules, provide all the tools that are needed from the JavaScript side.

However, for the view part of our components, we face some limitations. Although HTML supports great flexibility in terms of composability because the DOM tree is nothing else than a big composition, we have no way to reuse these compositions. We can only create one large composition, which is the page itself. HTML being only the final view that was delivered from the server, this was never really a real concern. Today's applications are much more demanding, and we need to have a fully-encapsulated component running in the browser, which also consists of a partial view.

We face the same problem with CSS. There is no real modularization and encapsulation while writing CSS, and we need to use namespaces and prefixes in order to segregate our CSS styles. Still, the whole cascading nature of CSS can easily destroy all encapsulation that we try to bring in place using CSS structuring patterns.

Time for new standards

Web standards have been evolving immensely in the last couple of years. There are so many new standards, and the browser became such a big multimedia framework, that it's hard for other platforms to compete with this.

I'd even go as far as to say that web technology will actually replace other frameworks in the future, and it probably will be renamed to multimedia technology or something similar. There's no reason why we need to use different native frameworks to create user interfaces and presentations. Web technologies embed so many features that it's hard to find a reason not to use them for any kind of application. Just look at the Firefox OS or the Chrome OS, which are designed to run with web technologies. I think it's only a matter of time until more operating systems and embedded devices make use of web technologies to implement their software. This is why I believe that at some point it will be questionable whether the term *web technologies* is still appropriate or whether we should replace it with a more general term.

Although we usually just see new features appear in browsers, there is a very open and long-winded standardization process behind them. It's very important to standardize features, but this takes a lot of time, especially when people disagree about different approaches to solving problems.

Coming back to the concept of components, this is something where we really need support from web standards to break the current limitations. Fortunately, the W3C (World Wide Web Consortium) thought the same, and a group of developers started to work on specifications under the hood of an umbrella specification called *web components*.

The following topics will give you a brief overview over two specifications that also play a role in Angular components. One of Angular's core strengths is that it acts more like a superset of web standards rather than being a complete isolated framework.

Template elements

Template elements allow you to define regions within your HTML, which will not be rendered by the browser. You can then instantiate these document fragments with JavaScript and then place the resulting DOM within your document.

While the browser is actually parsing the template content, it only does so in order to validate the HTML. Any immediate actions that the parser would usually execute will not be taken. Within the content of template elements, images will not be loaded and scripts won't be executed. Only after a template is instantiated will the parser take the necessary actions, as follows:

```
<body>
<template id="template">
  <h1>This is a template!</h1>
</template>
</body>
```

This simple HTML example of a template element won't display the heading on your page. As the heading is inside a template element, we first need to instantiate the template and add the resulting DOM into our document:

```
var template = document.querySelector('#template');
var instance = document.importNode(template.content, true);
document.body.appendChild(instance);
```

Using these three lines of JavaScript, we can instantiate the template and append it into our document.

 Template elements are used by Angular in order to instantiate dynamic parts of your user interface. This will be the case while conditionally rendering parts of your template using the `ngIf` directive, or by repeating a template using the `ngFor` directive.

Shadow DOM

This part of the web components specification was the missing piece to create proper DOM encapsulation and composition. With shadow DOM, we can create isolated parts of the DOM that are protected against regular DOM operations from the outside. Also, CSS will not reach into shadow DOM automatically, and we can create local CSS within our component.

 If you add a `style` tag inside shadow DOM, the styles are scoped to the root within the shadow DOM, and they will not leak outside. This enables a very strong encapsulation for CSS.

Content insertion points make it easy to control content from the outside of a shadow DOM component, and they provide some kind of an interface to pass in content.

At the time of writing this book, shadow DOM is supported by most browsers, although it still needs to be enabled in Firefox.

Angular's component architecture

For me, the concept of directives from the first version of Angular changed the game in frontend UI frameworks. This was the first time that I felt that there was a simple yet powerful concept that allowed the creation of reusable UI components. Directives could communicate with DOM events or messaging services. They allowed you to follow the principle of composition, and you could nest directives and create larger directives that solely consisted of smaller directives arranged together. Actually, directives were a very nice implementation of components for the browser.

In this section, we'll look into the component-based architecture of Angular and how the things we've learned about components will fit into Angular.

Everything is a component

As an early adopter of Angular and while talking to other people about it, I got frequently asked what the biggest difference is to the first version. My answer to this question was always the same. Everything is a component:

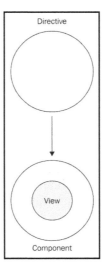

Within the Angular architecture, a component is a directive with an additional view

For me, this paradigm shift was the most relevant change that both simplified and enriched the framework. Of course, there are a lot of other changes with Angular. However, as an advocate of component-based user interfaces, I've found that this change is the most interesting one. Of course, this change also came with a lot of architectural changes.

Angular supports the idea of looking at the user interface holistically and fosters composition with components. However, the biggest difference to its first version is that now, your pages are no longer global views; they are simply components that are assembled from other components. If you've been following this chapter, you'll notice that this is exactly what a holistic approach to user interfaces demands. No more pages, but systems of components.

 Angular still uses the concept of directives, although directives are now really what the name suggests. They are orders for the browser to attach a given behavior to an element. Components are a special kind of directive that come with a view.

Your first component

Keeping up the tradition, before we start building a real application together, we should write our first `hello world` component with Angular:

```
import {Component} from '@angular/core';

@Component({
  selector: 'hello-world',
  template: '<div>Hello {{name}}</div>'
})
class HelloWorldComponent {
  name: string = 'World';
}
```

This is already a fully-working Angular component. We used ECMAScript 6 classes to create the necessary encapsulation required for a component. You can also see a meta-annotation that is used to declaratively configure our component. This statement, which looks like a function call that is prefixed with an *at* symbol, actually comes from the ECMAScript 7 decorator proposal. For the moment, you can think of decorators as a way to attach metadata to our component class.

ECMAScript 7 decorators are still very experimental at the time of writing this book. We're using TypeScript in the examples of this book, which is already implementing the decorator proposal with a slight twist. The Angular core team has decided to go with this experimental technology, since it reduces the overall amount of code and introduces an aspect oriented flavor to the Angular API.

It's important to understand that an element can only be bound to one single component. As a component always comes with a view, there is no way that we can bind more than one component to an element. On the other hand, an element can be bound to many directives, as directives don't come with a view—they only attach behavior.

In the Component decorator, we need to configure everything that is relevant to describe our component for Angular. This, of course, also includes our template for the view. In the preceding example, we are specifying our template directly within JavaScript as a string. We can also use the templateUrl property to specify a URL where the template should be loaded from.

The second configuration, applied using the selector property, allows us to specify a CSS selector, which is used by Angular to attach the component to certain elements within our view. Every time Angular encounters an element which matches the component's selector, it will render the given component into that element.

Now, let's enhance our example a little bit so that we can see how we can compose our application from smaller components:

```
import {Component} from '@angular/core';

@Component({
  selector: 'shout-out',
  template: '<strong>{{words}}</strong>'
})
class ShoutOutComponent {
  @Input() words: string;
}

@Component({
  selector: 'hello-world'
  template: '<shout-out words="Hello, {{name}}!"></shout-out>'
})
class HelloWorldComponent {
  name: string = 'World';
}
```

You can see that we have now created a small component that allows us to shout out words as we like. In our *Hello World* application, we make use of this component to shout out **Hello, World!**

Within the template of our hello world component, we are including the shouting component by placing an HTML element which matches the CSS element selector of the shouting component.

Over the course of this book and while writing our task management application, we will learn a lot more about the configuration and implementation of components. However, before we start with this in the Chapter 2, *Ready, Set, Go!*, we should take a look at some tools and language features that we'll use during this book.

Angular NgModule

Organizing an application solely by composing components comes with some challenges. Angular supports the concept of application modules, which essentially are just containers around components that help structure your application.

The concept of NgModule was introduced to mainly solve the following issues:

- **Explicit template parsing**:
  With the use of modules and by declaring all components, directives, pipes, and providers which are used inside of your application module, Angular is able to parse HTML templates very explicitly. This is really helpful when it comes to debugging. Let's say you're including an element within one of your component templates which does not match any of the selectors specified by the components within your module. Angular can now assert an error because you explicitly told it what components are available within your module. Without telling Angular which components belong to your application module, it would not be able to know if you're including a non-existing component within your template.

- **Simpler dependency resolution**:
  Since Angular can now simply resolve your main application module to find out what components are present within your application, things get simplified a lot. Imagine you have a very complex application existing of hundreds of components. Without modules, Angular would need to follow each individual component to find out how they are dependent on each other. With modules, Angular can simply check what components are declared inside of the module to find all components.

- **Lazy loading with the Angular router**:
  The router of Angular is able to load parts of your application lazily when required. This is a very powerful feature, but it requires that you declare a bundle of application artefacts like components or directives, to be loaded asynchronously after your main application has started. NgModule comes in very handy at this point. By creating a separate module using NgModule, you can now define a part of your application consisting of new components and other artefacts. Within the build of your application, this module is then built separately into its own JavaScript resource, which can be loaded asynchronously at runtime by the router.

Your application requires at least one main module, which is declaring all your application components. Let's look at a very simple example and build the main module for our HelloWorld component:

```
import {BrowserModule} from '@angular/platform-browser';
import {NgModule} from '@angular/core';
import {HelloWorldComponent} from './hello-world.component';
import {ShoutOutComponent} from './shout-out.component';

@NgModule({
  declarations: [HelloWorldComponent, ShoutOutComponent],
  imports: [BrowserModule],
  bootstrap: [HelloWorldComponent]
})
export class HelloWorldAppModule { }
```

Similar to a component definition, we're using an ES6 class and a decorator to define an Angular module. The NgModule decorator of our main application module has three configuration properties:

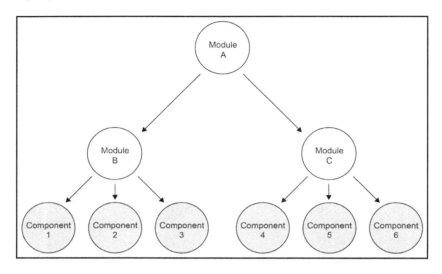

A module dependency tree: Module A importing module B and C so that all components are available to module A

The declarations property is used to tell Angular what components, directives, and pipes are present within this module. If our application consists of 30 components, we need to add them all to the declarations of the NgModule. Every time you create a new component, you will also need to add it to the declarations array within your application module.

Within the array of the imports property, we can tell Angular to import other NgModule. This way, you can compose your application modules from many smaller modules if you like. However, there's no real benefit of structuring your application into submodules, unless you're exporting a submodule as a library, or if you're using the lazy loading feature of the router, as discussed earlier. It's crucial that you always import the Angular BrowserModule within your main application module. The BrowserModule contains all the Angular core components, directives, and other dependencies which are required in order to run your application within a browser environment.

Finally, the bootstrap property is telling Angular which of your components should be rendered first. You should specify your main application component here, which is representing the root component of your application. In the second chapter of this book, we'll take a closer look at the bootstrapping mechanism of Angular.

JavaScript of the future

It was not so long ago that somebody asked me whether we should really use the bind function of ECMAScript 5.1, as then we'd probably run into browser compatibility issues. The web moves very fast, and we need to keep up the pace. We can't write code that does not use the latest features, even if this would cause issues in old browsers.

The fantastic people from TC39, the technical committee that is responsible for writing the ECMAScript specification, have done a great job progressively enhancing the JavaScript language. This, and the fact that JavaScript is so flexible, allows us to use so-called polyfills and shims to make our code run in older browsers.

ECMAScript 6 (also referred to as ECMAScript 2015) was published in June 2015, exactly four years after its predecessor. There is a massive amount of new API additions as well as a whole bunch of new language features. The language features are syntactic sugar, and ECMAScript 6 can be transpiled to its previous version where it runs perfectly in older browsers. At the time of writing this book, none of the current browser versions have fully implemented ECMAScript 6, but there's absolutely no reason not to use it for production applications.

 Syntactic sugar is a design approach where we evolve a programming language without breaking backwards compatibility. This allows language designers to come up with new syntax, which enriches developer experience but does not break the web. Every new feature needs to be translatable to the old syntax. This way, so-called transpilers can be used to convert code to older versions.

I speak JavaScript, translate, please!

While compilers compile from a higher-level language to a lower-level language, a transpiler or transcompiler acts more like a converter. It is a source-to-source compiler that translates code to run in a different interpreter.

Recently, there's been a real battle among new languages that are transpiled to JavaScript and can run in the browser. I used Google Dart for quite some time, and I must admit, I really loved the language features. The problem with nonstandardized languages is that they depend heavily on community adoption and the hype. Also, it's almost certain that they will never run natively within the browser. This is also the reason why I prefer standard JavaScript, and the JavaScript of the future using transpilers and polyfills.

Some people argue that transpilers introduce code that isn't very performant and, therefore, recommend that you do not use ECMAScript 6 and transpilers at all. I don't agree with this for many reasons. Usually, this is about performance in micro or even nanosecond areas where this often really does not matter for most applications.

I don't mean that performance doesn't matter, but performance always needs to be discussed within a context. If you're trying to optimize a loop within your application by reducing processing time from 10 microseconds to five microseconds where you'd never iterate over more than 100 items, then you're probably spending your time on the wrong things.

Also, a very important fact is that transpiled code is designed by people who understand micro performance optimization much better than I do, and I'm sure their code runs faster than mine. On top of this, a transpiler is probably also the right place where you'd want to do performance optimization because this code is automatically generated and you don't lose maintainability of your code through performance quirks.

I'd like to quote Donald Knuth here and say that premature optimization is the root of all evil. I really recommend that you read his paper on this topic (Donald Knuth, December 1974, *Structured Programming with go to Statements*). Just because the `goto` statements got banished from all modern programming languages, it doesn't mean this is less of a good read.

Later on in this chapter, you'll learn about tools that help you use transpilers easily within your project, and we'll take a look at the decisions and directions Angular went with regarding their source code.

Let's look at a few language features that come with ECMAScript 6 and make our life much easier.

Classes

Classes were among one the most requested features in JavaScript, and I was one of the people voting for it. Well, coming from an OOP background and being used to organizing everything within classes, it was hard for me to let go. Although, after working with modern JavaScript for some time, you'll reduce their use to the bare minimum and to exactly what they are made for—inheritance.

Classes in ECMAScript 6 provide you with syntactic sugar to deal with prototypes, constructor functions, super calls, and object property definitions in a way that you have the illusion that JavaScript could be a class-based OOP language:

```
class Fruit {
  constructor(name) { this.name = name; }
}
const apple = new Fruit('Apple');
```

As we learned in the previous topic about transpilers, ECMAScript 6 can be de-sugared to ECMAScript 5. Let's take a look at what a transpiler will produce from this simple example:

```
function Fruit(name) { this.name = name; }
var apple = new Fruit('Apple');
```

This simple example can easily be built using ECMAScript 5. However, once we use the more complex features of class-based object-oriented languages, the de-sugaring gets quite complicated.

ECMAScript 6 classes introduce simplified syntax to write class member functions (static functions), the use of the super keyword, and inheritance using the `extends` keyword.

If you would like to read more about the features in classes and ECMAScript 6, I highly recommend that you read the articles of Dr. Axel Rauschmayer (http://www.2ality.com/).

Modules

Modules provide a way to encapsulate your code and create privacy. In object-oriented languages, we usually use classes for this. However, I actually believe that this is an anti-pattern rather than a good practice. Classes should be used where inheritance is desired and not just to structure your code.

I'm sure that you've encountered a lot of different module patterns in JavaScript already. One of the most popular ones that creates privacy using a function closure of an **immediately invoked function expression (IIFE)** is probably the revealing module pattern. If you'd like to read more about this and maybe other great patterns, I recommend the book *Learning JavaScript Design Patterns*, by Addy Osmani.

Within ECMAScript 6, we can now use modules to serve this purpose. We simply create one file per module, and then we use the import and export keywords to connect our modules together.

Within the ECMAScript 6 module specification, we can actually export as many things as we like from each module. We can then import these named exports from any other module. We can have one default export per module, which is especially easy to import. Default exports don't need to be named, and we don't need to know their name when importing them:

```
import SomeModule from './some-module.js';
var something = SomeModule.doSomething();
export default something;
```

There are many combinations on how to use modules. We will discover some of these together while working on our task management application during the upcoming chapters. If you'd like to see more examples on how to use modules, I can recommend the Mozilla Developer Network documentation (`https://developer.mozilla.org`) on the `import` and `export` keywords.

Template strings

Template strings are very simple, but they are an extremely useful addition to the JavaScript syntax. They serve three main purposes:

- Writing multiline strings
- String interpolation
- Tagged template strings

Before template strings, it was quite verbose to write multiline strings. You needed to concatenate pieces of strings and append a new-line character yourself to the line endings:

```
const header = '<header>\n' +
' <h1>' + title + '</h1>\n' +
'</header>';
```

Using template strings, we can simplify this example a lot. We can write multiline strings, and we can also use the string interpolation functionality for our title variable that we used to concatenate earlier:

```
const header = `
  <header>
    <h1>${title}</h1>
  </header>
`;
```

Note the back ticks instead of the previous single quotes. Template strings are always written between back ticks, and the parser will interpret all characters in-between them as part of the resulting string. This way, the new-line characters present in our source file will also be part of the string automatically.

You can also see that we have used the dollar sign, followed by curly brackets to interpolate our strings. This allows us to write arbitrary JavaScript within strings and helps a lot while constructing HTML template strings.

You can read more about template strings on the Mozilla Developer Network.

TypeScript

TypeScript was created in 2012 by Anders Hejlsberg with the intention to implement the future standard of ECMAScript 6 but also to provide a superset of syntax and features that were not part of the specification.

There are many features in TypeScript that are a superset to the ECMAScript 6 standard, including, but not limited to the following:

- Optional static typing with type annotations
- Interfaces
- Enum types
- Generics

It's important to understand that all of the features that TypeScript provides as a superset are optional. You can write pure ECMAScript 6 and not take advantage of the additional features that TypeScript provides. The TypeScript compiler will still transcompile pure ECMAScript 6 code to ECMAScript 5 without any errors.

 Most of the features that are seen in TypeScript are actually already present in other languages, such as Java and C#. One goal of TypeScript was to provide language features that support workflows and better maintainability for large-scale applications.

The problem with any nonstandard language is that nobody can tell how long the language will be maintained and how fast the momentum of the language will be in the future. In terms of support, the chances are high that TypeScript, with its sponsor, Microsoft, will actually have a long life. However, there's still no guarantee that the momentum and trend of the language will keep moving at a reasonable pace. This problem does obviously not exist for standard ECMAScript 6 because it's what the web of the future is made of and what browsers will speak natively.

Still, there are valid reasons to use the extended features of TypeScript if you'd want to address the following concerns that clearly outweigh the negative implications of an uncertain future in your project:

- Large applications that undergo a huge amount of changes and refactoring
- Large teams that require a strict governance while working on code
- Creation of type-based documentation which would otherwise be difficult to maintain

Today's version of Angular is purely based on TypeScript and therefore it's your best option if you're starting to use Angular as your framework. There are also ways to use Angular with pure ECMAScript even without using a transpiler, however, you'll be missing some great language features and support.

 Within this book, we're using TypeScript for all examples as well as to create our task management system. Most of the features we're going to be using have already been or will be explained to you within this chapter. The typing system of TypeScript is pretty self-explanatory, however, if you'd like to know more about TypeScript and its features, I highly recommend that you visit the TypeScript documentation on their official website: `https://www.typescriptlang.org`.

History with TypeScript in Angular

When the Angular project was developed, it was important for the core team to include the best language support they could get. While evaluating different languages, they have actually considered Google Dart and TypeScript as potential candidates to implement the framework. However, there was one major feature missing in the superset which TypeScript provided. Let's look again at our first Angular component, which we wrote in a previous section:

```
@Component({
  selector: 'hello-world',
```

```
    template: '<div>Hello World</div>'
})
class HelloWorld {}
```

An Angular component always consists of an EMCAScript 6 class as well as the `@Component` decorator which is used to configure our component. At the time when Google started developing the Angular project, there was no such thing as the ECMAScript 7 decorator proposal and TypeScript did not support something similar. Still, the Angular team didn't want to miss out on such a great language feature which can simplify and ease the use of their framework API. This marked the birth of AtScript. AtScript was created by the Angular core team as a fork of TypeScript which added the possibility to write meta annotations using an at symbol. At the same time, the ECMAScript 7 decorator proposal was created to propose a similar feature to the JavaScript standard. It was only a few months later with TypeScript's Version 1.5 that Microsoft announced that they would include experimental support for decorators in the TypeScript transpiler.

Today, Angular has switched completely to TypeScript and AtScript as well as Dart, which is no longer supported in the core project. They have changed their code to run with the experimental decorator support of TypeScript and no longer rely on a custom solution.

From this rather long-winded history, you can get that the Angular core team has fought hard to be able to use a decorator language feature. And they have succeeded. Given the importance of this feature, we'll talk a bit about the possibilities we have with ECMAScript 7 decorators within the next section.

Decorators

Decorators are not part of the ECMAScript 6 specification, but they were proposed to the ECMAScript 7 standard for 2016. They provide us with a way to decorate classes and properties during design time. This allows a developer to use meta-annotations while writing classes, and declaratively attach functionality to the class and its properties.

Decorators are named after the decorator pattern that was initially described in the book *Design Patterns: Elements of Reusable Object-Oriented Software,* by Erich Gamma and his colleagues, also known as the **Gang of Four (GoF)**.

The principle of decoration is that an existing procedure is intercepted and the decorator has the chance to either delegate, provide an alternative procedure, or do a mix of both:

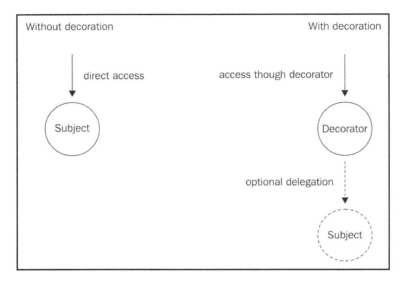

Visualization of decoration in a dynamic environment with the example of a simple access procedure

Decorators in ECMAScript 7 can be used to annotate classes and class properties. Note that this also includes class methods, as class methods are also properties of the class prototype object. Decorators get defined as regular functions, and they can be attached to classes or class properties with the *at* symbol. Our decorator function will then be called with contextual information about the location of inclusion every time that the decorator is placed.

Let's take a look at a simple example that illustrates the use of a decorator:

```
function logAccess(obj, prop, descriptor) {
  const delegate = descriptor.value;
  descriptor.value = function() {
    console.log(`${prop} was called!`);
    return delegate.apply(this, arguments);
  };
}

class MoneySafe {
  @logAccess
  openSafe() {
    this.open = true;
  }
```

```
}
const safe = new MoneySafe();
safe.openSafe(); // openSafe was called!
```

We have created a `logAccess` decorator that will log all function calls that are tagged with the decorator. If we look at the `MoneySafe` class, you can see that we have decorated the `openSafe` method with our `logAccess` decorator.

The `logAccess` decorator function will be executed for each annotated property within our code. This enables us to intercept the property definition of the given property. Let's take a look at the signature of our decorator function. Decorator functions that are placed on class properties will be called with the target object of the property definition as a first parameter. The second parameter is the actual property name that is defined, followed by the last parameter, which is the descriptor object that is supposed to be applied to the object.

The decorator gives us the opportunity to intercept the property definition. In our case, we use this ability to exchange the descriptor value (which is the annotated function) with a proxy function that will log the function call before calling the origin function (delegation). For simplification purposes, we've implemented a very simple yet incomplete function proxy. For real-world scenarios, it would be advisable to use a better proxy implementation, such as the ECMAScript 6 proxy object.

Decorators are a great feature to leverage aspect-oriented concepts and declaratively add behavior to our code at design time.

Let's look at a second example where we use an alternative way to declare and use decorators. We can treat decorators like function expressions where our decorator function is rewritten as a factory function. This form of usage is especially useful when you need to pass along configuration to the decorator, which is made available in the decorator factory function:

```
function delay(time) {
  return function(obj, prop, descriptor) {
    const delegate = descriptor.value;
    descriptor.value = function() {
      const context = this;
      const args = arguments;
      return new Promise(function(success) {
        setTimeout(function() {
          success(delegate.apply(context, arguments));
        }, time);
      });
```

```
    };
  };
}

class Doer {
  @delay(1000)
  doItLater() {
    console.log('I did it!');
  }
}

const doer = new Doer();
doer.doItLater(); // I did it! (after 1 second)
```

We have now learned how ECMAScript 7 decorators can help you write declarative code that has an aspect-oriented twist to it. This simplifies development a lot because we can now think of behavior that we add to our classes during design time when we actually think about the class as a whole and write the initial stub of the class.

Decorators in TypeScript are slightly different than the decorators from ECMAScript 7. They are not limited to classes and class properties, but they can be placed on parameters within the class methods. This allows you to annotate function parameters, which can be useful in some cases:

```
class TypeScriptClass {
  constructor(@ParameterDecorator() param) {}
}
```

Angular uses this feature to simplify dependency injection on class constructors. As all directive, component, and service classes get instantiated from Angular dependency injection and not by us directly, these annotations help Angular find the correct dependencies. For this use case, function parameter decorators actually make a lot of sense.

 Currently, there are still issues with the implementation of decorators on class method parameters, which is also why ECMAScript 7 does not support it. The TypeScript compiler has worked around this issue but is currently not compliant to the ECMAScript 7 proposal.

Tools

In order to make use of all these future technologies, we need some tools to support us. We were already talking about ECMAScript 6 and decorators, where we actually prefer TypeScript decorators, as they support the constructor parameter decorators that are used by Angular. Although the ECMAScript 6 syntax supports modules, we still need some sort of module loader that will actually load the required modules in the browser or help us generate an executable bundle.

Node.js and npm

Node.js is JavaScript on steroids. Initially, a fork of the V8 JavaScript engine from the Google Chrome browser, Node.js was extended with more functionality, specifically to make JavaScript useful on the server-side. File handling, streams, system APIs, and a huge ecosystem of user-generated packages are just some of the facts that make this technology an outstanding partner for your web development.

The node package manager, NPM, is a door to over 200,000 packages and libraries that can help you build your own application or library. The Node.js philosophy is very similar to the UNIX philosophy, where packages should stay small and sharp, but they should use composition to achieve greater goals.

To build our application, we will rely on Node.js as the host for the tools that we're going to use. We should, therefore, make sure that we install Node.js on our machine so that we are prepared for the next chapter, where we will start to craft our task management application.

 The code within this book was written using Node.js 8.9.0. Please make sure you're installing an equivalent Node.js version on your system. You can get Node.js from their website at https://nodejs.org, and it should be a breeze to install this on any kind of operating system by following the instructions on their website.

Once you've installed Node.js, we can perform a simple test to check whether everything is up and running. Open a Terminal console and execute the following command:

```
node -e "console.log('Hello World');"
```

Angular CLI

There are many ways to start out with a new Angular project. The most convenient one is probably to use the Angular CLI. The CLI, as the name already suggests, is a command-line interface to create new projects as well as new artefacts within an existing project.

The following instructions are guiding you through the creation of your first Angular project using the Angular CLI tool.

1. Let's start by installing the Angular CLI on your system. Execute the following command on your command line:

   ```
   npm install -g @angular/cli@6.0.8
   ```

2. After you've installed the Angular CLI tool, you can now use it to scaffold a new Angular project. You can access the tool executable by typing ng in your terminal. Let's open another Terminal window and create a new Angular project using the Angular CLI tool:

   ```
   ng new my-first-app --prefix mac
   ```

3. The previous step will take a while since all dependencies of your project need to be installed first. After completion, we can now use the CLI tool to start a local development server:

   ```
   cd my-first-app
   ng serve
   ```

4. You can now launch your favourite browser and open up the address `http://localhost:4200`, where you should see the message welcome to mac.

Congratulations! You've just created your first Angular application using the Angular CLI tool! As I already told you, the convenience level of starting an Angular project like this is really great.

The CLI tool can be viewed as a scaffolding tool which helps you set up the necessary tooling as well as the structure of your project. Let's take a look at the most important features you'll get for free when you're using the CLI to give birth to your project:

- **TypeScript**: Maybe obvious, but in order to use a transpiler, there will be many manual steps involved for you to set up the necessary tooling.

- **Webpack**: This massive power tool is solving a lot of problems you probably haven't even though about yet. Along with TypeScript transpilation, its main concern is to load ECMAScript modules and provides you with a development server to preview and work on your project. Finally, it's also the tool which helps you to create an optimized bundled version of your project for production use.
- **Karma, Jasmine, and Protractor**: This trio is unbeatable when it comes to testing! While Karma runs your executable specifications, Jasmin helps you write your tests. Protractor, on the other hand, can be used to create full end-to-end, integrational tests.

 You could also use the ECMAScript 5 style of writing Angular applications, which would allow you to develop your application right away without additional tooling. However, if you want to leverage the full potential of Angular, you should write your application in TypeScript rather than JavaScript. The Angular API is optimized to use features from future JavaScript versions and TypeScript, in order to provide the best ease of development.

Please go ahead and explore the source code that has been generated using the Angular CLI. Over the course of the chapters in this book, we will gain more in-depth knowledge, which will help you understand and put all of those pieces together. For the moment, we were just concerned about the installation of the Angular CLI and gave it a quick dry run.

Summary

In this chapter, we looked at a component-based approach to structure user interfaces. We talked about the necessary background to understand why we are moving in this direction with the web standard and frameworks, such as Angular. We also ensured that we are prepared with all the technology that we will use in the upcoming chapters in this book. You created your first simple Angular application using the Angular CLI tool. Now, we are ready to start building our task-management system using a component-based architecture to its full potential.

In the next chapter, we're going to start building our task management application using Angular components. We'll look at the initial steps that are required to create an Angular application from scratch and flesh out the first few components in order to build a task list.

Ready, Set, Go! 2

In this chapter, we will start building our task management application. We'll jump right into the core of the application and create the initial components required to manage a simple task list.

In the process of going through this chapter, you'll learn about the following topics:

- Introduction to `NgModule`
- Bootstrapping an Angular application using a main module
- Component input and output
- Host property binding
- Styling and view encapsulation
- Using `EventEmitter` to emit custom events
- Component life cycle

Managing tasks

After picking up the basics from the previous chapter, we will now go on and create a task management application together in the upcoming chapters. You'll learn about some concepts during these chapters and then use them with practical examples. You'll also learn how to structure an application using components. This begins with the folder structure and ends with setting up the interaction between components.

Vision

The task management application, which we're going to create during the course of this book, should enable users to manage tasks easily and help them organize small projects. Usability is the central aspect of any application; therefore, you'll need to design a modern and flexible user interface that will support the users managing their tasks:

A preview of the task management application we are going to build

Our task management application will consist of components that will allow us to design a platform, providing a great user experience for the purpose of managing tasks. Let's define the core features of our application:

- Managing tasks within multiple projects and providing a project overview
- Simple scheduling as well as a time-and-effort-tracking mechanism
- Overviewing the DASHBOARD using graphical charts
- Tracking activities and providing a visual audit log
- A simple commenting system that will work across different components

The task management application is the main example in this book. Therefore, the building blocks within this book should only contain the code that is relevant to the theme of this book. Of course, other than components, an application needs other functionalities, such as visual design, data, session management, and other important parts, to work. While the required code for each chapter can be downloaded online, we'll only discuss the code that is relevant to the topics that we will be learning about in this book.

Starting from scratch

Let's start out by creating a new Angular project using the Angular CLI. We'll name it `mastering-angular-components`:

1. Open a console window and navigate to a proper workspace for our project. Let's use the Angular CLI to create our initial project structure:

```
ng new mastering-angular-components --prefix=mac
```

2. After the project has been successfully created, let's move into the project folder and start serving using the `ng serve` command:

```
cd mastering-angular-components
ng serve
```

After following the preceding steps, you should be able to open up your browser and point it to `http://localhost:4200`. You should be able to see the generated application app with a welcome message saying **Welcome to mac!**.

It's recommended that you leave the serving mode of the CLI running all the time while in development. Since the underlying webpack will use caching when recompiling the output bundles, it will speed up your development process quite a lot. I recommend that you always have a second command-line window open and start Angular CLI in serve mode there.

Let's examine what the Angular CLI tool has created for us so far. Along with a lot of files that we'll cover in later chapters, the Angular CLI tool has created the core files that are needed in order to assemble a simple Angular application. The following directory listing shows all the critical files, which you'll also find within your generated project folder:

```
mastering-angular-components
├───── node_modules
├───── package.json
```

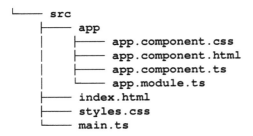

```
└─── src
    ├──── app
    │      ├─── app.component.css
    │      ├─── app.component.html
    │      ├─── app.component.ts
    │      └─── app.module.ts
    ├──── index.html
    ├──── styles.css
    └──── main.ts
```

Let's take a quick look at these dependencies, development dependencies, and their purpose:

File(s)	Description
package.json node_modules	Since the Angular CLI uses Node.js for tooling, our project contains a package.json to store all required dependencies and their versions. Node dependencies get installed within the node_modules folder. If you want to check which version of Angular has been installed along with your project, you can check the dependencies within the package.json file.
src/index.html	The main HTML file of your project. Within this file, you'll find the host element of your root component. This is the place where you root or main component will be rendered. Just open the file and you'll notice an element called <mac-root>. Since we've specified the prefix mac when creating our project using the Angular CLI, all our components and therefore all our component host elements contain this prefix.
src/main.ts	This is the main entry file of our TypeScript project code. It contains all the necessary code to start Angular and bootstrap our main application module.
src/styles.css	Any global CSS styles we'd like to apply to our application website go here.
src/app/app.module.ts	The main NgModule of your Angular project. This module is bootstrapped when your application is starting up. It contains references to your project components and specifies your main entry component, which should be rendered at startup.

`src/app/app.component.ts`
`src/app/app.component.html`
`src/app/app.component.css`
	The main component of your Angular application. This component represents the outermost component, sometimes just called app or root component. The TypeScript, HTML, and CSS code is separated into different files by default. This can also be changed so that everything is embedded within the TypeScript file. However, following a good separation practice, it makes absolute sense to have all concerns about the component in individual files.

Main application component

Let's take a look at our main application component. You can think of it as the outermost component of your application. It's called the main component because it represents your whole application. This is where your component tree has its roots and therefore it's sometimes also called the root component.

First, let's look at the component TypeScript file located in `src/app/app.component.ts`:

```
import {Component} from '@angular/core';

@Component({
  selector: 'mac-root',
  templateUrl: './app.component.html',
  styleUrls: ['./app.component.css']
})
export class AppComponent {
  title = 'mac';
}
```

There's nothing different here from what we already know about structuring a component, something that we learned in the previous chapter. However, there are two main differences here compared to how we created the components before. Instead of using the `template` property to write our HTML template inline, we're using the `templateUrl` property to tell Angular to load the HTML from the specified file. The second thing which we've not covered yet is how to load CSS for your component. The `styleUrls` property allows us to specify an array of URLs which get resolved to assemble the styles of our component. Similar to the HTML template mechanism, we could also use a property called `styles` to write our styles inline within the component TypeScript file.

For our application, we'd like to change the behaviour slightly on how we handle styling. The default way of organizing styles when creating components is that each component contains its own encapsulated styles. However, for our project, we want to use the global `styles.css` file to add all our component styles. This will make it much easier to work with the books source repository and eliminates the need to include CSS code excerpts within this book.

By default, Angular uses a Shadow DOM emulation on our components, which is preventing styles within a component to leak outside and influence other components. However, this behaviour can be changed easily by configuring the view encapsulation on components.

Angular has three ways to handle view encapsulation and each way has its own pros and cons. Let's look at the different settings:

Encapsulation type	Description
`ViewEncapsulation.Emulated`	If a component is set to emulated view encapsulation, it will emulate style encapsulation by attaching the generated attributes to the component element and modifying CSS selectors to include these attribute selectors. This will enable certain forms of encapsulation, although the outer styles can still leak into the component if there are other global styles. This view encapsulation mode is the default mode, if not specified otherwise.
`ViewEncapsulation.Native`	Native view encapsulation is supposed to be the ultimate goal of the view encapsulation concept within Angular. It makes use of Shadow DOM, as described in the previous chapter, to create an isolated DOM for the whole component. This mode depends on the browser to support Shadow DOM natively, and therefore, can't always be used. It's also important to note that global styles will no longer be respected and local styles need to be placed within the component in inline style tags (or use the `styles` property on the component annotation).

`ViewEncapsulation.None`	This mode tells Angular not to provide any template or style encapsulation. Within our application, we rely on styles coming from a global CSS; therefore, we use this mode for most of the components. Neither Shadow DOM, nor attributes will be used to create style encapsulation; we can simply use the classes specified within our global CSS file.

Let's change the view encapsulation of our main component to use the `ViewEncapsulation.None` mode. Since we're going to put all our styles in the global `src/styles.css` file, we can also remove the `styleUrls` property from our component configuration completely:

```
import {Component, ViewEncapsulation} from '@angular/core';

@Component({
  selector: 'mac-root',
  templateUrl: './app.component.html',
  encapsulation: ViewEncapsulation.None
})
export class AppComponent {
  title = 'mac';
}
```

Resource download

The goal of the first few chapters of this book is to build our application from scratch. There's some code which is necessary to build an application, which does not exactly meet the topic of this book, to master the creation of a solid component architecture. One of those things is CSS styling. Although an integral part of everything built with web technology, it's definitely not something to be bothered too much by in this book.

For this purpose, I've prepared all the CSS styling which is used within the components created throughout this book. Before you continue working on your application, you should download these styles and apply them to your project. Please find the exact download link in the download section of `Chapter 11`, *Task Management Application Source Code*.

Place the downloaded StyleSheet into the `src` folder of your project where it will replace the existing `styles.css` file.

Main application NgModule

Let's also take a look at the main NgModule generated by the Angular CLI. You can find it in the path src/app/app.module.ts:

```
import {BrowserModule} from '@angular/platform-browser';
import {NgModule} from '@angular/core';
import {AppComponent} from './app.component';

@NgModule({
  declarations: [AppComponent],
  imports: [BrowserModule],
  bootstrap: [AppComponent],
  providers: []
})
export class AppModule { }
```

If you've been following the section *Angular NgModule*, about NgModule within the first chapter of this book, there should not be any surprises when looking at our generated main application module.

Our application currently only consists of one component, the AppComponent, which we're declaring within our AppModule. We also specify that this component should be bootstrapped when this module is being bootstrapped.

Bootstrapping

The starting point of our project is located within the src/main.ts file. This file is responsible for bootstrapping the Angular framework and starting our applications main module.

We can go ahead and bootstrap our Angular application by providing our main application module, AppModule.

In order to bootstrap an Angular module, we first need to create a platform. There are many ways for different platforms and environments to create a platform. If you'd like to create a browser platform, which is the default platform for browser environments, we need to import the platform factory function `platformBrowserDynamic` from the `@angular/platform-browser-dynamic` module. Simply by calling the platform factory function, we will receive an instance of the newly created platform. On the platform instance, we can then call the `bootstrapModule` function, passing our main application module as a parameter:

```
import {platformBrowserDynamic} from '@angular/platform-browser-dynamic';
import {AppModule} from './app/app.module';

platformBrowserDynamic().bootstrapModule(AppModule)
  .catch(err => console.log(err));
```

Let's take a closer look at the steps involved in the bootstrapping mechanism of Angular. We should try to understand how our root component is getting rendered in the right place by calling the `bootstrapModule` function on the platform instance:

1. First, we call the `bootstrapModule` function on our platform instance, passing our main application module as a parameter
2. Angular will examine our main application module metadata and find the `AppComponent` listed in the `bootstrap` property of the `NgModule` configuration
3. By evaluating the metadata on the `AppComponent`, looking at the `selector` property, Angular will know where to render our root component
4. The `AppComponent` is rendered as our root component into the host element found within the `index.html` file matching the CSS selector in the `selector` property on the component metadata

Running the application

To make sure our modifications to the main component, `AppComponent`, are working as expected and we didn't break anything, let's start our application using the Angular CLI. Open a command line and point it to your project directory. Then, start the CLI in serve mode:

```
ng serve
```

If everything goes well, you will have an open web browser that shows **Welcome to mac!**.

Recap

Let's recap what we have done so far:

1. We initialized a new project using Angular CLI
2. We modified our main application component in
   `src/app/app.component.ts` to include `ViewEncapsulation.None` for
   enabling global styles
3. We've looked at the generated `MainModule` as well as the bootstrapping
   happening within our main entry file `src/main.ts`
4. Finally, we used the Angular CLI to start our application

Creating a task list

Now that we have our main application component set up, we can go on and start fleshing
out our task management application. The second component that we're going to create
will be responsible for listing tasks. Following the concept of composition, we'll create a
task list component as a subcomponent of our main application component.

Let's create a new component for our task list by using the Angular CLI generator
functionality. We already want to structure our application by area, where we put all task-
relevant components into a `tasks` subfolder:

```
ng generate component --spec false -ve none tasks/task-list
```

Using the `--spec false` option while generating our component, we can skip creating test
specifications. Since we're going to cover testing in a later chapter, we're skipping this
process for the moment. Also, by using the `-ve none` parameter, we can tell Angular to
create the component using `ViewEncapsulation.None` as a default encapsulation setting.

If you're using the Angular CLI tool to generate components, they will be
automatically added to your main module. This is really handy and
offloads a lot of boilerplate work on your side. If you're creating a
component manually, you should never forget to include the newly
created component within your `NgModule` declarations.

Let's open the generated file `src/app/tasks/task-list.ts` and do some modifications to it:

```
import {Component, ViewEncapsulation} from '@angular/core';

@Component({
  selector: 'mac-task-list',
  templateUrl: './task-list.component.html',
  encapsulation: ViewEncapsulation.None
})
export class TaskListComponent {
  tasks = [
    {id: 1, title: 'Task 1', done: false},
    {id: 2, title: 'Task 2', done: true}
  ];
}
```

We've created a very simple task list component that has a list of tasks stored internally. This component will be attached to HTML elements that match the CSS element selector `mac-task-list`.

Now, let's create a view template for this component to display the tasks. As you can see from the `templateUrl` property within the component metadata, we are looking for a file called `task-list.component.html`.

Let's change the content of this file to match the following excerpt:

```
<div *ngFor="let task of tasks">
  <input type="checkbox" [checked]="task.done">
  <div>{{task.title}}</div>
</div>
```

We use the `NgFor` directive to repeat the outermost DIV element for as many tasks as we have on the task list of our component. The `NgFor` directive in Angular will create a template element from its underlying content and instantiate as many elements from the template as the expression evaluates to. We currently have two tasks in our task list component, so this will create two instances of our template.

All that's left to do in order to make our task list work is include the task list component within the main application component. We can go ahead and modify our `src/app/app.component.html` file and change its content to match the following:

```
<mac-task-list></mac-task-list>
```

This was the last change we needed to make in order to make our task list component work. To view your changes, you can start the serving mode of Angular CLI, if you don't have it running already.

Recap

Let's look at what we did in the previous building block. We achieved a simple listing of tasks within an encapsulated component by following these steps:

1. We created the component TypeScript file that contains the logic of our component
2. We created the component's view within a separate HTML file
3. We included the component HTML element within our main application view template

The right size of components

Our task list is displayed correctly and the code we used to achieve this looks quite okay. However, if we want to follow a better approach for composition, we should rethink the design of our task list component. If we draw a line at enlisting the task list's responsibilities, we would come up with things such as listing tasks, adding new tasks to the list, sorting or filtering the task list; however, operations are not performed on an individual task itself. Also, rendering the task itself falls outside of the responsibilities of the task list. The task list component should only serve as a container for tasks.

If we look at our code again, we will see that we're violating the single responsibility principle and rendered the whole task body within our task list component. Let's take a look at how we can fix this by increasing the granularity of our components.

The goal now is to do a code refactoring exercise, also known as extraction. We are pulling our task's relevant template out of the task list template and creating a new component that encapsulates the tasks.

Let's use the Angular CLI to create a new task component. Open a command line and enter the root folder of our application. Execute the necessary code to create the task component:

```
ng generate component --spec false -ve none tasks/task
```

This will generate a new folder which includes all the code for our new task component. Now, let's open the HTML template on the path `src/app/tasks/task/task.component.html` and change the content to represent a single task:

```
<input type="checkbox" [checked]="task.done">
<div>{{task.title}}</div>
```

The content of our new `task.component.html` file is pretty much the same as what we already have within our task list component. However, within the newly created task component, we're only concerned about what a task looks like and not about the whole list of tasks.

Let's change the task component TypeScript file located on the path `src/app/tasks/task/task.component.ts`:

```
import {Component, Input, ViewEncapsulation} from '@angular/core';

@Component({
  selector: 'mac-task',
  templateUrl: './task.component.html',
  encapsulation: ViewEncapsulation.None
})
export class TaskComponent {
  @Input() task: any;
}
```

In the previous chapter of this book, we spoke about encapsulation and the preconditions to establish a clean encapsulation for UI components. One of these preconditions is the possibility to design proper interfaces in and out of the component. Such input and output methods are necessary to make the component work within compositions. That's how a component will receive and publish information.

As you can see from our task component implementation, we are now building such an interface using the @Input decorator on a class instance property. In order to use this decorator, we will first need to import it from the angular core module.

Input properties in Angular allow us to bind expressions in our templates to class instance properties on our components. This way, we can pass data from the outside of the component to the component inside, using the component's template. This can be thought of as an example of one-way binding, from the view of a parent component to the child component instance.

If we're using property binding on a regular DOM property, Angular will create a binding of the expression directly to the element's DOM property. We're using such a type of binding to bind the task completed flag to the `checked` property of the checkbox's `input` element:

Usage	Description
`@Input() inputProp;`	This allows us to bind the `inputProp` attribute to the component element within the parent component. Angular assumes that the attribute on the host element has the same name as that of the `input` property.
`@Input('inp') inputProp;`	You can also override the name of the attribute that should be mapped to this input. Here, the `inp` attribute of the component's host element is mapped to the component's input property, `inputProp`.

The last missing piece so that we can use our newly created task component is the modification of the existing template of the task list.

We include the task component within our task list template by using a `<mac-task>` element, as specified in the selector within our task component. Also, we need to create an input binding on the task component to pass the `task` object from the current `NgFor` iteration to the `task` input of the `task` component. We need to replace all the existing content in the `src/app/tasks/task-list/task-list.component.html` file with the following lines of code:

```
<mac-task *ngFor="let task of tasks"
          [task]="task"></mac-task>
```

Congratulations! You've successfully refactored your task list by extracting the task into its own component and established a clean composition, encapsulation, and single responsibility. Also, we can now say that our task list is a composition of tasks.

If you think about maintainability and re-usability, this was actually a very important step in the process of building our application. You should constantly look out for such composition opportunities, and if you feel something could be arranged into multiple subcomponents, you should probably go for it. Of course, you can also overdo this. There's simply no golden rule to determine what granularity of composition is the right one.

The right granularity of composition and encapsulation for a component architecture always depends on the context. My personal tip here is to use known principles from OOP, such as single responsibility, to lay the groundwork for a good design of your component tree. Always make sure your components are only doing things that they are supposed to do as their names suggest. A task list has the responsibility of listing tasks and providing some filters or other controls for the list. The responsibility of operating on individual task data and rendering the necessary view clearly belongs to a task component and not the task list.

Recap

In this building block, we cleaned up our component tree and established clean encapsulation using subcomponents. Then, we set up the interfaces provided by Angular using input bindings. We performed these actions by following the ensuing steps:

1. We created a task subcomponent
2. We used the task subcomponent with the task list component
3. We used input bindings and DOM element property bindings to establish one-way data binding in the task component

Adding tasks

Our task list looks nice already, but it would be quite useless if the user is unable to add new tasks to the list. Let's create a component for entering new tasks together. Let's create a new component with the responsibilities of handling all the UI logic necessary for entering a new task to our list.

Let's use the Angular CLI tool to create a new component stub:

```
ng generate component --spec false -ve none tasks/enter-task
```

Open up the template of the newly created component located at `src/app/tasks/enter-task/enter-task.component.html` and apply the following changes:

```
<input type="text"
       placeholder="Enter new task title..."
       #titleInput>
<button (click)="enterTask(titleInput)">
  Add Task
</button>
```

This template consists of an input field as well as a button to enter a new task. If you take a closer look at the input field, you can see that we've added a special attribute called `#titleInput`. This is called a local view reference and we can use this reference within the current component view, or query for the element within our component code.

In this case, we are actually using the local view reference to pass the input field DOM element to the `enterTask` function that we call on a click event on the `Add Task` button. All local view references are available as variables within expressions in the view of a component.

Let's take a look at the implementation of our component class for entering a new task. For this, we need to replace the generated code in the `src/app/tasks/enter-task/enter-task.component.ts` file with the following code:

```
import {Component, Output, ViewEncapsulation, EventEmitter} from
'@angular/core';

@Component({
  selector: 'mac-enter-task',
  templateUrl: './enter-task.component.html',
  encapsulation: ViewEncapsulation.None
})
export class EnterTaskComponent {
  @Output() outEnterTask = new EventEmitter<string>();
  enterTask(titleInput: HTMLInputElement) {
    this.outEnterTask.emit(titleInput.value);
    titleInput.value = '';
    titleInput.focus();
  }
}
```

For this component, we've chosen a design approach where we use a loose relation to our task list where the actual task will be created. Although this component is closely related to the task list, it's better to keep the components as loosely coupled as possible.

One of the simplest forms of inversion of control, a callback function or event listener is a great principle to establish loose coupling. In this component, we are using the @Output decorator to create an event emitter. The output properties need to be instance properties that hold an event emitter within the component. On the component's host element, we can then use event bindings to capture any events emitted. This gives us a great flexibility that we can use to create a clean application design, where we glue components together through the binding within the view:

 Most of the time, your output names will clash with your component instance methods names. For this purpose, it's advised that you stick to some naming conventions when naming your outputs and methods which will trigger the outputs. Within this book, we are sticking to the naming convention of prefixing all output names with the prefix "out". This way, we can avoid name clashes and still keep names similar.

Usage	Description
@Output() outputProp = new EventEmitter();	When outputProp.emit() is called, a custom event with the name outputProp will be emitted on the component. Angular will look for event bindings on the component's HTML element (where the component is used) and execute them: `<my-comp (outputProp)="doSomething()">` Within the expressions in event bindings, you will always have access to a synthetic variable called $event. This variable is a reference to the data emitted by the event emitter.
@Output('out') outputProp = new EventEmitter();	Use this way of declaring your output properties if you'd want to name your events differently from what your property name is. In this example, a custom event with the name out will be fired when outputProp.emit() is called: `<my-comp (out)="doSomething()">`

Okay, let's use our newly created component to add new tasks to our task list component. First, let's modify the existing template of the task list component. Open the task list template file, src/app/tasks/task-list/task-list.component.html. We need to add the enter-task component to the template and also handle the custom event that we're going to emit, once a new task is entered:

```
<mac-enter-task (outEnterTask)="addTask($event)"></mac-enter-task>
<div class="tasks">
  <mac-task *ngFor="let task of tasks"
            [task]="task"></mac-task>
</div>
```

Since the output property within the enter task component is called outEnterTask, we can bind it with the event binding attribute (outEnterTask)="" on the host element of the component.

Within the event binding expression, we then call a function on our task list component called addTask. We also use the synthetic variable $event, which contains the task title emitted from the enter task component. Now, whenever we push the button in our enter task component and an event gets emitted from the component, we catch the event in our event binding and handle it within the task list component.

We also need to make some minor changes to the task list component's TypeScript file. We need to implement the addTask function, which gets called within the template of the task list component. Let's open src/app/tasks/task-list/task-list.component.ts and modify it with the following changes:

```
import {Component, ViewEncapsulation} from '@angular/core';

@Component({
  selector: 'mac-task-list',
  templateUrl: './task-list.component.html',
  encapsulation: ViewEncapsulation.None
})
export class TaskListComponent {
  tasks = [
    {id: 1, title: 'Task 1', done: false},
    {id: 2, title: 'Task 2', done: true}
  ];

  addTask(title: string) {
    this.tasks.push({
      title, done: false
    });
  }
}
```

We have created a function, addTask, which will add a new task to our task list with a title that is passed to the function. Now, the loop is closed and our event from the enter task component is forwarded to this function within the view of the task list component.

Now is a good time to preview your changes if you haven't already. Try adding new tasks to the list and relate the behaviour to the changes you've applied to the code.

Recap

We have added a new enter task component which is responsible for providing the UI logic to add new tasks. We have covered the following topics:

- We created a child component that is loosely coupled using output properties and event emitters
- We learned about the @Output decorator and how to use it to create output properties
- We used event bindings to react on component output and execute actions

Custom UI elements

The standard UI elements in the browser are great, but sometimes, modern web applications require smarter and more complex input elements than the ones available within the browser.

We'll now create two specific custom UI elements that we'll use within our application going forward in order to provide a nice user experience:

- **Checkbox**: There's already a native checkbox input in the browser, but sometimes, it's hard to fit it into the visual design of an application. Native checkboxes are limited in their styling possibilities, and therefore, it's hard to make them look great. Sometimes, it's those minor details that make an application look appealing.
- **Toggle buttons**: This is a list of toggle buttons, where only one button can be toggled within the list. They can also be represented with a native radio button list. However, like with native checkboxes, radio buttons are sometimes not really the nicest visual solution to the problem. A list of toggle buttons that also represent a select-one-user input element is much more modern and provides the visual aspect that we are looking for. Besides, who doesn't like to push buttons?

Let's create our custom checkbox UI element first. As we'll probably come up with a few custom UI elements, we will introduce a new top-level UI folder. By calling the Angular CLI generator with the right parameter, we can create the stub for our checkbox component in the right folder:

```
ng generate component --spec false -ve none ui/checkbox
```

Let's start with the template of our new component and change the content of `src/app/ui/checkbox/checkbox.component.html`:

```html
<label class="label">
  <input class="input" type="checkbox"
         [checked]="checked"
         (change)="check($event.target.checked)">
  <span class="text">{{label}}</span>
</label>
```

On the checkbox input, we have two bindings. First, we have a property binding for the `checked` property on the DOM element. We are binding the DOM property to the `checked` member field on our component, which we are going to create in a moment.

Also, we have an event binding on the input element where we listen for the checkbox change DOM event and call the method `check` on our component instance. We use the synthetic variable `$event` to pass the `checked` property of the checkbox DOM element where the change event originated.

Moving on to our component class implementation, let's edit the TypeScript file on the path `src/app/ui/checkbox/checkbox.component.ts`:

```typescript
import {Component, Input, Output, ViewEncapsulation, EventEmitter} from
'@angular/core';

@Component({
  selector: 'mac-checkbox',
  templateUrl: './checkbox.component.html',
  encapsulation: ViewEncapsulation.None
})
export class CheckboxComponent {
  @Input() label: string;
  @Input() checked: boolean;
  @Output() outCheck = new EventEmitter<boolean>();

  check(checked: boolean) {
    this.outCheck.emit(checked);
  }
}
```

There's nothing special about this component class. It uses an input property to set the checked state from the outside, and it also has an output property with an event emitter that allows us to notify the outer component about the changes of the checked state.

Let's integrate our checkbox in the task component to replace the native checkbox input we're currently using there. For this purpose, we need to modify the `src/app/tasks/task/task.component.html` file by replacing its previous content with the following code:

```html
<mac-checkbox [checked]="task.done"
              (outCheck)="task.done = $event"></mac-checkbox>
<div class="title">{{task.title}}</div>
```

You should now already be able to see the changes in your browser and our nice custom checkbox component in action. As a next step, we'd like to apply some styling changes when a task is marked as done. This gives us better visual feedback than just the tick of the checkbox. For this, we're looking at a new concept to manipulate the host element of a component. Let's open the task component class on the path `src/app/tasks/task/task.component.ts` and add the following code to the body of the `TaskComponent` class:

```typescript
@HostBinding('class.done')
get done() {
  return this.task && this.task.done;
}
```

Using the `@HostBinding` decorator, we can create property bindings on the component host element based on the members of our component. Let's use this decorator in order to create a binding that will conditionally set a class with the name `done` on the component's HTML element. This is used to make some visual distinctions of finished tasks within our styles.

This is a good time to check your result and play around with these large new checkboxes in the task list. Isn't that much more fun to do than activating regular checkboxes? Don't underestimate the effect of a user interface that is pleasing to use. This can have a very positive impact on the usage of your product:

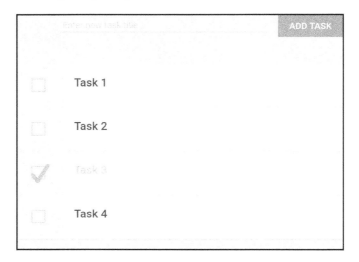

Our task list after adding our custom checkbox component

Recap

In this section, you learned how to build custom UI components that are generic and loosely coupled so that they can be used in other components as subcomponents. We also completed the following tasks:

- We created a subcomponent that is loosely coupled using output properties and event emitters
- We learned what the @Output decorator is and how to use it to create output properties
- We used event bindings to link the behaviour together from the view of a component

Task data service

We have already learned a lot about building basic components and how to compose them together in order to form larger components. In the previous building block, we created a reusable checkbox UI component, which we've used to enhance the usability of our task list.

In this topic, we will use the toggle button component to create a filter for our task list. But before we start to introduce more complexity into our application, we're going to refactor our application by introducing data services. As our application gets larger, it's crucial to centralize our data manipulation and streamline our data flow. Services come in very handy since they allow us to store state which is accessible in all our components using Angular's dependency injection.

Going forward, we'll deal with quite a lot of data within our application. TypeScript supports us very well when it comes to building type-safe data structures. So far, we've treated our task data as object literals, and TypeScript was extracting type information from there. However, as we start to use our data in different areas of our application, it makes sense to model our data in a central location. For this purpose, we're going to create our first TypeScript interface for representing our task data. In TypeScript, we can not only use interfaces for implementing classes and polymorphism, we can also use it to solely add type safety to our object literals and operations on objects. This is considered a very useful practice and will save us from a lot of potential bugs in the future.

Let's create a new TypeScript file on the path `src/app/model.ts` and add the following content to the file:

```
export interface Task {
  id?: number;
  title: string;
  done: boolean;
}
```

So far, we have stored our task list data directly within the task list component, but let's change that here and use a service that will provide task data for us. It's generally never a good idea to store data directly within a component. Refactoring our data into services is only the first step toward a clean component architecture, and we will learn about different methods about how to store our state and data in later chapters of this book.

In order to use the service we're about to create, we're going to make use of Angular's dependency injection for the first time. The Angular CLI comes in handy here, too. We can use it to generate a stub service for us:

```
ng generate service --spec false tasks/task
```

This will generate a file for us located on the path `src/app/tasks/task.service.ts`. Let's open this file in an editor and edit it with the following changes:

```
import {Injectable} from '@angular/core';
import {Task} from '../model';

@Injectable()
export class TaskService {
  private tasks: Task[] = [
    {id: 1, title: 'Task 1', done: false},
    {id: 2, title: 'Task 2', done: false},
    {id: 3, title: 'Task 3', done: true},
    {id: 4, title: 'Task 4', done: false}
  ];

  getTasks(): Task[] {
    return this.tasks.slice();
  }

  addTask(task: Task) {
    this.tasks.push({
      ...task,
      id: this.tasks.length + 1
    });
  }

  updateTask(task: Task) {
    const index = this.tasks
      .findIndex((t) => t.id === task.id);
    this.tasks[index] = task;
  }
}
```

We've moved all our task data into the newly created service. In order to make our service class injectable, we need to decorate it with the `@Injectable` decorator.

We're also using the `Task` interface for our tasks so that we have better type safety when working with task objects. In order to keep our data encapsulated and safe, we're going to create a clone of the internal tasks list when we're exposing it to any consumers. In JavaScript, we can simply call `Array.prototype.slice` in order to create a copy of an existing array.

Before we can use our task service within components, we need to provide it as a dependency. Dependencies are typically provided on the application level. In order to provide a dependency on the application level, we need to do some modifications to our main application module located on the path `src/app/app.module.ts`. The changes to the module are highlighted in the following code excerpt. The ellipsis character indicates that there's more code in the existing file, which is irrelevant for the changes we are applying:

```
...
import {TaskService} from './tasks/task.service';
...
@NgModule({
...
 providers: [TaskService],
 ...
})
export class AppModule {
}
```

Since we've provided our task service to the main module as a dependency, it will now be available for injection from the application injector.

Now, we can go ahead and modify our task list component to consume our task service. All our tasks are now stored in the task service and we need to remove the data which we previously embedded into the task list component.

Let's apply the changes to our task list component and modify the `src/app/tasks/task-list/task-list.component.ts` file. The following excerpt contains the whole code for the task list component. The changed and new sections are highlighted:

```
import {Component, ViewEncapsulation} from '@angular/core';
import {TaskService} from '../task-list.service';
import {Task} from '../../model';

@Component({
  selector: 'mac-task-list',
  templateUrl: './task-list.component.html',
  encapsulation: ViewEncapsulation.None
})
```

```
export class TaskListComponent {
  tasks: Task[];

  constructor(private taskService: TaskService) {
    this.tasks = taskService.getTasks();
  }

  addTask(title: string) {
    const task: Task = {
      title, done: false
    };
    this.taskService.addTask(task);
    this.tasks = this.taskService.getTasks();
  }

  updateTask(task: Task) {
    this.taskService.updateTask(task);
    this.tasks = this.taskService.getTasks();
  }
}
```

Instead of storing all our tasks within the task list component, we're now just declaring the `tasks` member. On the constructor of our component, we're using dependency injection to inject our newly created task service. Within the constructor body, we're retrieving task data by calling the `getTasks` method on our service. The resulting list is then stored within the `tasks` member of our component.

Within the `addTask` method, we're no longer directly modifying our task list. Instead, we're using the service to add a new task. After that, we need to get the updated list from the service by calling `getTasks` again.

We've also created a method called `updateTask` to update our tasks using our task service. Until now, we have updated the task data directly within our task component. The output binding on our checkbox was modifying the task's state on updates directly from within the view. While we're shaping our application, it becomes critical that we modify the state of our application in a more controlled manner. Imagine that you have dozens of components within your application, where each of them is modifying the state of your application. This would be a true maintenance hell.

So, how should we best approach this problem? The answer is delegation. We will delegate state manipulation to our parent components until we reach a component which is supposed to handle the manipulation. Component output is perfect for this use-case. We can tell our parent component about a change by emitting an output value. In our case, this means the following flow should occur:

1. The checkbox component will tell the task component that the checkbox was ticked
2. The task component will tell the task list component that the task should be updated
3. The task list component will call the service to update the task data

First, we're going to fix the state manipulation which is happening within the task component. Open up the task component template located at `src/app/tasks/task/task.component.html` and perform the following changes:

```
<mac-checkbox [checked]="task.done"
              (outCheck)="updateTask($event)"></mac-checkbox>
<div class="title">{{task.title}}</div>
```

Now, we're adding a new output to our task component and implementing the `updateTask` method in `src/app/tasks/task/task.component.ts`:

```
...
export class TaskComponent {
  @Input() task: Task;
  @Output() outUpdateTask = new EventEmitter<Task>();
  ...

  updateTask(done: boolean) {
    this.outUpdateTask.emit({
      ...this.task,
      done
    });
  }
}
```

Great! All whats left to do now is to catch the `outUpdateTask` output in the task list component template and call the `updateTask` method, which we've already added to the component class. Let's edit the file `src/app/tasks/task-list/task-list.component.html`:

```
<mac-enter-task (outEnterTask)="addTask($event)"></mac-enter-task>
<div class="tasks">
  <mac-task *ngFor="let task of filteredTasks"
            [task]="task"
            (outUpdateTask)="updateTask($event)"></mac-task>
</div>
```

Now is a good time to preview your changes in the browser. Our task list should be fully functional again. Try adding new tasks and marking tasks as done. Our task list component is already much cleaner since we're not storing any data within the component. Instead, we're using a service which can also be used in other components.

Recap

Within this section, we've not created anything new in the user interface of our application. However, it was still one of the more important sections of this chapter. We've learned about clean data flow, data and state best practices, and have created and integrated our first Angular service:

1. We have created a task service to store and manipulate our task data
2. We've delegated state manipulation from our task component to the task list component which was then interacting with our service
3. We have learned about `@Injectable` and how to provide dependencies at the application level
4. We've injected our task service in the constructor of our task list component where we use it to obtain data

Filtering tasks

In this section, we're going to implement some filter functionality for our task list. In order to control the active filter criteria, we are first building a toggle button list component. Let's go ahead and create a new component using the Angular CLI:

```
ng generate component --spec false -ve none ui/toggle
```

After running the Angular CLI generator command on your console, let's edit the HTML template of the newly created component in `src/app/ui/toggle/toggle.component.html`:

```
<button class="toggle-button"
        *ngFor="let button of buttonList"
        [class.active]="button === activeButton"
        (click)="activate(button)">{{button}}</button>
```

Nothing special here, really! We repeat a button by iterating over an instance field called `buttonList` using the `NgFor` directive. This button list will contain the labels of our toggle buttons. Conditionally, we set a class called `active` using a property binding and check it against our current button within the iteration against an instance field called `selectedButton`. When the button is clicked, we call a method, `activate`, on our component instance and pass the current button label from the iteration.

Now, let's change the code of our component class on the path `src/app/ui/toggle/toggle.component.ts`:

```
import {Component, Input, Output, ViewEncapsulation, EventEmitter, OnInit}
from '@angular/core';

@Component({
  selector: 'mac-toggle',
  templateUrl: './toggle.component.html',
  encapsulation: ViewEncapsulation.None
})
export class ToggleComponent implements OnInit {
  @Input() buttonList: string[];
  @Input() activeButton: string;
  @Output() outActivate = new EventEmitter<string>();

  ngOnInit() {
    if (!this.activeButton) {
      this.activeButton = this.buttonList[0];
    }
  }

  activate(button: string) {
    this.outActivate.emit(button);
  }
}
```

Within our toggle component, we rely on the `buttonList` input to be an array of button label strings. We are using this array within our template on a `NgFor` directive.

The `activeButton` input is expected to be set to the button label string which is currently active within the toggle list. We also create an output named `outActivate` to notify the outside world about state changes of the active toggle button.

Within the `activate` function, we are only emitting the `outActivate` output. From the binding outside of the component, we then expect the `activeButton` input to be updated accordingly. It's important to understand that our toggle component is only communicating to the parent component about a button that got activated. It's not updating any state, really. We're expecting that the parent component which uses our toggle component will then update the `activeButton` input accordingly.

The `ngOnInit` method is called by Angular automatically within the life cycle of directives and components. This is also the reason why our toggle component class is implementing the life cycle hook interface `OnInit`. In the case where the `activeButton` input property was not specified, we'll add a check and select the first button from the available button list. Since `activeButton`, as well as `buttonList`, are input properties, we need to wait for them to be initialized in order to execute this logic. It's important not to perform this initialization within the component constructor. Only within the life cycle hook `OnInit` do we have the guarantee that our input properties have been set already. It is invoked only once for each component which is created.

 Angular will call any life cycle hooks that have been implemented in your component automatically. The interfaces which are available for each life cycle hook are only helpful in the sense that they ensure you have implemented all desired callbacks for the individual life cycle hooks.

The following diagram illustrates the life cycle of an Angular component. Upon component construction, all the life cycle hooks will be called as per the order which is shown in the diagram, except the `OnDestroy` hook, which will be called upon component destruction.

Change detection will also start a subset of life cycle hooks, where some of the hooks which are called during creation are skipped:

- `doCheck`
- `afterContentChecked`
- `afterViewChecked`
- `onChanges (if any changes are detected)`

A detailed description of the life cycle hooks and their purposes is available on the Angular documentation website at `https://angular.io/guide/lifecycle-hooks`:

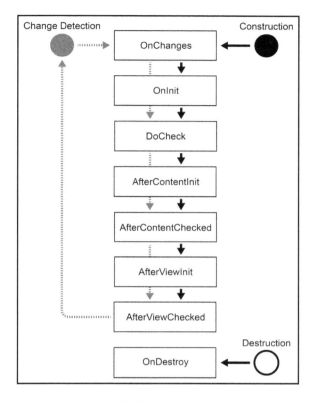

An illustration of the life cycle of an Angular component

Alright! We have created a new UI component to render a toggle button list. Now, it's time to move on with our main goal within this chapter, implementing a filtering system in our task list component.

First, we should think about the model for our filter. We'd want to include three states, all, open, and done, which should each result in a different view of our task list. Let's open up our model file located at `src/app/model.ts` and add the following changes:

```
export interface Task {
  id?: number;
  title: string;
  done: boolean;
}

export type TaskListFilterType = 'all' | 'open' | 'done';
```

We're defining a type alias, which represents a list of valid filter types. TypeScript type aliases are really helpful in order to make certain things more type safe. Especially when you're dealing with string types, you can use type aliases to create string literal types. By creating a type alias `TaskListFilterType`, and later using it in the context of the filter, we can specify which strings are valid while filtering. This will prevent any typos when dealing with task filter type strings within our application.

Now, it's time to implement our filter functionality. Let's open the task list component file located at `src/app/tasks/task-list/task-list.component.ts` and apply some code changes. Again, changed parts of the code are highlighted, to make it easier for you to see the effective changes:

```
import {Component, ViewEncapsulation} from '@angular/core';
import {TaskService} from '../task.service';
import {Task, TaskListFilterType} from '../../model';

@Component({
  selector: 'mac-task-list',
  templateUrl: './task-list.component.html',
  encapsulation: ViewEncapsulation.None
})
export class TaskListComponent {
  tasks: Task[];
  filteredTasks: Task[];
  taskFilterTypes: TaskListFilterType[] = ['all', 'open', 'done'];
  activeTaskFilterType: TaskListFilterType = 'all';

  constructor(private taskService: TaskService) {
    this.tasks = taskService.getTasks();
    this.filterTasks();
  }

  activateFilterType(type: TaskListFilterType) {
    this.activeTaskFilterType = type;
    this.filterTasks();
  }

  filterTasks() {
    this.filteredTasks = this.tasks
      .filter((task: Task) => {
        if (this.activeTaskFilterType === 'all') {
          return true;
        } else if (this.activeTaskFilterType === 'open') {
          return !task.done;
        } else {
          return task.done;
```

```
      }
    });
  }

  addTask(title: string) {
    const task: Task = {
      title, done: false
    };
    this.taskService.addTask(task);
    this.tasks = this.taskService.getTasks();
    this.filterTasks();
  }

  updateTask(task: Task) {
    this.taskService.updateTask(task);
    this.tasks = this.taskService.getTasks();
    this.filterTasks();
  }
}
```

Within the component, we want to store a list of types the task filter can have. This list will serve as input for our toggle button list. If you recall the input properties on our toggle button, we have a buttonList input that accepts a list of button labels. To store the currently selected filter type, we use an instance field called activeTaskFilterType.

The last piece that we need to add to our task list component is the actual filtering of tasks. For this, we're introducing a new member called filteredTasks, which will always be updated with the currently filtered subset of tasks. Within the filterTasks method, we are computing the subset of filtered tasks by evaluating the active filter criteria stored in activeTaskFilterType. The result of the filtering will be stored in our filteredTasks member.

We've also created a method, activateFilterType, which we can call to switch the active filter criteria. This method will then call the filterTasks method to update our filtered subset of tasks.

Okay, that's all we are going to change in our component class. We still need to change our view template, though. We need to render our toggle component and execute our filtering on filter criteria changes. Since we want to render the filtered subset of tasks instead of the whole task list, we also need to change the source for the NgFor, which repeats our tasks in the view. Let's open the template file src/app/tasks/task-list/task-list.html and modify it with the following changes:

```
<mac-toggle [buttonList]="taskFilterTypes"
            [activeButton]="activeTaskFilterType"
```

```
                        (outActivate)="activateFilterType($event)">
</mac-toggle>
<mac-enter-task (outEnterTask)="addTask($event)"></mac-enter-task>
<div class="tasks">
    <mac-task *ngFor="let task of filteredTasks"
              [task]="task"
              (outUpdateTask)="updateTask($event)"></mac-task>
</div>
```

Let's discuss the changes quickly. First, we are binding the `taskFilterTypes` property where we store a list of possible filter types within the task list component class, to the toggle component `buttonList` input property. This will make the toggle component render all filter types as toggle buttons.

We also bind the `activeTaskFilterType` instance field of the task list to the `activeButton` input property of the toggle component. This way, changes to the `activeTaskFilterType` property will be reflected in the toggle component. At the same time, when a user changes the active toggle button inside the toggle component, we capture the `outActivate` output of the toggle component and call the `activateFilterType` method on the task list component.

That's it, congratulations! You've successfully added a filtering mechanism to your task list by using our newly created toggle component. Preview the changes in your browser; you should see a fully functional task list where you can mark tasks as done, add new tasks, and filter the list by activating our nice toggle buttons:

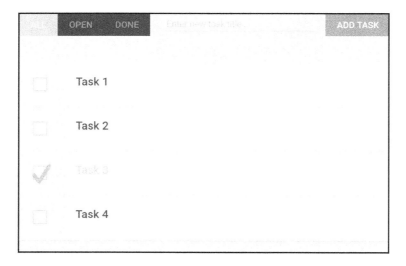

Screenshot of the task list with the newly added toggle button component for filtering the task state

Recap

In this section, we've built a filtering system into our task list component. We have also created an additional UI component to render toggle buttons, which we're presenting to the user for selecting the filter criteria:

- We created a new toggle component to render a set of toggle buttons
- We used the `@HostBinding` decorator to create property bindings declaratively from within our component class
- We learned about the Angular component life cycle and how we can use the `OnInit` life cycle hook to initialize the component after the input has been processed for the first time

Summary

In this chapter, you learned a lot of new concepts on building UI component-based applications with Angular. We also built the core component of our task management application, which is the task list itself. You learned about the concept of input and output properties and how to use them to establish proper component communication.

We also covered the basics of the Angular component life cycle and how to use life cycle hooks to execute post-initialization steps within the `OnInit` hook.

As the last step, we integrated a toggle button list component within our task list to filter the task states. We refactored our task list component to use a service in order to obtain task data. For this, we used Angular's dependency injection.

Within the next chapter, we're going to look at ways how to improve our handling of data and state. There are plenty of ways how to deal with application state and we're going to learn how to best tackle this issue.

Dealing with Data and State

3

In this chapter, we will go one step further in structuring our application and work on the data architecture that serves as the base for our task management system. So far, we've obtained task data synchronously from the task service which we created in the previous chapter. However, in real-world scenarios, this will rarely be the case. In a real application, we would obtain data in an asynchronous way where we need to manage client state, and we need to ensure the integrity of our state and data at all times. In this chapter, we'll look at how we can restructure our application to deal with a RESTful interface using the HTTP client module which comes with Angular. We will use an in-memory database to simulate our HTTP backend. Furthermore, we will be looking at some critical concepts like reactive programming, immutability, and "pure" components to help us build a data architecture that shines on both a small as well as large scale.

In this chapter, we will look at the following topics:

- Reactive programming, the basics of RxJS, and its operators to deal with asynchronous data
- Restructuring our application to deal with simulated HTTP calls to an in-memory database
- The concept of immutability
- Using pure components in Angular
- The introduction of container components to separate our user interface from application state
- Using `ChangeDetectionStrategy.OnPush` for pure components

Reactive programming with RxJS

So far, we have used simple array data structures in the task list that we created. That is not really what we'll find in real-world scenarios. In real applications, we have to deal with asynchronous data coming from a server.

Handling data in applications behaves very similarly to streams. You take input, transform it, combine it, merge it, and finally, write it into the output. In systems such as this, it's also very likely that input is in a continuous form and sometimes even of infinite duration. Just take a live feed as an example; this type of data flows continuously, and the data also flows infinitely. Functional and reactive programming are paradigms to help us deal with this kind of data more cleanly:

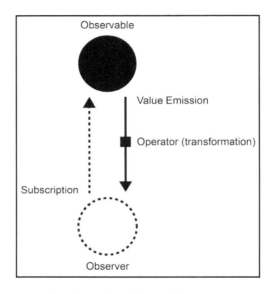

A simple observable subscription with value emission and a transformation

Angular is reactive at its very core, and the whole change detection and bindings are built using a reactive architecture. The input and output of components, which we've learned about in the previous chapter, is nothing but a data flow that is established using a reactive event-driven approach. Angular uses RxJS, a functional and reactive programming library for JavaScript, to implement this data flow. In fact, the EventEmitter, which we've used to send output from within our components, is just a wrapper around a RxJS observable.

Before we mess around with RxJS within our task management system, let's take a look at a straightforward RxJS example first to see how we can deal with observable streams in general:

```
import {from} from 'rxjs';
import {map, filter} from 'rxjs/operators';

from([1, 2, 3, 4])
  .pipe(
```

```
    map((num) => num * num),
    filter((num) => num < 10)
  )
  .subscribe((num) => console.log(num));

// This script is finishing with the following output on the console:
// 1
// 4
// 9
```

This simple script will generate an observable sequence from an array of numbers. We pass each number through the observable stream, item by item. We're using two simple operators before we subscribe to the observable and print the resulting items to the console. The map operator is squaring each number, which flows through the observable stream. The filter operator is then filtering out items which are greater or equal to 10.

Observables provide a large number of so-called operators that allow you to transform the data stream that originated at the source observable. You might already know about some of these functional operators from the ECMAScript 5 array extra functions, such as map and filter. Using operators, you can model a whole transformation flow until you finally subscribe to the data.

I often use the analogy of water pipes when talking about RxJS observables. If you think of your transformation operators as pieces within a pipeline, then the subscribe function is the final drain valve within the pipe. If you don't open the drain of a water pipe, no water will flow. The behaviour of RxJS is very similar. Without the final subscribe call, RxJS will not perform any of the operators. Only if you subscribe to an observable will it become active. Within the subscribe callback, you can then use the resulting items which flow through the stream.

Now, building pipelines come with a significant advantage. A transformation system which is built like a pipe is expecting input, and it will deliver some output. However, we don't perform anything immediately. Instead, we're setting up a system which knows how to deal with the data, when there's data flowing through it. This pipeline system is entirely stateless and reactive—reactive in the sense that it will react to incoming data and produce a new output of each input.

We can treat any source which emits items over time as an observable. Let's take a look at another example:

```
import {fromEvent} from 'rxjs';
import {throttleTime, map} from 'rxjs/operators';

fromEvent(window, 'mousemove')
```

```
.pipe(
  throttleTime(200),
  map((event: MouseEvent) => `Move(${event.screenX}, ${event.screenY})`)
)
.subscribe((move) => console.log(move));
```

In this example, we're using the `fromEvent` observable helper to create an observable source from the mouse move event on the window object. For each mouse move event, the event object will be emitted through the observable stream. We will then use the `throttleTime` operator to limit the amount of event emitted by the stream. This operator will block subsequent emissions within a given time frame, therefore throttling the steam. Within a `map` operator, we then format the emitted mouse event and finally subscribe to write the results to the console.

Using only a few lines of code, we've implemented an excellent little pipeline which transforms a source into a usable result. There lies the power of observables, reactive programming, and RxJS. We can solve difficult problems regarding building a reactive system in a very lovely and declarative way.

HTTP client and in-memory web APIs

At the beginning of this chapter, we decided that we'd like to change the way how we handle data within our application. Currently, our task data is embedded within our task service and retrieving as well as manipulating are both happening synchronously. Going forward, we want to change that and come as close as possible to a real-world situation. At the same time, we should keep an eye on the complexity costs of our solution.

Angular comes with a very nice utility for these use cases. Using the in-memory web API module, we can create a mock back-end service which will allow us to use a RESTful interface the same way as if we would connected to a real server. All remote calls using the Angular HTTP client will, however, be redirected to our local in-memory database. The way we deal with our data will be entirely authentic. At some point, we could even create a real backend server and connect our application to it, while our frontend code would stay the same.

Let's look into the necessary changes in order to implement our data layer using the in-memory web API. As a first step, we need to install the package using npm. Open a command line and navigate to your project directory. Then, execute the following command:

```
npm install --save angular-in-memory-web-api@0.5.1
```

Running this command will install the in-memory web API package and save it to our project `package.json` file. As a next step, we want to create our application's in-memory database. We're creating a new TypeScript file on the path `src/app/database.ts` and adding the following content:

```
import {InMemoryDbService} from 'angular-in-memory-web-api';
import {Task} from './model';

export class Database implements InMemoryDbService {
  createDb() {
    const tasks: Task[] = [
      {id: 1, title: 'Task 1', done: false},
      {id: 2, title: 'Task 2', done: false},
      {id: 3, title: 'Task 3', done: true},
      {id: 4, title: 'Task 4', done: false}
    ];
    return {tasks};
  }
}
```

Using the Angular in-memory web API, we can create a class which holds all our initial data. The class is implementing the `InMemoryDbService` interface, which demands that we create a method named `createDb`. Within this function, we can create resources which will be made available for use with the Angular HTTP client in a RESTful style.

Next, we're going to update our main application module located in the path `src/app/app.module.ts`, and set up our application for using the in-memory web API with our newly created database. You should only add the highlighted parts of the following code excerpt. The ellipsis character is indicating that there's more code existing, which is irrelevant for the changes you need to apply to your code:

```
...
import {HttpClientModule} from '@angular/common/http';
import {HttpClientInMemoryWebApiModule} from 'angular-in-memory-web-api';

import {Database} from './database';
...
```

```
@NgModule({
  ...
  imports: [
    BrowserModule,
    HttpClientModule,
    HttpClientInMemoryWebApiModule.forRoot(Database, {
      delay: 0
    })
  ],
  ...
})
export class AppModule {
}
```

We've added two more modules to the import section of our main application module. We've added the Angular HTTP client module which we'll use to call our simulated REST endpoint in our database. As discussed earlier, this library would also be used in the same way if we were to call a remote server.

The second module we are importing is the HTTP client adapter of the in-memory web API module. This module will intercept all HTTP calls executed by the Angular HTTP client and redirect the requests to our local database. We're using the factory method `HttpClientInMemoryWebApiModule.forRoot` to configure the adapter module before we import it. In the first argument to the factory function, we're passing the database class we've created. In the second argument, we can provide some additional options for the adapter. In our case, we're setting the delay to zero. Using higher values will artificially delay the responses from our database, which is nice if you want to simulate a network delay.

Using behaviour subjects

The HTTP client is using RxJS to return observable streams for all HTTP request methods. The response body will then be emitted through the observable streams, and we can subscribe to the streams to retrieve the results:

```
this.http.get<Task[]>('/api/tasks')
  .subscribe((tasks) => console.log(tasks));
```

Since we know how to deal with observable streams within our components, we could go ahead and directly return the observable resulting from the HTTP client call.

However, instead, we want to make use of a RxJS class called `BehaviorSubject`. The problem with directly returning the observable from the HTTP client is that we're always returning a new observable when the tasks are loaded from the server. That would be impractical, and after reloading tasks when performing updates or adding new tasks, we'd like to be able to reuse the same observable stream to re-emit the updated task list. This way, all components of our system will be notified when we reload our tasks. You can use a behaviour subject whenever you want to create your own source of an observable stream. You can control what should be emitted and when. Let's look at a simplified example of how a behaviour subject can be used:

```
const subject = new BehaviorSubject<number>(0);
subject.asObservable().subscribe(num => console.log(`Item: ${num}`));
// console output -> Item: 0

subject.next(1);
// console output -> Item: 1

subject.next(2);
// console output -> Item: 2

subject.asObservable().subscribe(num => console.log(`Second subscription:
${num}`));
// console output -> Second subscription: 2
```

Within the constructor of a behaviour subject, we can specify the initial value or item which will be emitted initially to all subscribers. Behaviour subjects are also always emitting the most recent item they have to their new subscribers.

A behaviour subject is both an observer as well as an observable. Therefore, it would be possible to directly call the `subscribe` method on the subject. However, if you'd like to convert your subject into a plain observable again, you can use the `asObservable` method. This is especially useful for encapsulation. When you're returning your observable stream to be used outside of your immediate program logic, you don't want to give the outside world the power to emit items. It should only be possible to observe the stream.

Finally, whenever you want to emit a new item through the observable stream, you can use the `next` method on the subject.

Loading data in the task service

It's time to change our task service and make use of the Angular HTTP client to obtain the task data from our database. Let's open up the `src/app/tasks/task.service.ts` file and change the file content to the following:

```
import {Injectable} from '@angular/core';
import {HttpClient} from '@angular/common/http';
import {BehaviorSubject} from 'rxjs';
import {Task} from '../model';

@Injectable()
export class TaskService {
  private tasks = new BehaviorSubject<Task[]>([]);

  constructor(private http: HttpClient) {
    this.loadTasks();
  }

  private loadTasks() {
    this.http.get<Task[]>('/api/tasks')
      .subscribe((tasks) => this.tasks.next(tasks));
  }

  getTasks() {
    return this.tasks.asObservable();
  }

  addTask(task: Task) {
    return this.http
      .post<Task>('/api/tasks', task)
      .subscribe(() => this.loadTasks());
  }

  updateTask(task: Task) {
    return this.http
      .post(`/api/tasks/${task.id}`, task)
      .subscribe(() => this.loadTasks());
  }
}
```

We are injecting the Angular HTTP client into our constructor so we can use it within our service. In the `loadTasks` method, we're executing a GET call on the RESTful tasks resource which is provided by our database.

The `tasks` member of our service is holding a behaviour subject which is initialised with an empty array. Whenever we call the internal `loadTasks` method, the resulting task list array is emitted through our behaviour subject by calling the next method.

The `loadTasks` method is first called within the service constructor. That will ensure that the resulting task list obtained from the HTTP call is initially emitted through our behaviour subject. We also call the `loadTasks` method right after we've completed the POST requests within the `addTask` and `updateTask` methods. That will guarantee that we're reloading the updated task list from the "server" and emitting it through our behaviour subject.

Within the `getTasks` method, we're converting our subject to an observable and returning it. This way, we can ensure that no one outside of the service will have the power to emit items through our subject. Using the observable of our behaviour subject, we can have hundreds of components subscribing, which will all receive the most recent task list whenever there is a change in our data.

The in-memory web API will automatically generate IDs for our tasks when we add new tasks by executing a post request to the tasks resource. This means that when we call the `addTask` method with a task object, we can skip adding the ID property and the in-memory database will take care of finding the next possible ID value for us.

Now, let's use our updated task service in the task list component. Open up the `src/app/tasks/task-list/task-list.component.ts` file and apply the following changes. Again, effective changes are in bold:

```
import {Component, ViewEncapsulation} from '@angular/core';
import {TaskService} from '../../tasks/task.service';
import {Task, TaskListFilterType} from '../../model';
import {Observable, combineLatest, BehaviorSubject} from 'rxjs';
import {map} from 'rxjs/operators';

@Component({
  selector: 'mac-task-list',
  templateUrl: './task-list.component.html',
  encapsulation: ViewEncapsulation.None
})
export class TaskListComponent {
  tasks: Observable<Task[]>;
  filteredTasks: Observable<Task[]>;
  taskFilterTypes: TaskListFilterType[] = ['all', 'open', 'done'];
  activeTaskFilterType = new BehaviorSubject<TaskListFilterType>('all');

  constructor(private taskService: TaskService) {
```

```
    this.tasks = taskService.getTasks();

  this.filteredTasks = combineLatest(this.tasks,
this.activeTaskFilterType)
    .pipe(
      map(([tasks, activeTaskFilterType]) => {
        return tasks.filter((task: Task) => {
          if (activeTaskFilterType === 'all') {
            return true;
          } else if (activeTaskFilterType === 'open') {
            return !task.done;
          } else {
            return task.done;
          }
        });
      })
    );
  }

  activateFilterType(type: TaskListFilterType) {
    this.activeTaskFilterType.next(type);
  }

  addTask(title: string) {
    const task: Task = {
      title, done: false
    };
    this.taskService.addTask(task);
    // Two lines got removed from there
  }

  updateTask(task: Task) {
    this.taskService.updateTask(task);
    // Two lines got removed from there
  }
}
```

We have changed the type of our `tasks` member, which is now holding an observable with
a task array generic type. In TypeScript, RxJS makes use of generics to specify what type of
items will be emitted through the observable stream. The `tasks` member will store the
observable stream which we obtain by calling our task service. It will make the basis for our
filtering inside of the component.

In the constructor of our task list component, we're still calling the `getTasks` method of our service. However, this time, we won't receive a list of tasks synchronously. Instead, we're an observable stream which will emit a list of tasks when we subscribe. Since we're using a behaviour subject inside of the task service, we will never need to call the task service again to obtain tasks. If there are updates to the task list data, we will receive a new item through the connected observable stream containing the most recent task list.

We have also changed our `activeTaskFilterType` member to a behavior subject. That will help us in building a consistent reactive data flow within our component. Instead of storing the active filter type directly, we're using a subject to emit the filter type. Within the `activateFilterType` method, we do precisely this. When this method is called from our view, as a filter toggle button is clicked, we will emit the new active filter type using the behavior subject.

Our `tasks` observable will always emit the latest list when the underlying data is changed. Also, the `activeTaskFilterType` subject is emitting an item when we change the active task filter. Now, we can combine both streams to implement our filter logic reactively. Again, think of a pipeline system. Instead of filtering immediately, we are building a network of pipes which will filter whenever new data arrives. So, how can we combine two observable streams into one? There are many ways to do this using the broad variety of operators RxJS provides. However, in our current situation, the `combineLatest` operator will work best.

Let's look at a small illustration of how this operator combines multiple observable streams into one single observable stream:

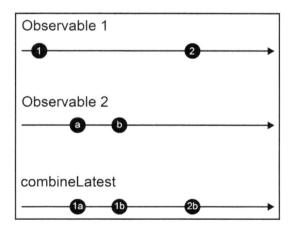

Combining two observables into one by using the combineLatest operator

The `combineLatest` operator is combining two or more input observables into a single output observable. The first item will be emitted on the output observable when all input observables have emitted at least one item. The emitted item on the output observable is always an array which contains the most recent, or latest items of all input observables. In the preceding example, you can see that the first item is emitted when **Observable 2** emits its item labelled with **(a)**. The emitted item is an array containing both values **(1)** from **Observable 1** and **(a)** from **Observable 2**. After the first combined item was emitted, if one of the input streams is emitting a new item, the output observable by `combineLatest` will emit an updated item which again contains the latest items of all input observables.

This is exactly the behaviour we're looking for when we're building our filter observable. Just switch **Observable 1** from the preceding example with our tasks observable and **Observable 2** with our active filter type. Now, if we either input an observable, the tasks observable, the active filter subject, or emit a new item, our filtered output observable will also produce a new item. This is reactive programming at its best. We never need to be concerned about updating our state anymore. It's all taken care of using reactive streams.

Since `combineLatest` will just produce an array of all the latest values emitted by the input observables, we need to use an additional map operator to provide the desired filtered list output. We're destructuring the value pair emitted by `combineLatest` into a `tasks` and `activeTaskFilterType` variable and performing the filtering based on that data. The resulting filtered list is returned and will be emitted by the output observable of the map operator.

Subscribing in the view using the async pipe

We have learned about RxJS observables and that they will not start to emit items if we don't subscribe to them. You can compare this to the analogy of the drain valve of a water pipe. If you don't open the drain, the water will not flow.

Within our updated task list component, we now have a `filteredTasks` observable to which we can subscribe to and obtain the latest filtered tasks. However, there's a slightly better way to handle RxJS subscriptions, which we're going to take a look at now.

The problem with subscriptions is that they always want to be cleaned up too. Imagine your subscription is causing many event handlers to be added and other resources which might get allocated for observing your stream. Calling the subscribe method will return a subscription object, and on that subscription object, you will find a method called unsubscribe. Usually, it's always a good idea to call this method when you don't need the observable subscription anymore. In the case of Angular components, we can say that when a component gets removed from the view, it's a good time to clean up the observable subscriptions.

Luckily, there's a life cycle hook called OnDestroy for detecting when a component is removed from the view. We can use this hook to clean up any subscriptions to RxJS observables. Let's take a look at a straightforward example of a component subscribing to an observable and unsubscribing within the OnDestroy life cycle hook:

```
import {OnDestroy} from '@angular/core';
import {Observable, Subscription, fromEvent} from 'rxjs';

...
export class MousePositionComponent implements OnDestroy {
  mouseObservable: Observable<MouseEvent> = fromEvent(window, 'mousemove')
    .map(e => `${e.screenX}, ${e.screenY}`);
  mousePosition: string;
  mouseSubscription: Subscription = this.mouseObservable
    .subscribe((position: string) => this.mousePosition = position);

  ngOnDestroy() {
    this.mouseSubscription.unsubscribe();
  }
}
```

In the preceding example, we're creating an observable stream from the mouse move events on the window object. All we'd like to do is display the most recent mouse position, which was emitted by the observable stream, within our component view. You can immediately see that this is quite a bit of code just for dealing with one observable. We need to store three things for each observable:

- The observable itself
- A property to store the most recent emitted item by the stream
- The subscription object which allows us to unsubscribe and clean up when our component gets destroyed

This might be okay if we're only dealing with one single observable, however, imagine if your component needs to deal with several observables at the same time. This is going to be quite a mess.

Another problematic thing is that we need to manually unsubscribe when our component gets destroyed using the OnDestroy life cycle hook. This is a manual, error-prone process and we can lose track over our subscriptions quite easily.

Luckily, Angular comes with a genius solution for this problem. Instead of dealing with the subscription manually, we will use a view pipe with the name AsyncPipe to subscribe directly within the view of our component. This means that we don't need to subscribe in our component class and extract the latest emitted item manually. Instead, the async pipe will extract the item for us and update our view automatically whenever there's a new item coming through the stream. The async pipe will also store the subscription internally and automatically unsubscribe for us if it detects that the component has been destroyed.

Let's look at the same example from before, but now using the async pipe. The component class would look like this:

```
import {Observable, fromEvent} from 'rxjs';

...
export class MousePositionComponent implements OnDestroy {
  mouseObservable: Observable<MouseEvent> = fromEvent(window, 'mousemove')
    .map(e => `${e.screenX}, ${e.screenY}`);
}
```

Wow! That's a radical simplification, isn't it? All we need to store now is the observable itself. Extracting the latest emitted item as well as unsubscribing from the stream is all handled by the async pipe. Let's take a look at how we would need to change our view to use the async pipe:

```
<strong>Mouse position:</strong>
<p>{{mouseObservable | async}}</p>
```

How cool is that! By only using the async pipe in our view, we can create a subscription to the observable, render the latest item emitted by the stream, and unsubscribe when our component gets destroyed. Additionally, from a functional and reactive standpoint, we also enhanced our code in a way that we don't create any side effects within our component class. We don't hold any intermediate state, and all we store is the observable stream itself. The async pipe is an excellent addition to your toolset when dealing with asynchronous data, and you should always make use of it when working with RxJS observables.

Okay, I hope you felt the power and simplicity of using the async pipe within the previous example. Now, we'll use that knowledge and refactor our task list component to use the async pipe to subscribe to our observables within the component view.

Since we've already updated our component logic to expose an observable to emit our filtered task list, we can go directly to the view of our task list component and apply the changes to use the async pipe. Let's open the `src/app/tasks/task-list/task-list.component.html` file and implement the following changes:

```
<mac-toggle [buttonList]="taskFilterTypes"
            [activeButton]="activeTaskFilterType | async"
            (outActivate)="activateFilterType($event)">
</mac-toggle>
<mac-enter-task (outEnterTask)="addTask($event)"></mac-enter-task>
<div class="tasks">
  <mac-task *ngFor="let task of filteredTasks | async"
            [task]="task"
            (outUpdateTask)="updateTask($event)"></mac-task>
</div>
```

We've added two async pipes. The first one is to subscribe to our `activeTaskFilterType` behaviour subject. The async pipe will create a subscription directly from the view, and it will update our binding automatically whenever there's a new item emitted through the stream.

The second async pipe is used directly in the binding of the `NgFor` directive. We're subscribing to our `filteredTasks` observable, which will always emit the latest result of our filtered task list.

Recap

Congratulations! We've successfully updated our code to establish a reactive data flow within our application using the in-memory web API and the Angular HTTP client. We are using RxJS observables, transforming them using operators, and resolving our data directly within the view using the Angular async pipe. This refactoring was quite a technical but significant change. We're now following a very clean approach on how to react to application state changes. Our observable streams are router down directly into the view where we then subscribe using the async pipe. If Angular destroys our task list component, the async pipe will also take care of the necessary unsubscriptions. We've learned about the following topics:

- The Angular in-memory API to simulate a RESTful backend and using HTTP client to obtain data
- RxJS basics, basic operators, as well as behaviour subject and the `combineLatest` operator
- Using the async pipe to subscribe from the view of our components
- Establishing an end-to-end reactive data architecture within our application

Immutability

Within this section, we're going to learn about the concept of immutability. This knowledge will help us for the upcoming refactoring exercises of our application.

Immutable data has initially been a core concept of functional programming. This section will not cover immutable data in much depth, but it will explain the core concept so that we can talk about how to apply this idea to Angular components.

Immutable data structures force you to create a full copy of the data before you modify it. You'll never operate on the data directly, but on a copy of this same data. This approach has many benefits over mutable data operations, the most obvious probably being clean application state management. When you always operate on new copies of data, there's no chance that you're messing up data that you didn't want to modify.

Let's take this simple example, which illustrates the issues object references can cause:

```
const list = [1, 2, 3];
console.log(list === list.reverse()); // true
```

Although this seems odd at first, it makes sense that the output of this case is valid. `Array.reverse()` is a mutable operation, and it will modify the innards of the array. The actual reference will stay the same because JavaScript will not create a copy of the array to reverse it. Although technically this makes a lot of sense, this is not what we expected in the first place when we looked at this code.

We can quickly change this example to an immutable procedure by creating a copy of the array before we reverse it:

```
const list = [1, 2, 3];
console.log(list === list.slice().reverse()); // false
```

The issue with references is that they can cause a lot of unexpected side effects. Also, if we come back to our encapsulation topic from Chapter 1, *Component-Based User Interfaces*, object references are entirely against the concept of encapsulation. Although we might think that it would be safe to pass complex data types into a capsule, it's not. As we're dealing with references here, the data can still be modified from the outside, and our capsule will not have complete ownership. Consider the following example:

```
class Sum {
  constructor(data) {
    this.data = data;
    this.data.sum = data.a + data.b;
  }
  getSum() {
    return this.data.sum;
  }
}

const data = {a: 5, b: 8};
var sum = new Sum(data);
console.log(sum.getSum()); // 13
console.log(data.sum); // 13
```

Even if we only wanted to store the data internally in our `Sum` class, we would have created the unwanted side effect of referencing and modifying the data object which is outside the instance. Multiple `sum` instances would also share the same data from outside and cause more side effects. As a developer, you've learned to treat object references correct, but they still can cause a lot of problems.

We don't have these problems with immutable data, which can be illustrated easily with primitive data types in JavaScript. Primitive data types don't use references, and they are immutable by design:

```
let originalString = 'Hello there!';
let modifiedString = originalString.replace(/e/g, 3);
console.log(originalString); // Hello there!
console.log(modifiedString); // H3llo th3r3!
```

There's no way we can modify an instance of a string. Every modification that we perform on a string will generate a new string, and this prevents the unwanted side effects.

So, why do we still have object references within programming languages, even though they cause so many issues? Why aren't we performing all these operations on immutable data, and why aren't we only dealing with values rather than object references?

Of course, mutable data structures also come with their benefits, and it always depends on the context if immutable data brings value.

One of the main reasons that is often used against immutable data is its lousy performance. Of course, it costs some performance if we need to create tons of copies of our data every time we want to modify it. However, there are significant optimization techniques which eliminate the performance issues that we would usually expect from immutable data structures. Using a tree data structure that allows internal structural sharing, copies of the data will be shared internally. This technique allows for very efficient memory management, which in some situations even outperforms mutable data structures. I can highly recommend the paper by Chris Okasaki about *Purely Functional Data Structures* if you would like to read more about performance in immutable data structures.

JavaScript does not support immutable data structures out of the box. However, you can use libraries, such as Immutable.js by Facebook, which provide you with an excellent API to deal with immutable data. Immutable.js even implements structural sharing and makes it a perfect power tool if you decide to build on an immutable architecture in your application.

As with every paradigm, there are pros and cons, and depending on the context, one concept may fit better than another one. In our application, we won't use immutable data structures that are provided by third-party libraries, but we'll borrow some of the benefits that you get from immutable data by going by the following immutable idioms:

- **It's much easier to reason about immutable data**: You can always tell why your data is in a given state because you know the exact transformation path. This may sound irrelevant, but in practice, this is a huge benefit not only for humans to write code but also for compilers and interpreters to optimize it.
- **Using immutable objects makes change detection much faster**: If we rely on immutable patterns to treat our data, we can rely on object reference checks to detect change. We no longer need to perform complex data analysis and comparison for dirty checking, and can fully rely on checking references. We have the guarantee that object properties don't change without the object identity changing as well. This makes change detection as easy as `oldObject ===` `newObject`.

Immutability with TypeScript

With TypeScript 2, new type features were added which help you to embrace immutable operations. Using the `readonly` type modifier, we can achieve a compile-time immutability guard.

Let's look at the following example of how to use the `readonly` modifier to define some immutable data structures:

```
export interface Person {
  readonly firstName: string;
  readonly lastName: string;
}

let person: Person = {
  firstName: 'Peter',
  lastName: 'Griffin'
};

// This will result in a compile time error
person.firstName = 'Mag';
```

As you can see from the preceding example, we can use the `readonly` modifier to prevent object properties from being modified. Instead, if we'd like to modify the `person` object, we'll need to create a copy of that object. There are many ways to do this, however, using the object property spread operator is probably the most convenient of all. Let's see how we can update our person object in an immutable way using the object property spread operator:

```
export interface Person {
    readonly firstName: string;
    readonly lastName: string;
}

let person: Person = {
    firstName: 'Peter',
    lastName: 'Griffin'
};

person = {
  ...person,
  firstName: 'Mag'
};
```

Using the object property spread operator, we can spread all existing properties and their values of the existing person object into a new object literal. In the same step, we can then override any properties, right after the spread operation. This allows us to easily create a copy of an existing object and add or override specific properties. The preceding code could also be written by using `Object.assign`:

```
person = Object.assign({}, person, {
  firstName: 'Meg'
});
```

Actually, this is how the object spread operator is desugaring to JavaScript. However, it's much more convenient to use the spread operator than `Object.assign`. The object spread operator is proposed to the future JavaScript standard and is currently at stage 3.

Pure components

The idea of a "pure" component is that its whole state is represented by its inputs, where all inputs are immutable. This is effectively a stateless component, but additionally, all the inputs are immutable.

I like to call such components "pure" because their behaviour can be compared to the concept of pure functions in functional programming. A pure function is a function which has the following properties:

- It does not rely on any state outside of the function scope
- It always behaves the same and returns the same result if input parameters don't change
- It never changes any state outside the function scope (side effect)

With pure components, we have a simple guarantee. A pure component will never change without its input parameters being changed. Sticking to this idea about components gives us several advantages. Besides having a complete trust in your component state, we can also gain some performance benefits by optimizing the change detection of Angular. We know that a component will render exactly the same if its inputs don't change. This means that we can ignore all components and their subcomponents in change detection if there are no input changes.

It's very easy to reason about pure components. Their behaviour can be predicted very easily. Let's look at a simple illustration of a component tree with only pure components:

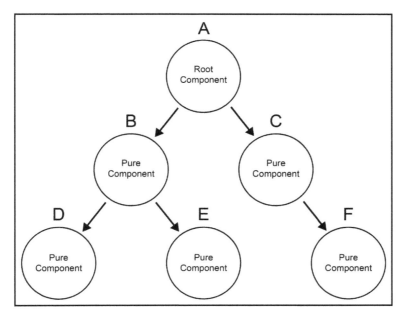

A component tree with immutable components

Usually, Angular performs change detection for every single binding in all of your components within the component tree. It does that on every browser event, which could change your system state. This eventually comes with a large performance overhead.

If we have the guarantee that each component in our tree has a stable state until an immutable input property changes, we can safely ignore change detection that would usually be triggered by Angular. The only way that such a component could change is if an input of the component changes. Let's say that there's an event that causes the root component (**A**) to change the input binding value of component (**B**), which will change the value of a binding on component (**E**). This event and the resulting procedure would mark a certain path in our component tree to be checked by change detection:

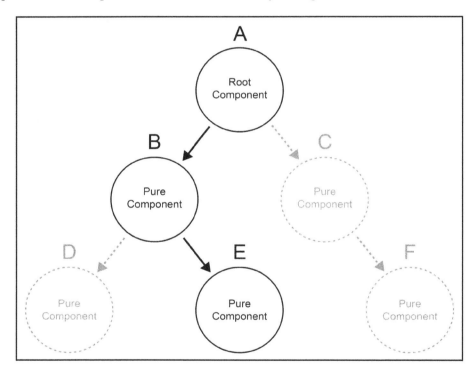

A marked path for change detection (in black) with "pure" components

Although the state of the root component changed, which also changed input properties of the subcomponents on two levels, we only need to be concerned about a given path when thinking about possible changes in the system. Pure components give us the promise that they will not change if their inputs don't change. Immutability plays a big role here. Imagine that you're binding a mutable object to component (**B**), and component (**A**) would change a property of this object. As we use object references and mutable objects, the property would also be changed for component (**B**). However, there's no way for component (**B**) to notice this change and it would leave our component tree in an unstable state. Basically, we'd need to go back to the regular dirty checking of the whole tree again.

By knowing that all our components are pure and that their inputs are immutable, we can tell Angular to disable change detection until an input property value changes. This makes our component tree very efficient, and Angular can optimize change detection effectively. When thinking about large component trees, this can make the difference between a stunningly fast application and a slow one.

The change detection of Angular is very flexible, and each component gets its own change detector. We can configure the change detection of a component by specifying the `changeDetection` property of the component decorator.

Using `ChangeDetectionStrategy`, we can choose from two strategies that apply for the change detection of our component. In order to tell Angular that our component should only be checked if an immutable input was changed, we can use the `OnPush` strategy. This change detection mode is specifically designed for the purpose of pure components.

Let's take a look at the two different configuration possibilities of component change-detection strategies and some possible use cases:

Change-detection strategy	Description
OnPush	This strategy tells Angular that a given component subtree will only change under one of the following conditions: • One of the input properties changes where changes need to be immutable. Inputs are always checked for reference changes (using the triple-equals operator ===) • An event binding within the component subtree is receiving an event. This condition tells Angular that there might be a change inside of the component itself and it will trigger change detection, even if none of the inputs have changed.
Default	The default strategy of Angular's change detection will perform change detection for every single browser event which occurs within your application.

Introducing container components

The main topic of this book is to learn how to create scalable user interfaces using Angular components. You can probably already see a trend within this chapter. From a simple task list component holding its own state, we're slowly moving into a more serious and maintainable application architecture. We've already been going through some major refactorings which can be summarized as follows:

- Creating a simple task list component to list some tasks coming from a simple list of plain objects
- Splitting the task list component into various subcomponents and finding the right size for our components (task list, task, checkbox, toggle)
- Introducing a service in order to store our task data and remove any data which was directly embedded into our components
- Using the Angular HTTP client and the in-memory web API to simulate asynchronous data fetching and using RxJS observables in our service and components

Within this section, we're going to learn about another concept which will enhance our maintainability even further. The concept of container components helps us to separate our user interface from our application state. This might sound difficult at the beginning but it's actually a concept which blends really nicely into our existing approach. With the introduction of container components, we're setting clear responsibilities when it comes to state management. Let's look at the following illustration to see the concept in action:

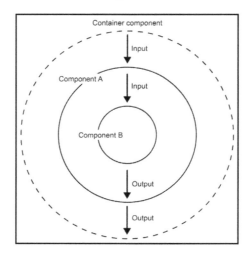

Container component and interactions with regular UI components

Container components are in charge of your application state. They are the only components of your system which are allowed to manipulate state and data. They are passing this state and data down into your user interface component through component input. Within the preceding illustration, we have a container component surrounding **Component A**. **Component A** is again consisting of a subcomponent, **B**. Data is flowing down from our container component into component **A** and **B**. Whenever the container provides new data, that data is seeping down into your user interface components through their inputs.

Now, here comes the tricky part of this concept. User interface components, like component **A** and **B** within our illustration, are never, ever manipulating data directly. They will always delegate to their parent component. I often explain this concept as a kind of **inversion of control (IoC)**. Instead of performing the action which was triggered by a user controlling the user interface directly, we just delegate to the parent component and tell it to perform this action. If the parent component is a simple UI component too, we delegate again. This goes on until we reach a container component. The container component then has the ability to effectively perform the desired operation on the application state. Once performed, the updated data will then seep back down the component tree. This approach of building user interfaces comes with an amazing list of positive effects on your application architecture:

- **All your data manipulation is handled in a central location**:
  This is really beneficial since we can always go to one single place if we need to change the way we manipulate our state and data.
- **All user interface components can be "pure"**:
  Since we won't have any user interface components which manipulate data directly, and they are only dependent on the data which is flowing down the component tree into their inputs, we can build "pure" components in most cases. This gives all the benefits of "pure" components, including the performance boost.
- **Container components act as adapter layers**:
  Since the container components are the only components which interact with your data services, database, state machine, or whatever else you're using to manage your state and data, we can see them as adapters of your application user interface to your data layer. When you decide to go differently about your state management and data sources, the only place where you need to apply changes is your container components.

- **Separation of state and user interface**:
  The separation of your application's state from your user interface is underestimated by far. By building a simple UI component which just accepts data through its inputs, we can build highly flexible and reusable components. If we would like to include them in a completely different context of state and data, we simply create another container component.

Purifying our task list

In the previous three sections, we looked into the basics of using immutable data structures and that Angular can be configured to assume that components only change when their input changes. We learned about the concept of "pure" components and how we can configure Angular's change detection to gain some performance benefits. We also learned about the concept of container components to separate our UI components from our application state.

Within this section, we would like to refactor our application to include our newly learned skills about immutability, "pure" components, and container components.

Let's start with our existing task list component. Currently, this component is directly interacting with data coming from the task service. However, we have learned that "pure" UI components should never directly retrieve or manipulate the state or data of our application. Instead, they should only depend on their inputs to retrieve data.

Open up the `src/app/tasks/task-list/task-list.component.ts` file and apply the following changes. The code changes are highlighted in bold:

```
import {Component, ChangeDetectionStrategy, EventEmitter, Input, Output,
ViewEncapsulation} from '@angular/core';
import {Task, TaskListFilterType} from '../../model';

@Component({
  selector: 'mac-task-list',
  templateUrl: './task-list.component.html',
  encapsulation: ViewEncapsulation.None,
  changeDetection: ChangeDetectionStrategy.OnPush
})
export class TaskListComponent {
  @Input() taskFilterTypes: TaskListFilterType[];
  @Input() activeTaskFilterType: TaskListFilterType;
  @Input() tasks: Task[];
  @Output() outAddTask = new EventEmitter<string>();
  @Output() outActivateFilterType = new EventEmitter<TaskListFilterType>();
```

```
@Output() outUpdateTask = new EventEmitter<Task>();

addTask(title: string) {
  this.outAddTask.emit(title);
}

activateFilterType(filterType: TaskListFilterType) {
  this.outActivateFilterType.emit(filterType);
}

updateTask(task: Task) {
  this.outUpdateTask.emit(task);
}
}
```

You can immediately see that our component is now much simpler. Instead of it containing all the filter logic, we're just relying on the tasks passed to the component using the `tasks` input. Our task list component is now assuming that the tasks coming into the component input are already filtered and that it's no longer in control of the filtering itself. It still renders the filters, however, as you can see from the `activateFilterType` method, we're now using output properties to delegate the filter action to the parent component. We've also added outputs for adding a task as well as for updating a task. We've learned from the previous section about container components that our UI components use inversion of control. That's exactly what is happening here. We're no longer manipulating our state, but instead delegating the manipulation to our parent component using output properties. The `addTask` method, as well as the `updateTask` method, are both just emitting output, nothing else.

The same principle which we used for the tasks is also applied to the filter type list and the active filter type. We're using the input properties `taskFilterTypes` and `activeTaskFilterType` so that we can pass this information down from the parent component. The task list is no longer in charge of controlling the state of the active filter type and we can control this state from the parent container component.

Since we're now assuming that tasks passed into the component using the task's input property are already filtered, we need to apply a small change to our component template, too. Also, we no longer need the async pipe in our task list component, since our component will receive the resolved array of filtered tasks directly. We'll let our container component deal with the observables. Let's open the `src/app/tasks/task-list/task-list.component.html` file and apply some changes. Changed code is highlighted in bold and the ellipsis symbol is indicating more hidden but irrelevant code:

```
...
<div class="tasks">
  <mac-task *ngFor="let task of tasks"
            [task]="task"
            (outUpdateTask)="updateTask($event)"></mac-task>
</div>
```

That's already it in our task list component. We're now only relying on input properties for obtaining the data required to render our component. This makes our component so much simpler, doesn't it?

Let's continue with the container component for our task list. We're creating a new component using the Angular CLI. This time, we're creating the component into a separate subfolder called `container`. As our application grows, and we have more container components that need to be created, we will put them all into this folder.

Also, note that we're now starting to use the `-cd onpush` option for generating components using the Angular CLI. This will add the change detection strategy `OnPush` onto our generated component stubs for us:

```
ng generate component --spec false -ve none -cd onpush container/task-list-container
```

The task list container is now responsible for dealing with the data necessary to render a task list component. It will also perform all the state and data manipulation required to cover the behaviour of our task list. Let's open the generated component class file:

```
import {ChangeDetectionStrategy, Component, ViewEncapsulation} from
'@angular/core';
import {TaskService} from '../../tasks/task.service';
import {Task, TaskListFilterType} from '../../model';
import {Observable, combineLatest, BehaviorSubject} from 'rxjs';
import {map} from 'rxjs/operators';

@Component({
  selector: 'mac-task-list-container',
  templateUrl: './task-list-container.component.html',
```

```
  encapsulation: ViewEncapsulation.None,
  changeDetection: ChangeDetectionStrategy.OnPush
})
export class TaskListContainerComponent {
  tasks: Observable<Task[]>;
  filteredTasks: Observable<Task[]>;
  taskFilterTypes: TaskListFilterType[] = ['all', 'open', 'done'];
  activeTaskFilterType = new BehaviorSubject<TaskListFilterType>('all');

  constructor(private taskService: TaskService) {
    this.tasks = this.taskService.getTasks();

    this.filteredTasks = combineLatest(this.tasks,
this.activeTaskFilterType)
      .pipe(
        map(([tasks, activeTaskFilterType]) => {
          return tasks.filter((task: Task) => {
            if (activeTaskFilterType === 'all') {
              return true;
            } else if (activeTaskFilterType === 'open') {
              return !task.done;
            } else {
              return task.done;
            }
          });
        })
      );
  }

  activateFilterType(type: TaskListFilterType) {
    this.activeTaskFilterType.next(type);
  }

  addTask(title: string) {
    const task: Task = {
      title, done: false
    };
    this.taskService.addTask(task);
  }

  updateTask(task: Task) {
    this.taskService.updateTask(task);
  }
}
```

When looking at the code of our new task list container component, you should notice something. The code is an exact copy of the code we had in our task list component before we turned it into a "pure" UI component. Well, does this look right? If you look at the code again, now that we have learned about separating the user interface concerns from our application state, you will notice that none of this code is actually the responsibility of a UI task list component. It's code that is mainly concerned with data manipulation and retrieval. It should actually never have been part of our task list UI component. This code clearly belongs to a container component.

The next step is to create the view template of our container component. A container component should actually never contain much code in the template. Ideally, the only thing you want to do within the view of a container component is to render the UI component which you're concerned with in that specific container. Let's open the `src/app/container/task-list-container/task-list-container.component.html` file and change its content to the following:

```
<mac-task-list
  [tasks]="filteredTasks | async"
  [taskFilterTypes]="taskFilterTypes"
  [activeTaskFilterType]="activeTaskFilterType | async"
  (outUpdateTask)="updateTask($event)"
  (outActivateFilterType)="activateFilterType($event)"
  (outAddTask)="addTask($event)">
</mac-task-list>
```

As you will have noticed, the only things we're concerned about in the view of our task list container component is to render a task list UI component. We're passing the list of filtered tasks into the task list component. Since we're using an observable within our container component, we use the async pipe again to subscribe and resolve to the most recently filtered task list. Similarly, we're passing the list of filter types and the currently active filter, which we both now store in our container, down into the task list component.

On the other hand, we're binding the outputs of the task list UI component and calling the necessary method within the container when we get notified about updated tasks, filter changes, and newly added tasks. The task list UI component just tells us **what** to do, and inside of the container component, that we know **how** to do it.

Summary

In this chapter, we have learned how to deal with data and application state in a way which is best for the maintainability of our application. We have switched our task service from synchronous operations on tasks stored within the service directly to using the Angular in-memory web API and the HTTP client.

We learned about how we can profit from concepts, such as reactive programming, observable data structures, and immutable objects, in order to make our application perform better, and most importantly, simple and easy to reason about.

We have also learned about the separation of user interface from application state and implemented the concept of container components into our application.

In the next chapter, we're going to organize our application on a larger scale. By introducing a new project layer, we can start organizing tasks within projects. We will create the necessary state and UI components in order to view and edit tasks within projects.

4
Thinking in Projects

It's time to think bigger. So far, we've created everything within our application around the concept of a simple task list. However, we want to build something bigger than that. Users should be able to organize their tasks into projects. Within this chapter, we're going to introduce a frame around our task list and make it feel like a full-blown application. With the introduction of a project component, the main navigation, tabbed interfaces, and a user area, we are moving a big step closer to our final application look.

We will create a reusable in-place editor component, which we will put into action on many existing areas within our application. With the help of this editor, the user experience of our system will increase tremendously, and our users will start to feel the underlying reactive architecture.

During this chapter, we will also create a commenting system that we build in a way that allows us to place it anywhere we'd like for our users to put comments.

Application security and proper user management are not within the scope of this book. However, we're going to create a dummy user service that will help us simulate a logged-in user. This service will be used by the commenting system, and we'll refactor our existing component to make use of it too.

We'll cover the following topics in this chapter:

- Introduction of a new project component and additional container components
- Two new RxJS operators called `switchMap` and `take`
- Creating a tabbed interface component for project detail navigation
- Using content projection to create a navigation UI component
- Using `contenteditable` to create an in-place editor
- Using `@HostBinding` and `@HostListener` to bind component members to host element properties and events
- Obtaining view elements using the `@ViewChild` decorator

- Performing DOM operations by using the `ElementRef` DOM abstraction
- Creating a commenting system that allows us to gather user comments in different areas of our application
- Summarizing a simple pipe to format relative time intervals using the third-party library Moment.js
- Creating an editor that enables users to edit text fields in-place

Moving into projects

Within this topic, we're going to implement the changes needed to move our simple task list into a structure that is organized by projects. For this purpose, we need to modify the main layout of our components as well as introduce a new component that represents our projects.

Project service

First, let's update our application model to include project data. For this, we're going to create a new model for a project as well as update the model of our tasks to add a project ID.

Open up the `src/app/model.ts` file and apply the following changes:

```
export interface Task {
  readonly id?: number;
  readonly projectId?: number;
  readonly title: string;
  readonly done: boolean;
}

export type TaskListFilterType = 'all' | 'open' | 'done';

export interface Project {
  readonly id?: number;
  readonly title: string;
  readonly description: string;
}
```

Each task is now including a reference to a project. The project entities are consisting of an ID, individual title, and description property. Let's also update our in-memory web API database. Open the `src/app/database.ts` file and apply the following changes:

```
import {InMemoryDbService} from 'angular-in-memory-web-api';
import {Project, Task} from './model';

export class Database implements InMemoryDbService {
  createDb() {
    const projects: Project[] = [
      {id: 1, title: 'My first project', description: 'This is your first
project.'},
      {id: 2, title: 'My second project', description: 'This is your second
project.'}
    ];

    const tasks: Task[] = [
      {id: 1, projectId: 1, title: 'Task 1', done: false},
      {id: 2, projectId: 1, title: 'Task 2', done: false},
      {id: 3, projectId: 1, title: 'Task 3', done: true},
      {id: 4, projectId: 1, title: 'Task 4', done: false}
    ];

    return {projects, tasks};
  }
}
```

We've added two projects to our database as well as updated all the tasks to include a reference to the first of the two projects.

Now, we are going to need a service to access our projects, and we should also update our task service to include a method that allows us to query for tasks that belong to a specific project.

First, let's apply the changes to the existing task service. Open up the `src/app/tasks/task.service.ts` file and implement the following changes. Effective changes are marked in bold, and the ellipsis character is indicating more code that is irrelevant for the changes to be applied:

```
import {Injectable} from '@angular/core';
import {HttpClient} from '@angular/common/http';
import {BehaviorSubject} from 'rxjs';
import {map} from 'rxjs/operators';
import {Task} from '../model';

@Injectable()
```

```
export class TaskService {
  ...

  getProjectTasks(projectId: number) {
    return this.tasks
      .asObservable()
      .pipe(
        map((tasks) => tasks.filter((task) => task.projectId ===
projectId))
      );
  }
}
```

The added `getProjectTasks` method is providing a mapped observable that takes our source tasks subject and maps each tasks array to produce a filtered tasks array that only includes tasks of a specific project.

Alright, now we need to create a new service that allows us to obtain information about the projects from our in-memory web API database. Let's use the Angular CLI to create a new service:

ng generate service --spec false project/project

The Angular CLI should have created our service on the path `src/app/project/project.service.ts`. Let's open that file and replace its content with the following code:

```
import {Injectable} from '@angular/core';
import {HttpClient} from '@angular/common/http';
import {BehaviorSubject, Observable, combineLatest} from 'rxjs';
import {map} from 'rxjs/operators';
import {Project} from '../model';

@Injectable()
export class ProjectService {
  private projects = new BehaviorSubject<Project[]>([]);
  private selectedProjectId = new BehaviorSubject<number>(1);
  private selectedProject: Observable<Project>;

  constructor(private http: HttpClient) {
    this.loadProjects();
    this.selectedProject = combineLatest(this.projects,
this.selectedProjectId)
      .pipe(
        map(([projects, selectedProjectId]) =>
        projects.find((project) => project.id === selectedProjectId)
      )
```

```
    );
  }

  private loadProjects() {
    this.http.get<Project[]>('/api/projects')
      .subscribe((projects) => this.projects.next(projects));
  }

  selectProject(id: number) {
    this.selectedProjectId.next(id);
  }

  getSelectedProject() {
    return this.selectedProject;
  }
}
```

Let's discuss the preceding code changes briefly. Our project service contains three members:

- **projects: BehaviourSubject<Project[]>**
  The `projects` member behaviour subject is emitting our whole project list once loaded from our database. This subject is the basis for all operations within our service.

- **selectedProjectId: BehaviourSubject<number>**
  Since we will need to know which of the projects is currently selected within our application, we need to store this information in our service. We're using a behaviour subject for emitting the currently selected project ID. This allows us to simply emit a project ID through `selectedProjectId` if we wish to select a given project.

- **selectedProject: Observable<Project>**
  The `selectedProject` observable will always emit the currently selected project. We'll make use of `combineLatest` to make sure if either `projects` or `selectedProjectId` emits a change. We will re-emit the updated, selected project through the `selectedProject` observable stream.

Within the constructor of our service, we're first calling the `loadProjects` method to do the HTTP call to our in-memory web API database to obtain the list of projects. Within the `loadProjects` method, we're sticking to the same pattern from our task service. We're subscribing to the HTTP service observable and emitting the resulting items through our internal `projects` subject.

After executing the `loadProjects` method within our constructor, we will create the `selectedProject` observable. We will use `combineLatest`, which we've discussed already in the previous chapter, to combine the `projects` and the `selectedProjectId` subjects into a single observable stream. Whenever one of those two input observables emits an event, `combineLatest` will combine the latest result of both input observables into a single item that is emitted through the output observable stream. We're using the map operator to extract the selected project from the list of projects and returning it as an item into the observable output stream.

Finally, the `selectProject` method is merely emitting the new project ID through the `selectedProjectId` subject. Since we're using this subject within the `selectedProject` observable created with `combineLatest`, this change will cause the `selectedProject` observable to re-emit the currently selected project.

As the last step, we need to add our new service to the app module providers. Let's open the `src/app/app.module.ts` file and apply the following changes:

```
...
import {ProjectService} from './project/project.service';

...
  providers: [ProjectService, TaskService],
...
```

Now, that's it for our project service for the moment. We've created our service in a highly reactive way, where we store all state within RxJS behavior subjects and react to change, transform streams, and emit where updates need to be communicated.

Project component

We've already implemented all necessary changes to deal with the model, data, and state for our projects. Now, it's time to move on to the components that are required to display our projects and the tasks that belong to them.

Let's start by creating the project component using the Angular CLI:

```
ng generate component --spec false -ve none -cd onpush project/project
```

First, let's change the component class file located in
`src/app/project/project/project.component.ts` by replacing its content with the
following code:

```
import {ChangeDetectionStrategy, Component, Input, ViewEncapsulation} from
'@angular/core';
import {Project} from '../../model';

@Component({
  selector: 'mac-project',
  templateUrl: './project.component.html',
  styleUrls: ['./project.component.css'],
  encapsulation: ViewEncapsulation.None,
  changeDetection: ChangeDetectionStrategy.OnPush
})
export class ProjectComponent {
  @Input() project: Project;
}
```

Nothing special here. We've created a simple project component that accepts a project
object as input. Let's move on the template of our new component and change the content
of the file in `src/app/project/project.component.ts`:

```
<header class="header">
  <h2 class="title">{{project.title}}</h2>
  {{project.description}}
</header>
<mac-task-list-container>
</mac-task-list-container>
```

Within our template, we first render the project header, which consists of the title and the
description of our project. After the project header, we want to render all project tasks. We
can just include the task list container component to do so.

Updating the task list container

That's it for our project component. However, our task list container is still implemented in
such a way that it deals with all available tasks and does not know anything about projects.
Let's change that by modifying our component class located in
`src/app/container/task-list-container.component.ts`. Changes are highlighted
in bold while irrelevant parts are hidden under an ellipsis character:

```
...
import {Project, Task, TaskListFilterType} from '../../model';
```

```
import {map, switchMap, take} from 'rxjs/operators';
import {ProjectService} from '../../project/project.service';

@Component({
  selector: 'mac-task-list-container',
  templateUrl: './task-list-container.component.html',
  encapsulation: ViewEncapsulation.None,
  changeDetection: ChangeDetectionStrategy.OnPush
})
export class TaskListContainerComponent {
  selectedProject: Observable<Project>;
  ...

  constructor(private taskService: TaskService, private projectService:
ProjectService) {
    this.selectedProject = this.projectService.getSelectedProject();

    this.tasks = this.selectedProject.pipe(
      switchMap((project) => this.taskService.getProjectTasks(project.id))
    );

    ...
  }

  ...

  addTask(title: string) {
    this.selectedProject
      .pipe(
        take(1)
      )
      .subscribe((project) => {
        const task: Task = {
          projectId: project.id, title, done: false
        };
        this.taskService.addTask(task);
      });
  }

  ...
}
```

First of all, we're introducing a new member called selectedProject, which is an observable stream that we obtain from our project service. Within the constructor of our component, we're injecting the project service and receiving the observable by calling the getSelectedProject method on our service. If you remember from the previous topic, this observable will always emit the currently selected project within our application.

Within the constructor, we also need to change the way we obtain our task list. Going forward, the task list that we're going to use within our container is always dependent on the selected project. To make this happen, we're going to look at a new RxJS operator called `switchMap`.

Let me first try to explain how `switchMap` works in one sentence. It takes an observable stream and for every item emitted, it connects a different observable stream to the output. This might sound confusing, so for you to get a better grasp on that new concept, let's look at a simplified example:

```
import {from, interval} from 'rxjs';
import {switchMap} from 'rxjs/operators';

const o1 = interval(1000);
const o2 = from(['a', 'b']);

o1.pipe(
  switchMap(() => o2)
).subscribe((item) => console.log(item));
```

The preceding example uses `switchMap` to connect an observable **(o2)** to a new output observable, every time the source observable **(o1)** is emitting an item. We're using the `interval` helper to create an observable that is emitting an item every second. For the second observable **(o2)**, we're using the `from` helper to generate an observable sequence that is emitting the strings **a** and **b** as separate items. After that, we're using the `switchMap` operator, which will create a new output observable that connects our **(o2)** observable to the output, whenever there's a new item emitted by the source observable **(o1)**. The preceding example will, therefore, log the strings **a** and **b** to the console each second:

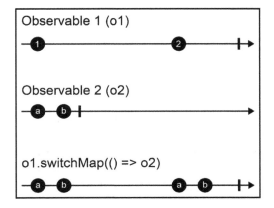

A stream diagram showing the behaviour of the switchMap operator

If you're used to Promises, then you can also think of the `switchMap` operator as building an asynchronous Promise chain by returning new Promises within the `then` function:

```
function timer(time) {
  return new Promise(resolve => setTimeout(resolve, time));
}

timer(1000)
 .then(() => timer(1000))
 .then(() => timer(1000))
 .then(() => timer(1000))
 .then(() => console.log('After 4 seconds!'));
```

By chaining Promises, we can perform four different asynchronous operations in sequence. The `switchMap` operator behaves almost the same, but instead, we could chain four different observables after each other:

```
import {timer} from 'rxjs';
import {switchMap} from 'rxjs/operators';

timer(1000).pipe(
  switchMap(() => timer(1000)),
  switchMap(() => timer(1000)),
  switchMap(() => timer(1000))
).subscribe((item) => console.log('After 4 seconds!'));
```

Okay, we have learned about the `switchMap` operator and how we can use it to chain multiple asynchronous operations in sequence. Now, let's go back to our task list container component and see how we can apply this concept to obtain project tasks. The following core excerpt is only showing the relevant part of the changes we have used already in our task list container component:

```
...
this.tasks = this.selectedProject.pipe(
  switchMap((project) => this.taskService.getProjectTasks(project.id))
);
...
```

In our case, we're using the `switchMap` operator to take the `selectedProject` observable as input and switch to the observable we're obtaining by the `getProjectTasks` call. This technique allows us to chain the two asynchronous operations, obtaining the selected project and receiving tasks, together in sequence. Within the callback of the `switchMap` operator, we are receiving the selected project object, and we use the ID of the project to obtain the observable of project tasks.

Now, every time the `selectedProject` observable is emitting a new value, our tasks observable will also emit the latest tasks of the selected project. Nice and reactive.

Alright! There's only one change left to discuss. Let's focus on the changes within the `addTask` method. Since our task model is now also including a `projectId` property, we need to make sure we're adding the correct project ID every time we create a task.

We make use of another unknown RxJS operator, `take`, within the code changes for the `addTask` method. Don't worry. The `take` operator works much more straightforward than the `switchMap` operator. Again, let's start with a simplification:

```
import {from} from 'rxjs';
import {take} from 'rxjs/operators';

from([1, 2, 3]).pipe(
  take(1)
).subscribe((item) => console.log(item));
```

The code in the preceding example will print the number one to the console. The numbers two and three will not be emitted by the output stream after the transformation using the `take` operator. The `take` operator will create a new observable stream that will only emit the number of items specified with the parameter passed to it. After the amount of items specified are emitted, the stream will close itself, even calling for unsubscription to all parent streams:

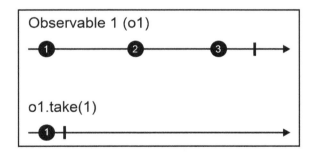

Input observable with three emissions is transformed to an output observable with one emission using the take operator

The `take` operator is especially impressive on our behaviour subjects, where you'd like to do some one-off actions on emitted items. Since behaviour subjects are always issuing the most recent item at a new subscription, we can use the take operator to immediately extract the latest value of the behaviour subject and do something with it.

Let's look at the code of our updated `addTask` method again to see how and why we're making use of the `take` operator there:

```
...
addTask(title: string) {
  this.selectedProject
    .pipe(
      take(1)
    )
    .subscribe((project) => {
      const task: Task = {
        projectId: project.id, title, done: false
      };
      this.taskService.addTask(task);
    });
}
...
```

First of all, we need to understand at which point in time the `addTask` method is getting called. This call happens whenever the user clicks on the add task button within the user interface. All we want to do now really is get the latest value of our `selectedProject` observable so that we can use the project ID to create our task associated with this project. However, if we'd subscribed to the `selectedProject` observable in a usual way, we'd keep those subscriptions within the `addTask` method active forever. This behaviour would mean that going forward when we call this method, let's say, ten times, on every change of the selected project, those ten subscriptions would fire again and create some unwanted duplicate tasks.

Using the `take` operator, we can prevent this behaviour. It allows us to create an observable stream that will be automatically unsubscribed once the desired amount of items have passed through. When we pass the number one as an item count parameter to the `take` operator, we can just take one item from the source stream and create a subscription that is only valid for this one item.

That's it for the changes within the task list container component. Till now, we have created a new project service, updated our existing task service, created a project component, and updated our task list container component to deal with the currently selected project. The last thing that is left to do is integrate our project component into the overall application as a top level component.

Integrating the project component

Within this topic, we're going to integrate the changes we've applied so far to our application. Currently, our root component is rendering a task list container component directly, which we will need to change to render our projects.

We could go ahead and render the project UI component directly within our application root component, however, we've learned that we should never include a top-level component without a container component to separate our state concerns from our user interface.

Let's fix this and use the Angular CLI to create a project container component:

```
ng generate component --spec false -ve none -cd onpush container/project-
container
```

After the component stub has been generated, open up the src/app/container/project-container/project-container.component.ts file and apply the following changes:

```
import {Component, ChangeDetectionStrategy, ViewEncapsulation} from
'@angular/core';
import {Observable} from 'rxjs';
import {Project} from '../../model';
import {ProjectService} from '../../project/project.service';

@Component({
  selector: 'mac-project-container',
  templateUrl: './project-container.component.html',
  styleUrls: ['./project-container.component.css'],
  encapsulation: ViewEncapsulation.None,
  changeDetection: ChangeDetectionStrategy.OnPush
})
export class ProjectContainerComponent {
  selectedProject: Observable<Project>;

  constructor(private projectService: ProjectService) {
    this.selectedProject = projectService.getSelectedProject();
  }
}
```

Nothing fancy here. We're using the project service to obtain the observable that is emitting the currently selected project. We're going to use this observable to render our project UI component. Let's open up the view template of our new container component located in `src/app/container/project-container/project-container.component.html` and replace the stub template with the following code:

```
<mac-project [project]="selectedProject | async">
</mac-project>
```

Also, the view template is ridiculously simple. However, we should not fall into the temptation of skipping a data container component just because things look too simple to be worth a wrapper. You should always bring up the discipline to stick to the rule that every top-level component needs a container component to handle the data and state concerns. It will save you a lot of time in the future.

Now, it's time to include the project container component in the view of our root component. At the same time, we'll also change the layout of our application slightly, and go one step further toward our final application look.

Let's open up the view template of our root component located in `src/app/app.component.html` and apply the following changes:

```
<aside class="side-nav"></aside>
<main class="main">
  <mac-project-container></mac-project-container>
</main>
```

We're adding two layout elements as well as our newly created project container component. That's it for our changes to integrate the project component into our application.

Recap

Congratulations! You've successfully implemented the first version of the project feature into our application. We've created a whole bunch of things in this topic. Besides building the model and database, services, and components, we have also integrated our feature successfully by creating and including a new project container component. Go ahead and preview our changes within your browser. I hope you're happy with the results and are looking forward to further enhancements.

Let's summarize what we did within this topic:

- Created and updated our model to include projects
- Implemented a new project service to obtain project data and updated the existing task service to deal with project tasks
- We've created a new project component as well as a project container component to separate our UI from state and data concerns
- We updated the task list container component to use the active project information to display only relevant project tasks
- We learned about the switchMap and take operators from RxJS and how to use them within our application
- Updated our root component view to include our project container component instead of the task list container

Creating a tabbed interface component

Let's introduce a new UI component to the project that will provide us with a tabbed interface that we can use for navigation purposes inside of the project component. We'd like to divide the project view into different areas that can be accessed through this tabbed interface:

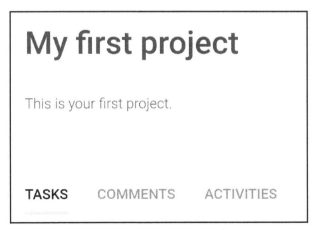

Screenshot of the tabbed interface we're going to create

Before we create a new component to render tabs, we will update our model to declare an interface that we're using to represent an individual tab. Open the `src/app/model.ts` file and apply the following changes:

```
...
export interface Tab {
  readonly id: any;
  readonly title: string;
}
```

Our tabs will always consist of a title and an ID, which will be useful later when we need to distinguish between individual tabs. Next, we're going to create our tabs component. Using the Angular CLI, we can create the stub of our new component:

```
ng generate component --spec false -ve none -cd onpush ui/tabs/tabs
```

Let's open up the component class located in `src/app/ui/tabs/tabs.component.ts` and add the following code:

```
import {
  ChangeDetectionStrategy, Component, EventEmitter, Input, Output,
ViewEncapsulation
} from '@angular/core';
import {Tab} from '../../model';

@Component({
  selector: 'mac-tabs',
  templateUrl: './tabs.component.html',
  styleUrls: ['./tabs.component.css'],
  encapsulation: ViewEncapsulation.None,
  changeDetection: ChangeDetectionStrategy.OnPush
})
export class TabsComponent {
  @Input() tabs: Tab[];
  @Input() activeTab: Tab;
  @Output() outActivateTab = new EventEmitter<Tab>();

  activateTab(tab: Tab) {
    this.outActivateTab.emit(tab);
  }
}
```

We're following the concept of simple and "pure" components and only using input to determine how we should render our tabs. Also, when a tab gets activated, we'll call the `activateTab` method that will then emit using the `outActivateTab` output. By now, you should be quite familiar with what you see in this component class and the concepts behind it. The `tabs` input is expected to be a list of tab objects, for which we've just created an interface within our model. Let's open the component view template located in `src/app/ui/tabs/tabs.component.html` and replace its content with the following code:

```
<ul class="tab-list">
  <li *ngFor="let tab of tabs"
      class="tab-list-item">
    <button class="tab-button"
            [class.tab-button-active]="activeTab?.id === tab.id"
            (click)="activateTab(tab)">{{tab.title}}</button>
  </li>
</ul>
```

We're repeating over our list of tabs and rendering a button as the effective tab element. On the tab button, we set a class based on the condition if the current tab from the repetition is the same tab that got passed into our component as an active tab. This will make our active tab look different from the rest. When the user clicks one of the tabs, we're calling the `activateTab` method and passing the clicked tab object as a parameter. Going back to the component code, you can see that we're then emitting this tab through the `outActivateTab` output.

Alright, that was already everything we need for our tabs component. Let's make use of our tabs in the project component and provide a tabbed interface to access the project's details.

First, let's open the project component class in `src/app/project/project/project.component.ts` and update our code with the following changes:

```
import {ChangeDetectionStrategy, Component, EventEmitter, Input, Output,
ViewEncapsulation} from '@angular/core';
import {Project, Tab} from '../../model';

...
export class ProjectComponent {
  @Input() project: Project;
  @Input() tabs: Tab[];
  @Input() activeTab: Tab;
  @Output() outActivateTab = new EventEmitter<Tab>();

  activateTab(tab: Tab) {
```

```
    this.outActivateTab.emit(tab);
  }
}
```

We're going to use the tabs component in our project component, and therefore we need to provide the necessary input and handle the output of the tabs component. For this reason, our project component will now also contain the inputs `tabs` and `activeTab`.

We've learned from the previous chapter, `Chapter 3`, *Dealing with Data and State,* that our UI components should always delegate output until they reach a container component. Following this concept will ensure we're separating our state and data manipulation from our UI components, which will significantly enhance the overall maintainability of our code. Since our tabs component will notify us of a change in the active tab, we will respond to this by delegating and merely re-emitting the `outActivateTab` output.

Alright, let's open up the project view template located in `src/app/project/project/project.comonent.html` and edit it with the following changes:

```
<header class="header">
  <h2 class="title">{{project.title}}</h2>
  {{project.description}}
</header>
<mac-tabs [tabs]="tabs"
          [activeTab]="activeTab"
          (outActivateTab)="activateTab($event)">
</mac-tabs>
<mac-task-list-container *ngIf="activeTab.id === 'tasks'">
</mac-task-list-container>
```

We're rendering our tabs component, passing down the tabs objects and the currently active tab we've received as input to the project component. We'll also listen for a tab activation output on the tabs component and call the `activateTab` method within the project component.

We're also using the information of the active tab to decide if we should render the task list container component or not. Only if the ID of the currently active tab equals to "tasks" will we render the task list.

Okay, now we need to make sure we're passing the data required for the tabs down to the project component. We also need to ensure that when a tab is activated, we're performing the necessary changes to our application state. The project container component renders the project component, so let's open up the component class located in `src/app/container/project-container/project-container.component.ts` and apply the following changes:

```
...
import {Project, Tab} from '../../model';

...
export class ProjectContainerComponent {
  selectedProject: Observable<Project>;
  tabs: Tab[] = [
    {id: 'tasks', title: 'Tasks'},
    {id: 'comments', title: 'Comments'},
    {id: 'activities', title: 'Activities'}
  ];
  activeTab: Tab = this.tabs[0];

  ...
  activateTab(tab: Tab) {
    this.activeTab = tab;
  }
}
```

Since we're now in a container component, it's okay to store state and perform actions on that state. We're adding a list of tab objects where we are already thinking a bit ahead. The **Comments** tab will be used to switch to our commenting system that we'll be building later in this chapter. The **Activities** tab will be used in a later chapter of this book.

We're also storing the currently active tab using the `activeTab` member and initializing it with the first tab within our tabs list.

The code within the `activateTab` method looks almost too simple to be right. All we're doing is accepting a tab object as a parameter and updating our `activeTab` member.

Now, all that's left to do for making use of our tabs component is updating the bindings within the project container component. Let's open the component view template located in `src/app/container/project-container/project-container.component.html` and apply the following changes:

```
<mac-project [project]="selectedProject | async"
             [tabs]="tabs"
             [activeTab]="activeTab"
             (outActivateTab)="activateTab($event)">
</mac-project>
```

That was easy, right? This last change was already everything required to provide a friendly tabbed interface to our project component. We'll make use of the `activeTab` property to activate more detail views of our project going forward. At the moment, the **Tasks** tab is the only tab enabling something within our user interface, but as continue adding features, we'll use the other two tabs for navigation too.

Building the main navigation

In this chapter, we've already added a project feature to our application. We've also added a tabbed interface to navigate the details of a project. However, there's still no way to navigate between projects. That's what we're going to change now. In this section, we will create components to build our main navigation. We will then integrate it and use it to navigate between all existing projects within the application:

Screenshot of the main navigation we're going to build in this section of the book

We are designing our navigation components in such a way that we can quickly make use of them in any situation. For achieving this goal, we're going to look at a new concept within Angular, which is called content projection. With the use of content projection, we can achieve a new level of component composition.

Composition using content projection

Content projection allows you to insert a view portion from a parent component into its child component. This concept is a potent tool when it comes to composition. With so-called content slots, we can mark a position within our child component where we'd like to give our parent components the opportunity to pass in a view portion.

Let's look at a simple content projection example that helps us understand what this is good for:

```
@Component({
  selector: 'mac-reveal-content',
  template: `
    <h2 (click)="showContent = !showContent">{{revealTitle}}</h2>
    <div *ngIf="showContent" class="content">
      <ng-content></ng-content>
    </div>
  `
})
export class RevealContentComponent {
  @Input() title: string;
  showContent = false;
}

@Component({
  selector: 'mac-root',
  template: `
    <mac-reveal-content revealTitle="Click to show more">
      <p>I'm the content which is shown or hidden when you click the above
title</p>
    </mac-reveal-content>
  `
})
export class AppComponent {}
```

The preceding example is showing a straightforward UI component called the reveal content component. It's showing a title that we can click on to show or hide content. This behaviour is advantageous in a lot of situations and is similar to the concept of an accordion or collapsible component.

There are two things in this example that are unique and should look unfamiliar to you. I've also highlighted those two lines of code for you so that you can see them popping out right away.

Within our reveal content component, we're using the `<ng-content>` element to mark the position for content to be projected from a parent component. This element is also called a content projection slot, and you can have multiples of those slots within your component view.

The second thing, which is something we've never done so far, is within the app component of the preceding example. We put some template code between the reveal content component open and close tags. Usually, a component will eliminate any template code that is put into its host element. However, before it does so, it first checks if the child component contains content projection slots. If there are content projection slots within the child component, it will project any view portion found in the host element into the child component at the designated position. This is the position we've marked using the `<ng-content>` element.

 Content projection and projection slots are concepts borrowed from the web components Shadow DOM specification. Angular does not yet use Shadow DOM by default, and therefore the behaviour is emulated. However, the concept is the same. If you're familiar with Angular.js, the first version of Angular, content projection is very similar to the idea of transclusion from Angular.js.

Additionally, we can use a select attribute on the `<ng-content>` element to set a CSS-like selector. This selector will be used to selectively choose that elements should be projected into the specific content slot. In this way, you can have multiple content slots that cover different requirements.

Elements from the component host element can only be projected once, and this content projection works by going through all the `<ng-content>` elements in sequential order by projecting any matching elements. If you have multiple competing content projection slots in your template, the first one will win and receive the elements that get projected into your component.

Let's look at another example that illustrates this behavior:

```
@Component({
  selector: 'mac-multi-projection',
  template: `
    <header class="title">
      <ng-content select="h1"></ng-content>
    </header>
    <main class="rest-content">
      <ng-content></ng-content>
    </main>
  `
```

```
})
export class MultiProjectionComponent {}

@Component({
  selector: 'mac-root',
  template: `
    <mac-multi-projection>
      <h1>This title will be projected in the first slot</h1>
      <p>Any other element will be projected into the second, generic
slot</p>
    </mac-multi-projection>
    `
})
export class AppComponent {}
```

The preceding example shows how we can use selective content projection using the
`select` attribute on a `<ng-content>` element. The `h1` title element is projected into the
first content projection slot since we're using a CSS selector that matches all `h1` elements.
The second content slot does not contain a `select` attribute and therefore accepts all other
elements that are projected into the component.

Creating navigation components

We will build our navigation from three separate components. Let's look at their purpose
real quick:

- **The navigation item component**: Represents one navigation item within our
  navigation. Its responsibility is to render the title of a navigation item as well as
  its behavior when an item is activated.
- **The navigation section component**: This is used to visually separate navigation
  items that belong together. We can use this component to group navigation items
  under a title. This grouping makes it easier for our users to find the navigation
  items they are looking for.
- **The navigation component**: This holds the full navigation together. It's just a
  container that contains our navigation section components together.

By using selective content projection, we can provide an excellent content-based API, which
makes it easy to use our navigation components in any situation. The benefit of building
content-based APIs is that we can compose our components together, only by including
them in a view template.

Let's start by creating the lowest of the three components, the navigation item:

```
ng generate component --spec false -ve none -cd onpush ui/navigation-
item/navigation-item
```

Let's open up the view templated located in `src/app/ui/navigation-item/navigation-item.component.html` and change its content with the following code:

```
{{title}}
```

Yes, I know, it looks too simple to be true. But that's all we need within the view of our navigation item component. Let's move on to the component class of the navigation item located in `src/app/ui/navigation-item/navigation-item.component.ts`:

```
import {
  ChangeDetectionStrategy, Component, EventEmitter, HostListener, Input,
Output,
  ViewEncapsulation
} from '@angular/core';

@Component({
  selector: 'mac-navigation-item',
  templateUrl: './navigation-item.component.html',
  styleUrls: ['./navigation-item.component.css'],
  encapsulation: ViewEncapsulation.None,
  changeDetection: ChangeDetectionStrategy.OnPush
})
export class NavigationItemComponent {
  @Input() title: string;
  @Input() navId: any;
  @Output() outActivateNavigationItem = new EventEmitter<any>();

  @HostListener('click')
  activateNavigationItem() {
    this.outActivateNavigationItem.emit(this.navId);
  }
}
```

Besides a `title` input, the component also takes an input, `navId`, to be used later during activation. This ID will help us in our parent component when detecting which of the navigation items was activated.

We are using a new decorator within our component that we haven't used before. The @HostListener decorator is a handy addition to our Angular toolset. With the help of host listeners, you can create event bindings on the component host element, but handle them within your component. Usually, the host element is not in direct control of our component. The host element always resides within the parent component where our component is placed. However, sometimes it's required to bind to properties or events of that element. Just like in our case, where we'd like to bind to the click event on the host element of our component. You can use the @HostListener decorator on a method to bind that method to a specific event on the host element. Pass the event name you'd like to bind to as a parameter to the decorator. In our case, we're binding to the click event on the navigation item host element. Each time the click event is fired, our activateNavigationItem method will be executed.

Inside the activateNavigationItem method, after a navigation item is clicked, we're emitting the ID of the specific navigation item through the outActivateNavigationItem output.

Alright, that's it for our navigation items. Let's move one level higher within our navigation component tree and create the navigation section component:

```
ng generate component --spec false -ve none -cd onpush ui/navigation-
section/navigation-section
```

The navigation section component is responsible for grouping navigation items together. Let's open the view template located in src/app/ui/navigation-section/navigation-section.component.html first and apply the necessary changes:

```
<div class="title">{{title}}</div>
<div class="item-list">
  <ng-content select="mac-navigation-item"></ng-content>
</div>
```

Each navigation section consists of a title as well as a list of navigation items. Now, we're making use of content projection, which we looked at in the previous section. We're marking a place within our view template where view portions from the parent component can be projected into the navigation section component. Since we know that we only want the navigation item component to be projected into our navigation section, we are using a select attribute on the <ng-content> element. By setting the select attribute to a value of mac-navigation-item, Angular will only project navigation item components into this content slot.

Let's also apply the changes to our navigation section component class located in `src/app/ui/navigation-section/navigation-section.component.ts`:

```
import {ChangeDetectionStrategy, Component, Input, ViewEncapsulation} from
'@angular/core';

@Component({
  selector: 'mac-navigation-section',
  templateUrl: './navigation-section.component.html',
  styleUrls: ['./navigation-section.component.css'],
  encapsulation: ViewEncapsulation.None,
  changeDetection: ChangeDetectionStrategy.OnPush
})
export class NavigationSectionComponent {
  @Input() title: string;
}
```

This component class is elementary. The only thing we do here is to provide a title input that is rendered within our navigation section view. The rest of our component logic is handled using content projection, which is providing us with a beautiful content-based API.

Now, we could already go ahead and use those two components in conjunction and arrange them in any view template within our application. As an example, we could write a navigation for accessing cute dog pictures:

```
<mac-navigation-section title="Dogs">
  <mac-navigation-item navId="pug" title="Pug"></mac-navigation-item>
  <mac-navigation-item navId="french-bulldog" title="French Bulldog"></mac-navigation-item>
  <mac-navigation-item navId="corgi" title="Corgi"></mac-navigation-item>
</mac-navigation-section>
```

That's the big strength of content-based APIs. Using content projection, we provide the ability to compose complex component trees and configure behaviour using only view templates. This comes with a significant ease of use. Not surprisingly, a lot of Angular UI libraries are using content projection to create their APIs, simply because it's just so much easier to configure everything you need declaratively using Angular templates.

Okay, now, let's create the last component of our three—the navigation component. The navigation component is putting a frame on our navigation and is grouping navigation sections together:

```
ng generate component --spec false -ve none -cd onpush
ui/navigation/navigation
```

First, let's open the view template of the navigation component located in `src/app/ui/navgiation/navigation.component.html` and change its content to the following code:

```
<nav>
  <ng-content select="mac-navigation-section"></ng-content>
</nav>
```

We're using content projection again to project elements into our navigation view. This time, we're selecting only navigation section components. Let's also change our component class in `src/app/ui/navigation/navigation.component.ts`:

```
import {Component, ViewEncapsulation} from '@angular/core';

@Component({
  selector: 'mac-navigation',
  templateUrl: './navigation.component.html',
  styleUrls: ['./navigation.component.css'],
  encapsulation: ViewEncapsulation.None
})
export class NavigationComponent {

}
```

Okay, this is as simple as a component class could be. The class is empty, and we're not providing any particular component configuration. You might wonder why we even need this component. Well, to decide about the right to exist for our components, we need to look at all parts that are defining the component. The component class might not contain any behavioral content. However, the styles and the component view could provide material that makes the component worth existing. If you're using content projection, you often end up with very little code within your classes, and that's fine. As long as the content projection or even only encapsulated styles provide us developers with a more convenient API, we should feel right about the architecture.

Coming back to the overall navigation component tree, things might start to get a bit confusing, which is normal when multiple levels are involved. Just to recap quickly:

- The navigation item is rendering a title and dealing with the behaviour when an item is getting activated
- The navigation sections render a section title and project navigation items
- The navigation solely projects navigation sections and acts as a container around our navigation

Now, we're ready to use our navigation components and put them into action within our application!

Providing a project navigation

Within this section, we're going to use the navigation components we've just created to provide a project navigation. For this, we're first going to introduce the necessary changes in the app component class located in `src/main/app/app.component.ts`. This is the first time we are dealing with the app or root component class. Since this is our root component, we're treating it like a container component, and it gets the privileges to deal with state and data:

```
import {Component, ViewEncapsulation} from '@angular/core';
import {Observable} from 'rxjs';
import {Project} from './model';
import {ProjectService} from './project/project.service';

@Component({
  selector: 'mac-root',
  templateUrl: './app.component.html',
  styleUrls: ['./app.component.css'],
  encapsulation: ViewEncapsulation.None
})
export class AppComponent {
  projects: Observable<Project[]>;
  selectedProject: Observable<Project>;

  constructor(private projectService: ProjectService) {
    this.projects = projectService.getProjects();
    this.selectedProject = this.projectService.getSelectedProject();
  }

  selectProject(id: number) {
    this.projectService.selectProject(id);
  }
}
```

We're storing two observables within our app component. Using the project service, we're obtaining an observable that emits the list of available projects. We're also storing the observable that emits the currently selected project.

The `selectProject` method is accepting a project ID as a parameter and delegates the call to our project service. This will then cause all observers who subscribed to the selected project observable to receive the newly selected project. If you remember, we're already using this observable within our task list container component.

Let's move on to the view template of our app component located in `src/app/app.component.html` and apply the following changes:

```
<aside class="side-nav">
  <mac-navigation>
    <mac-navigation-section title="Projects">
      <mac-navigation-item *ngFor="let project of projects | async"
                           [navId]="project.id"
                           [title]="project.title"
                           [class.active]="project.id === (selectedProject
| async).id"
(outActivateNavigationItem)="selectProject($event)">
      </mac-navigation-item>
    </mac-navigation-section>
  </mac-navigation>
</aside>
<main class="main">
  <mac-project-container></mac-project-container>
</main>
```

We're using our navigation components to create a project navigation in the space that is reserved for our main navigation. At the moment, we're rendering just one navigation section that belongs to our projects. By using the `NgFor` directive, we're repeating a navigation item component for each project within the list of available projects. We're binding the project ID to the `navId` input as well as the project title to the `title` input of our navigation item. Additionally, we're setting an active class on the navigation item component if the specific project is currently selected.

If one of the navigation items is activated, we call the `selectProject` method of our app component and pass the ID that is emitted by the `outActivgateNavigationItem` as `$event`.

That's it! You have successfully built a project navigation. It's a good time to preview your changes in the browser now. You should already be able to navigate between the two projects that were added into our database. Since our task list container is already making use of the selected project observable, the logic of switching between projects should already be seamless. You can try to navigate to the second project, which does not contain any tasks. Try adding tasks and switching between the two projects.

Recap

Within this section, we've created our navigation components and used them to create our project navigation. You have learned about the following concepts:

- Using content projection to build a content-based API for your components
- The idea of content projection slots and the use of `<ng-content>`
- Using the `select` attribute on content slots to selectively project content
- Using the `@HostListener` decorator to bind host element events to component methods

One editor to rule them all

We will be processing a lot of user input within our application. Therefore, it's crucial to provide a pleasant authoring experience to our users. Users need to be able to edit project titles, descriptions, and task titles. Within the commenting system, which we are creating later in this chapter, users also need to be able to edit their comments. We could use regular text area input and work with dialogue boxes to edit those fields, but this seems too old-fashioned for a modern user interface. Native input fields are fantastic, but sometimes they don't provide an outstanding user experience. What we're looking for is a way to edit stuff in-place:

A screenshot of our in-place editor in action, showing the save and cancel buttons

To build our in-place editor, we're going to use the contenteditable API that will enable a user to modify the content within HTML elements directly.

The following example illustrates how we can use the `contenteditable` attribute to make HTML elements editable:

```html
<h1 contenteditable>I'm an editable title</h1>
<p>I can't be edited</p>
```

Run the preceding example on a blank HTML page and click on the `h1` text. You will see that the element has become editable and you can type to modify its content.

Getting notified about changes within editable elements is relatively easy. There's an input event emitted on every DOM element that is editable, and this will allow us to react to change easily:

```js
const h1 = document.querySelector('h1');
h1.addEventListener('input', event => console.log(h1.textContent));
```

With this example, we have already created a naive implementation of an in-place editor where we're able to monitor changes applied by the user. Within this topic, we'll use this standard technology to build a reusable component that we can use wherever we want to make things editable.

Creating an editor component

First, let's create a new stub component for our editor using the Angular CLI:

```
ng generate component --spec false -ve none -cd onpush ui/editor/editor
```

After the files have been generated, so let's open up the component class located in `src/ui/editor/editor.component.ts` and apply the following code changes:

```ts
import {
  AfterViewInit, ChangeDetectionStrategy, Component, ElementRef,
EventEmitter, HostBinding, HostListener,
  Input, OnChanges, Output, SimpleChanges, ViewChild, ViewEncapsulation
} from '@angular/core';

@Component({
  selector: 'mac-editor',
  templateUrl: './editor.component.html',
  styleUrls: ['./editor.component.css'],
  encapsulation: ViewEncapsulation.None,
  changeDetection: ChangeDetectionStrategy.OnPush
})
export class EditorComponent implements OnChanges, AfterViewInit {
  @ViewChild('editableContentElement') editableContentElement: ElementRef;
```

```
@HostBinding('class.edit-mode') editMode = false;
@Input() content: string;
@Input() showControls: boolean;
@Output() outSaveEdit = new EventEmitter<string>();
@Output() outCancelEdit = new EventEmitter<never>();

ngOnChanges(changes: SimpleChanges) {
  if (changes.content && this.editableContentElement) {
    this.setEditableContent(this.content);
  }
}

ngAfterViewInit() {
  this.setEditableContent(this.content);
}

@HostListener('click')
focusEditableContent() {
  if (this.editMode) {
    this.editableContentElement.nativeElement.focus();
  }
}

saveEdit() {
  this.editMode = false;
  this.outSaveEdit.emit(this.getEditableContent());
}

cancelEdit() {
  this.editMode = false;
  this.setEditableContent(this.content);
  this.outCancelEdit.emit();
}

beginEdit() {
  this.editMode = true;
}

private getEditableContent() {
  return this.editableContentElement.nativeElement.textContent;
}

private setEditableContent(content: string) {
  this.editableContentElement.nativeElement.textContent = content;
}
}
```

Okay, that's quite a lot of new code. Let's dissect the different parts of the editor component and go through each part step by step.

Within our editor component, we'll need to interact with the native DOM element, which we make editable using the contenteditable API. The easiest and also the safest method to do this is to use the `@ViewChild` decorator to retrieve a DOM element by using local view references:

```
@ViewChild('editableContentElement') editableContentElement: ElementRef;
```

The `@ViewChild` decorator can be used to search our component view for a specific DOM element or a component instance. When we'd like to search our view for a particular component instance, we can just pass the component class as a parameter to the decorator. When searching for a DOM element, we need to pass a string that should match a local view reference on one of the elements within our component view. Angular returns a type called `ElementRef` when we're searching our view for DOM elements. This object is just a wrapper around native DOM elements, which you can then use to access the DOM element.

If we want to search the component subtree for one single DOM element or component instance, we can use the `@ViewChild` decorator. We can also search for a list of DOM elements or component instances using the `@ViewChildren` decorator:

Query decorator	Description
@ViewChildren (selector)	Will query the current component's view for either directives or components and return an object of the type `QueryList`. If the view is dynamically updated, the list will be updated as well. When the selector parameter is a directive or component type, the query decorator will search our component view for matching directives or components and return a list of directive or component instances. The selector parameter can also be a string that is then used as a local view reference name to find DOM elements containing this local view reference.
@ViewChild (selector)	Will query for only the first matching component or directive instance or a DOM element containing the specific local view reference.

If you need to communicate with view child components directly, you can use the @ViewChild and @ViewChildren decorators to get hold of those components. Sometimes, this is required, but this technique should be used carefully. Direct component communication only makes sense when you have requirements that can not be fulfilled by using component input and output.

 Sometimes, you need to run some initialization code on view children after your component is initialized. In such cases, you can use the AfterViewInit life cycle hook. While the view child properties of your component class will still be undefined within the constructor of your component, they will be populated and initialized after the AfterViewInit life cycle callback.

Let's move back to our editor component code. The next thing we're going to look at is another property in our editor component called editMode:

```
@HostBinding('class.edit-mode') editMode = false;
```

Our editor is functioning in two modes. The editMode property is used inside of our component to determine if the editor is in edit mode or display mode. The default mode of the editor component is the display mode. A user can then switch an editor to edit mode, where he/she will be able to edit the content within the editor. After he/she's done editing, he/she can save or discharge the changes. This action will also switch the component back into display mode (where editorMode is false again).

We are using the @HostBinding decorator to set the CSS class edit-mode on the component host element conditionally. This state class will help us to style our component differently, depending on the editor mode.

Next, let's take a look at the input properties of our component:

```
@Input() content: string;
@Input() showControls: boolean;
```

The content input property can be used to set the content of our editor from the parent components. This input is required to set the initial content that appears when our editor is in display mode.

The second input property, `showControls`, controls whether the editor should show the control functions. When this input is annoying to false, the editor does not show any controls and therefore acts in read-only mode. Three UI controls will be shown in our editor when this property is set to true:

- **Edit button**: If the editor is in display mode, the edit button is the only visible control on the editor. When a user clicks this button, the editor component will switch into edit mode by setting `editMode` to true.
- **Save button**: This control will only be shown if the component is in edit mode. It's there to save any changes performed by the user and switch the component back to display mode.
- **Cancel button**: This control is shown along with the save button when the component is in edit mode. If activated, the component will switch back to display mode, reverting any changes that were typed into the editor by the user.

Besides our input properties, we also need some output properties to notify the outer world about the changes within our editor. Let's quickly discuss the two output properties we're exposing on our component:

```
@Output() outSaveEdit = new EventEmitter<string>();
@Output() outCancelEdit = new EventEmitter<never>();
```

The `outSaveEdit` output is emitting the updated content once the user applies any changes to the editor content and has clicked the save button.

Our editor component works in a simple way. If the component is in edit mode, it shows an element that can be edited using the contenteditable API. However, once the editor switches back to display mode, we see a different element that cannot be edited. CSS controls the visibility within the modifier class, which is set by the host element property binding to the `editMode` flag.

Angular has no control over the content within our editable element. We control this content manually by using native DOM operations. Let's look at how we do this:

```
private getEditableContent() {
  return this.editableContentElement.nativeElement.textContent;
}

private setEditableContent(content: string) {
  this.editableContentElement.nativeElement.textContent = content;
}
```

These two private methods can be used inside of our editor component to obtain the content of our editable DOM element or to set its content, respectively.

We've already discussed the editableContentElement property of our editor component and how we obtain a reference to the editable element within our component view using the @ViewChild decorator.

Angular does not directly provide us with a DOM element reference but a wrapper object of the type ElementRef. It's a wrapper around the native DOM element, which holds additional information that is relevant to Angular. Using the nativeElement property, we can obtain a reference to the underlying native DOM element.

 The ElementRef wrapper plays an integral part in Angular's platform-agnostic architecture. It allows you to run Angular in different environments (for example, on a server, native mobile, web workers, or others). It's part of an abstraction layer between the components and their views.

Let's see how we set editable content within our component view using the setEditableContent method. First, we want to make sure that when our view is ready, we are initializing the editable content with the text present in our content component input. For this, we can use the AfterViewInit life cycle hook. We also needed a way to react to changes to the content input property, and update the editable content element based on that. We can use the life cycle hook OnChanges for this purpose:

```
ngOnChanges(changes: SimpleChanges) {
  if (changes.content && this.editableContentElement) {
    this.setEditableContent(this.content);
  }
}

ngAfterViewInit() {
  this.setEditableContent(this.content);
}
```

Within the ngOnChanges callback, once a change in the content input property is detected, we can reflect the changed content onto our editable element. It's important to check whether the editableContentElement input is already set before we call setEditableContent. Since the OnChanges life cycle hook is called before the AfterViewInit life cycle, the editableContentElement obtained by our @ViewChild query will not be available yet. Because of that, we also need to use the ngAfterViewInit callback to set the initial content of our editable element once our component view has initialized.

Okay, so far, we've looked at how we can reflect the content input of our component into the editable element within the view of the editor component. Now, let's take a look at the implementation of the three user actions within the editor. These are the three actions for the edit, save, and cancel buttons:

```
saveEdit() {
  this.editMode = false;
  this.outSaveEdit.emit(this.getEditableContent());
}

cancelEdit() {
  this.editMode = false;
  this.setEditableContent(this.content);
  this.outCancelEdit.emit();
}

beginEdit() {
  this.editMode = true;
}
```

When our editor is in display mode, a user can only activate edit mode. We are taking care of that using the `beginEdit` method. If a user clicks the edit button on our editor component, the only thing we need to do is switch our editor into edit mode. We can do that by merely setting the `editMode` property to `true`.

Whatever we've discussed thus far concerning the code is good enough for us to set up a fully functional component. However, the last part of the code, which we haven't discussed yet, relates to ensuring better accessibility of our editor. Since our editor component is a bit larger than the editable element, we also want to make sure that a click anywhere inside the editor component will cause the editable element to be focused. The following code makes this happen:

```
@HostListener('click')
focusEditableContent() {
  if (this.editMode) {
    this.editableContentElement.nativeElement.focus();
  }
}
```

Using the `@HostListener` decorator, we are registering an event binding on our component host element that calls the `focusEditableContent` method. Inside this method, we are using the reference to the editable DOM element and triggering a focus.

That was the last missing piece of code to discuss within our component class. Let's look at the template of our component, which is located within the `src/app/ui/editor/editor.component.html` file, to see how the code we've just created in our component class is related to the component view:

```
<div #editableContentElement
     class="editable-content"
     contenteditable="true"></div>
<div class="output">{{content || '-'}}</div>
<div *ngIf="showControls && !editMode"
     class="controls">
  <button (click)="beginEdit()" class="icon-edit"></button>
</div>
<div *ngIf="showControls && editMode"
     class="controls">
  <button (click)="saveEdit()" class="icon-save"></button>
  <button (click)="cancelEdit()" class="icon-cancel"></button>
</div>
```

The logic within the editor component template is quite straightforward. If you've been following the component code, you'll now be able to identify the different elements that compose this component's view.

The first element within the CSS class, `editable-content`, is our editable element that has the `contenteditable` attribute. The user will be able to type into this element when the editor is in edit mode. It's important to note that we've annotated it with a local view reference, `#editableContentElement`, which we're using in our view child queries.

The second element within the CSS class, `output`, is only to display the editor content and is only visible when the editor is in display mode. The visibility of both the elements is controlled using CSS, based on the `edit-mode` modifier class, which, if you recall from the component class code, is set through host property binding based on the `editMode` property.

The three control buttons are shown conditionally using the `NgIf` directive. The `showControls` input property needs to be `true`, and depending on the `editMode` flag, the view will either show the edit button or the save and the cancel buttons.

Integrating the editor component

Now, it's time to incorporate the editor component we've just created within our current project. We will use the editor component to make three areas in our application editable in-place:

- The titles of tasks within our task list
- The title of projects
- The description of projects

Let's start by integrating our in-place editor component into our task list component and making the titles of our tasks editable. Open up the file located in `src/app/tasks/task/task.component.html` and apply the following changes:

```
<mac-checkbox [checked]="task.done"
              (outCheck)="updateTask($event)"></mac-checkbox>
<div class="title">
   <mac-editor [content]="task.title"
               [showControls]="true"
               (outSaveEdit)="updateTitle($event)"></mac-editor>
</div>
```

Instead of just rendering the task title directly, we will now use our editor component to render the task title. We're binding the task title onto the `content` input property of our editor and calling a new method called `updateTitle` when the editor is emitting a `outSaveEdit` output. The `showControls` input property needs to be set to `true`, otherwise the editor will always stay in read-only mode.

Let's add the new `updateTitle` method in the task component class located in `src/app/tasks/task/task.component.ts`. The following code excerpt shows the added method in bold; unchanged code parts are hidden using the ellipsis character:

```
...
export class TaskComponent {
  ...
  updateTitle(title: string) {
    this.outUpdateTask.emit({
      ...this.task,
      title
    });
  }
}
```

The `updateTitle` method is very similar to the already present `updateTask` method. The difference is that we're emitting an updated task model which contains the updated title from out editor component. The `updateTask` method is emitting an updated task model where the done flag was updated.

The fact that we can re-use the `outUpdateTask` output makes our change to integrate the editor component very simple. To help you recall the data flow that is now happening within our component tree, let's look at all the different pieces involved once again:

1. A user clicks the edit button within the editor component inside a task component
2. After editing and clicking the save button, an `outSaveEdit` output with the updated title is emitted from the editor and our `updateTitle` method is called
3. The `updateTitle` method is emitting a new task object containing the updated title using the `outUpdateTask` output
4. The task list component is delegating the `outUpdateTask` output to its parent using an output with the same name.
5. The task list container component is catching the updated task and calls the `updateTask` method on our task list service
6. After the service has updated the data in our in-memory web API database, the updated task list will be passed down the component tree again until the task we've just updated arrives at the specific task component again, where it will also update the `content` input of our editor

Once again, our reactive and unidirectional data flow pays off when it comes to state architecture. With minimal changes, we've added a new feature to make our task titles editable in-place. Also, the way our data flows has not increased in complexity by implementing this change.

Let's apply similar changes to make our project title and description editable. Let's start by implementing changes to the template of our project component located in `src/app/project/project/project.component.html`. Again, changes are in bold and unchanged parts are hidden using the ellipsis character:

```
<header class="header">
  <h2 class="title">
    <mac-editor [content]="project.title"
                [showControls]="true"
                (outSaveEdit)="updateTitle($event)"></mac-editor>
  </h2>
  <mac-editor [content]="project.description"
              [showControls]="true"
```

```
                    (outSaveEdit)="updateDescription($event)"></mac-editor>
  </header>
  ...
```

This time, we're using two editors, one for our project title and one for the description. The rest of the changes are very similar to the changes we've applied to our task component. We're using two new methods called `updateTitle` and `updateDescription`, which we now need to add in the project component class located in `src/app/project/project/project.component.ts`:

```
...
export class ProjectComponent {
  ...
  @Output() outUpdateProject = new EventEmitter<Project>();

  activateTab(tab: Tab) {
    this.outActivateTab.emit(tab);
  }

  updateTitle(title: string) {
    this.outUpdateProject.emit({
      ...this.project,
      title
    });
  }

  updateDescription(description: string) {
    this.outUpdateProject.emit({
      ...this.project,
      description
    });
  }
}
```

Since we did not have anything to update in our project component as of yet, we first need to add a new output called `outUpdateProject` to notify our parent component about an updated project. The two methods `updateTitle` and `updateDescription` are both emitting an updated version of the project data using the updated information.

Now, we need to update our project container component to handle the newly introduced project updates. Let's start by changing the view template located in `src/app/container/project-container/project-container.component.html`:

```
<mac-project [project]="selectedProject | async"
             [tabs]="tabs"
             [activeTab]="activeTab"
```

```
                (outActivateTab)="activateTab($event)"
                (outUpdateProject)="updateProject($event)">
  </mac-project>
```

We're handing the new `outUpdateProject` output of our project component and calling a new method called `updateProject`. Let's look at the implementation of this method in the project container component class located in `src/app/container/project-container/project-container.component.ts`:

```
...
export class ProjectContainerComponent {
  ...
  updateProject(project: Project) {
    this.projectService.updateProject(project);
  }
}
```

Within the newly added method, we're calling the `updateProject` method on the project service and passing the project object that was initially emitted by the project UI component.

Finally, let's implement the `updateProject` method within our project service to update project data using the Angular HTTP service. Let's open the `src/app/project/project.service.ts` file and apply the following changes:

```
...
export class ProjectService {
  ...
  updateProject(project: Project) {
    this.http.post(`/api/projects/${project.id}`, project)
      .subscribe(() => this.loadProjects());
  }
}
```

Nothing new here. We're using the Angular HTTP service to execute a post request to the in-memory web API. After a successful call, we're calling the `loadProjects` method on our service, which will emit an updated project list using the `projects` behavior subject. This will cause all of our reactive subscriptions to receive the updated list of projects and update accordingly.

Congratulations! You've successfully created and integrated our editor component to make project titles, descriptions, and task titles editable. Now is a great time to preview your changes in the browser and play around with the editing capabilities we've added using the editor component. Using an in-place editor, we've simplified the authoring process within our application for our users. Also, by using a reactive data architecture, the editing feels very responsive and intuitive.

Recap

Within this building block, we have created an in-place editor component, which we can use to make things editable for any content within our application. It allows us to provide the user with contextual editing capabilities, which will result in a fantastic overall user experience.

We have also learned about the following topics:

- Using the `contenteditable` HTML5 attribute to enable in-place editing
- Using `@ViewChild` and `@ViewChildren` to query view child elements
- Using the `ElementRef` dependency to perform native DOM operations
- Implementing the logic, using the `OnChange` as well as the `AfterViewInit` life cycle hooks, to reflect data between Angular and content that is not in immediate control of Angular

Dealing with users

Going forward, we'll start dealing with user-generated content within our application and therefore require a minimal setup that allows us to deal with users correctly. We're creating a model to represent users as well as a simple user service that will tell us about the currently logged in user. Our service will just act as a mock user service and concerns like registration, login, and authentication are not within the scope of this book.

Let's stick to the practice we've established within this book and start by introducing the model for our users. Let's open the `src/app/model.ts` file and add the following interface at the end of the file:

```
export interface User {
  readonly id?: number;
  readonly name: string;
  readonly pictureUrl: string;
}
```

Let's keep this as minimal as possible. Our users will consist of only an ID, name, and a URL to a profile picture. As a next step, let's add a new users resource to our in-memory web API database. Open up the `src/app/database.ts` file and apply the following changes. Updated content is marked in bold while the ellipsis character indicates unchanged, hidden parts of the code:

```
import {InMemoryDbService} from 'angular-in-memory-web-api';
import {Project, Task, User} from './model';

export class Database implements InMemoryDbService {
  createDb() {
    const users: User[] = [
      {id: 1, name: 'You', pictureUrl: '/assets/user.svg'}
    ];

    ...

    return {users, projects, tasks};
  }
}
```

We've used our newly created user model to add a new users resource to the in-memory database. Currently, we'll only store one user within the users resource.

You can see from the `pictureUrl` inside of the added user object that we're referencing a path called `/assets/user.svg`. You can download this resource from this book's online resource repository. Please find the exact download link in the Download section of `Chapter 13`, *Task Management Application Source Code*.

You can also choose your personal profile picture instead of the generic profile picture that is available in the book resources. Either way, after preparing the image, you need to store it on the path `src/assets/` and set the filename to match what is specified in our user object within the in-memory database.

User service

Alright, we've prepared our model and database for handling users within our application. Now, we can create a new service that we are using in our container components to obtain the currently logged in user. Let's create a user service using the Angular CLI:

```
ng generate service --spec false user/user
```

Let's open the stub service generated on the `src/app/user/user.service.ts` path and replace its content with the following code:

```
import {Injectable} from '@angular/core';
import {HttpClient} from '@angular/common/http';
import {User} from '../model';

@Injectable()
export class UserService {
  constructor(private http: HttpClient) {

  }

  getCurrentUser() {
    return this.http.get<User>('/api/users/1');
  }
}
```

We're keeping things simple here. The only method we're providing from our service is the `getCurrentUser` method, which will execute a call to our in-memory web API and return the first user in the users resource.

That's already everything for our user service. Next up, we're going to create two simple UI components to display the logged in user within our application.

User area component

We've already created the data structures required to represent users within our application. We'll now make use of this to create a user area that shows the user profile of the currently logged in user. The user area will be placed above the main navigation within the left-hand side area in our application layout:

The user area component will be positioned above our main navigation

First of all, we will be creating a reusable component to render user profile pictures. Let's use the Angular CLI to generate the stub of our profile picture component:

```
ng generate component --spec false -ve none -cd onpush user/profile-
picture/profile-picture
```

Alright, let's open the component class file located in `src/app/user/profile-picture/profile-picture.component.ts` and change its content to the following code:

```
import {
  Component, ViewEncapsulation, ChangeDetectionStrategy, Input,
SimpleChanges,
  OnChanges
} from '@angular/core';
import {User} from '../../model';
import {DomSanitizer, SafeResourceUrl} from '@angular/platform-browser';

@Component({
  selector: 'mac-profile-picture',
  templateUrl: './profile-picture.component.html',
  styleUrls: ['./profile-picture.component.css'],
```

```
  encapsulation: ViewEncapsulation.None,
  changeDetection: ChangeDetectionStrategy.OnPush
})
export class ProfilePictureComponent implements OnChanges {
  @Input() user: User;
  pictureSafeUrl: SafeResourceUrl;

  constructor(private sanitizer: DomSanitizer) {

  }

  ngOnChanges(changes: SimpleChanges) {
    if (changes.user) {
      this.pictureSafeUrl = this.sanitizer
        .bypassSecurityTrustResourceUrl(this.user.pictureUrl);
    }
  }
}
```

Our profile picture component has one straightforward responsibility: to render the profile picture of a user. It accepts an input `user` of our model type `User`.

The Angular framework is concerned about security, and when we are rendering security relevant HTML, we need to tell Angular that this specific operation should be considered as trusted. In our case, we will render the image source attribute to display user profile pictures dynamically using Angular. Image source attributes are considered vulnerable because they execute get requests, can contain user-generated content, and therefore could also contain some attack vectors.

When we're using plain string URLs within HTML resource elements, like image, script, or link elements, Angular will raise an error. If we want to render an expression to an image source attribute within an Angular template, we need to use Angular's DOM sanitizer to create a trusted URL first.

Let's look at the different use cases for using the Angular `DomSanitizer` to mark vulnerable resources as trusted:

Use-case	Component class	Template usage

Render HTML	`safeHtml: SafeHtml =`
	`  bypassSecurityTrustHtml(`
	`    '<strong>Important</strong>'`
	`  );`
		`<div [innerHtml]="safeHtml">`
		`</div>`

Render Styles	`safeStyle: SafeStyle =`
	`  bypassSecurityTrustStyle(`
	`    'url(/assets/image.jpg)'`
	`  );`
		`<div`
		`[style.background]="safeStyle">`
		`</div>`

Render links	`safeUrl: SafeUrl = `
	`   bypassSecurityTrustUrl(`
	`      'https://google.com'`
	`   );`
		`<a [href]="safeUrl">Google</a>`

Resources	`safeUrl: SafeResourceUrl = `
	`   bypassSecurityTrustResourceUrl(`
	`      '/assets/image.jpg'`
	`   );`
		`<img [attr.src]="safeUrl" src="">`

 Note that bypassing security is not always a good solution. If you're rendering user-generated content that could contain attack vectors, you should consider sanitizing this content. The `DomSanitizer` of Angular provides a `sanitize` method that allows you to sanitize content for different contexts. It will strip out and escape security relevant parts of the content and return a sanitized version of it.

Inside of our profile picture component class, we are using the DOM sanitizer to create a trusted resource URL that we can then use within our template. We're sanitizing the user profile picture URL inside of the `OnChanges` life cycle hook. This way, if we're changing the user input, the trusted resource URL will also be updated.

Let's open the template of our profile picture component located in `src/app/user/profile-picture/profile-picture.component.html` and replace the content with the following code:

```
<img [attr.src]="pictureSafeUrl" src="">
```

This is all we need in our profile picture component template. We can now use the trusted picture URL inside the `src` attribute, binding on an image element.

Alright, let's move on to the main component we'd like to create for our user area within the left-hand side area of our application layout. We're using Angular CLI again to create the stub of our user area component:

```
ng generate component --spec false -ve none -cd onpush user/user-area/user-area
```

Let's jump right into the component class file located in `src/app/user/user-area/user-area.component.ts` and replace the content with the following code:

```
import {Component, ViewEncapsulation, ChangeDetectionStrategy, Input} from '@angular/core';
import {User} from '../../model';

@Component({
```

```
  selector: 'mac-user-area',
  templateUrl: './user-area.component.html',
  encapsulation: ViewEncapsulation.None,
  changeDetection: ChangeDetectionStrategy.OnPush
})
export class UserAreaComponent {
  @Input() user: User;
  @Input() openTasksCount: number;
}
```

Nothing special here. The user area component accepts a `user` input to render the profile information of a specific user. Also, we're adding an `openTasksCount` input to the component. This will be used to show a message about how many open tasks currently exist overall in the projects within the application.

Let's modify the user area component template located in `src/app/user/user-area/user-area.component.html` and replace the content with the following code:

```
<div class="profile">
  <mac-profile-picture [user]="user"></mac-profile-picture>
</div>
<div class="information">
  <p class="welcome-text">Hi {{user.name}}!</p>
  <p *ngIf="openTasksCount !== 0">You got
<strong>{{openTasksCount}}</strong> open tasks.</p>
  <p *ngIf="openTasksCount === 0">No open tasks. Hooray!</p>
</div>
```

First, we're rendering the users' profile picture by using our newly created profile picture component. We're just forwarding the user object that we provided as an input to our user area component down to the profile picture component.

Inside of the information container DIV element, we're rendering a welcome message for our user as well as a message to show the number of open tasks.

That wasn't too complicated. We've just created two UI components for our user feature. The user area UI component is rendering a section within the side area of our primary layout to show some profile information about the currently logged in user. We've also built a reusable profile picture component, which is rendering a user's profile image based on a user object.

Integrating the user area component

Now, it's time to incorporate our user component into our main layout. For this, we're going to modify our root application component, which is acting as our outermost container component.

Let's open the component class of our app component located in `src/app/app.component.ts` and apply the following changes:

```
...
import {map} from 'rxjs/operators';
import {UserService} from './user/user.service';
import {Project, Task, User} from './model';
...
export class AppComponent {
  openTasksCount: Observable<number>;
  user: Observable<User>;
  projects: Observable<Project[]>;
  selectedProject: Observable<Project>;

  constructor(taskListService: TaskService,
              userService: UserService,
              private projectService: ProjectService) {
    this.openTasksCount = taskListService.getTasks()
      .pipe(
        map((tasks: Task[]) => {
          return tasks
            .filter((task) => !task.done)
            .length;
        })
      );
    this.projects = projectService.getProjects();
    this.selectedProject = this.projectService.getSelectedProject();
    this.user = userService.getCurrentUser();
  }

  selectProject(id: number) {
    this.projectService.selectProject(id);
  }
}
```

We've introduced two new observables within our app component.

The `openTasksCount` observable is based on the task list observable we obtain by calling `getTasks` on our task list service. The task list observable is emitting the most recent list of all tasks within our application. Based on that, we're using the RxJS map operator to map the list of tasks as input to the count of open tasks as output. This results in an observable stream that always emits the most recent number of open tasks within our application.

The second observable, `user`, is obtained merely by calling the `getCurrentUser` method on our recently created user service.

Let's take a look at the changes within our app component template. Open the `src/app/app.component.html` file and apply the following changes. Effective changes are highlighted in bold while some unchanged code parts are hidden using the ellipsis character. Make sure that you only update the highlighted parts of your code:

```
<aside class="side-nav">
  <mac-user-area [user]="user | async"
                 [openTasksCount]="openTasksCount | async">
  </mac-user-area>
  ...
</aside>
...
```

We're rendering a user area component and passing the required inputs by subscribing to our observables directly in the view using the `async` pipe. Now, as soon as the logged in user or the amount of open tasks changes, our user area component will receive the updated values as input.

Well done! You've successfully created a user area component that you can now preview in your browser. Try to mark tasks as done and watch the user that is being updated based on the overall amount of open tasks.

Our main layout of the application is now complete, and all further enhancements will build on that basic layout.

Building a commenting system

In this chapter, we've created our main project components, a reusable editor component, and within the previous topic, we've created and integrated a user area component. Within this topic, we're going to create a commenting system that enables users to write comments on projects. The commenting system will use our editor component to make existing comments editable. We're also using our user feature and the profile picture component to visualize user comments. Based on the authoring user of comments, we will decide if existing comments are editable for the logged in user:

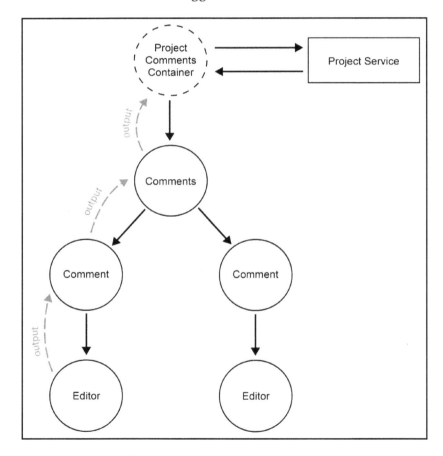

An illustration of the component subtree of our commenting system

The preceding diagram illustrates the architecture of the component tree within the commenting system that we are about to create.

The comments component will be responsible for listing all the existing comments, as well as creating new comments. A comment component represents each comment itself. Comment components use an editor that enables users to edit comments once they are created.

The editor component emits an output called `outSaveEdit` once editable content is saved using the control buttons of the editor. In the comment component, we will capture the output and propagate a new output upwards to our comments component. From there, we will delegate the output further to a new project comments container component that we're creating in this topic. The project comments container will be responsible for storing and retrieving comments using the project service.

The comments component will also be responsible for providing the necessary UI logic to create new comments. The creation of further comments will also be communicated to the project comments container using component output. There, we will use the project service to add the newly created comment.

Introducing a model for comments

Before we move on to creating more components within our application, let's first define the model and data we're using to represent comments.

Let's open up our model file located in `src/app/model.ts` and apply the following changes:

```
  ...

  export interface Project {
    readonly id?: number;
    readonly title: string;
    readonly description: string;
    readonly comments: Comment[];
  }

  ...

  export interface Comment {
    readonly time: number;
    readonly user: User;
    readonly content: string;
  }

  export interface CommentUpdate {
```

```
      readonly index: number;
      readonly comment: Comment;
}
```

We've added two new interfaces to represent our comments. The `Comment` interface consists of a `time` property that holds a number timestamp of the time the comment was created. We also store the user who commented and of course the comment itself using a property named `content`.

The `CommentUpdate` interface is used for communicating comment updates across components and services.

We've also updated the model of our projects to include an additional field called `comments`. That's where all project comments will be stored.

Since we're changing the `Project` interface to include a new property called `comments`, we also need to make sure our database is updated with this change. Let's open our database located in the `src/app/database.ts` file and apply the following changes:

```
import {InMemoryDbService} from 'angular-in-memory-web-api';
import {Project, Task, User} from './model';

export class Database implements InMemoryDbService {
  createDb() {
    ...

    const projects: Project[] = [
        {id: 1, title: 'My first project', description: 'This is your first
project.', comments: []},
        {id: 2, title: 'My second project', description: 'This is your second
project.', comments: []}
    ];

    ...
  }
}
```

The only difference in this file is that we've added the new `comments` property on our project objects. For both projects, we're just adding an empty array with no pre-existing comments.

Alright, that's all the changes required in our data and model for now. Let's move on to the creation of our commenting system.

Building the comment component

Let's start making our commenting system by fleshing out the comment component first. In addition to the comment itself, we'd like to display the user's profile, who commented, and the time of the comment.

To display the time, we will make use of relative time formatting, as this will give our users a better feel of time. Relative time formatting presents timestamps in the format "5 minutes ago" or "1 month ago", in contrast to absolute timestamps, such as "25.12.2015 18:00". Using a famous third-party library called Moment.js, we'll create a view pipe that we can use within component templates to convert timestamps and dates into a relative time format.

View pipes are a great way to enrich the template language of Angular. They allow you to create helper functions that you can then use within the view inside of your component templates. So far, we've only used one view pipe, the AsyncPipe, which was used to subscribe to observable streams directly inside of the component view. Within this section, we'll create our view pipe, which can be used to format dates using the Moment.js library.

First of all, we need to install Moment.js as a production dependency to our project. Open up a terminal within the root folder of your project and execute the following command:

```
npm install --save moment@2.19.3
```

After Moment.js is installed, we can go ahead and create our first view pipe. We can also use the Angular CLI to generate the stub code of our pipe for us:

```
ng generate pipe --spec false pipes/from-now
```

Alright, the Angular CLI should have created a new view pipe for us with the name fromNow. Let's open the view pipe code located in the src/app/pipes/from-now.pipe.ts file and change its content to the following code:

```
import {Pipe, PipeTransform} from '@angular/core';
import * as moment from 'moment';

@Pipe({
  name: 'fromNow'
})
export class FromNowPipe implements PipeTransform {
  transform(value: any) {
    return moment(value).fromNow();
  }
}
```

All view pipes need to be decorated using Angular's `@Pipe` decorator. Inside of the configuration object, we can pass this to the decorator factory, and specify the name of the pipe. This name is how we address the view pipe within our component templates.

View pipe classes should always implement an interface called `PipeTransform`. This interface will ensure that the mandatory method, `transform`, is implemented within our pipe class. The transform method is the central piece of every view pipe. This function will be called when a pipe is used within the view template of a component. Let's look at a basic example of how a view pipe is used inside of a template:

```
<div>{{name | toUpperCase}}</div>
```

In this essential case, we're using a view pipe with the name `toUpperCase`. Angular will take the value on the left-hand side of the expression and pass it to the `transform` method of the `toUpperCase` pipe as the first parameter. The value that is returned from the `transform` method is then evaluated and rendered into the view. We can also compose multiple view pipes by chaining them after each other:

```
<div>{{name | reverse | toUpperCase}}</div>
```

In this example, the name will be passed to the `transform` method of the `reverse` pipe. The returned value of the `reverse` pipe's `transform` method will then be passed as the first parameter to the `transform` method of the `toUpperCase` pipe. Like this, you can chain an indefinite amount of pipes onto each other to transform component properties directly in your component view template.

View pipes are treated as stateless by default. Angular uses this assumption to perform some optimizations in the background. If pipes and their `transform` methods can be considered stateless and pure, Angular can cache the results of pipe transformations and re-use the cached values later on. This behaviour is okay in most cases, and we don't want to miss out on that performance optimization. However, sometimes it's required to rely on some services or other sources of state to determine the result of a pipe transformation. In such a case, the `transform` method of a pipe is not pure, and therefore cannot be cached. To tell Angular that our pipe is not pure, you can use an additional configuration property on pipes called `pure`. If you set this property to false, your pipe transformations will not be cached, and Angular will execute your `transform` method every time your view is rendered.

Let's use our newly created `fromNow` pipe to format the timestamp of comments within our comment component. We're using the Angular CLI again to create the structure for the comment component:

```
ng generate component --spec false -ve none -cd onpush
comments/comment/comment
```

Let's open the component template file located in `src/app/comments/comment/comment.component.html` and replace its content with the following code:

```html
<div class="meta">
  <div class="user-picture">
    <mac-profile-picture [user]="comment.user"></mac-profile-picture>
  </div>
  <div class="user-name">{{comment.user.name}}</div>
  <div class="time">
    {{comment.time | fromNow}}
  </div>
</div>
<div class="main">
  <div class="content">
    <mac-editor [content]="comment.content"
                [showControls]="comment.user.id === user.id"
                (outSaveEdit)="updateComment($event)">
    </mac-editor>
  </div>
</div>
```

We're reusing our profile picture component to render the comment author user. To display the time of the comment in a relative format, we'll use the `fromNow` pipe that we created earlier.

Finally, we will make use of the in-place editor component to display the content of the comment and make it editable at the same time. We will bind the comment content property to the `content` input property of the editor. At the same time, we will listen for the `outSaveEdit` output of the editor and call the `updateComment` method on our comment component class.

We're also deciding if the currently logged in user passed into our component as `user` input is the authoring user of the given comment and then use this information to either enable or disable the controls on our editor using the `showControls` input property. This way, the current user is only allowed to edit a comment if he/she's also the author of that comment.

Let's also create our component class and open the
`src/app/comments/comment/comment.component.ts` file to replace its content with
the following code:

```
import {
  Component, ViewEncapsulation, ChangeDetectionStrategy, Input, Output,
EventEmitter
} from '@angular/core';
import {Comment, User} from '../../model';

@Component({
  selector: 'mac-comment',
  templateUrl: './comment.component.html',
  styleUrls: ['./comment.component.css'],
  encapsulation: ViewEncapsulation.None,
  changeDetection: ChangeDetectionStrategy.OnPush
})
export class CommentComponent {
  @Input() comment: Comment;
  @Input() user: User;
  @Output() outUpdateComment = new EventEmitter<Comment>();

  updateComment(content: string) {
    this.outUpdateComment.emit({
      ...this.comment,
      content
    });
  }
}
```

The component code is pretty straightforward. As input, we expect a user object that is
passed along to the `user` input property. This property represents the currently logged in
user and is used within our template to determine if a user should be able to edit the
comment. The `comment` input property is expected to be an object of type `Comment`. From
there, we gather the comment content, the time of creation, and the comment author user.

Going back to the view template of our comment component, we can observe that the
`outSaveEdit` output on the editor component will call the `updateComment` method in our
comment component. Inside of the `updateComment` method, we're creating a copy of our
comment object and updating its content with the editor output. This copy is then emitted
using the `outUpdateComment` output of the comment component.

That's all we need for our comment component. Next up, we're going to create the
comments component, which represents a list of comments and embraces the necessary UI
element to create new comments.

Building the comments component

The last missing piece of the puzzle for our commenting system is the comments component, which will list all the comments and provide the UI to create new comments:

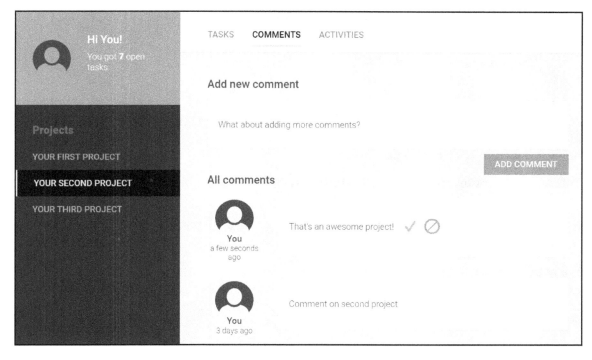

The comments component allows users to add comments to projects

Let's use the Angular CLI to create the structure for our comments component:

```
ng generate component --spec false -ve none -cd onpush
comments/comments/comments
```

First, let's edit the template of our comments component located in `src/app/comments/comments/comments.component.html`:

```
<div class="title">Add new comment</div>
<div class="add-comment-section">
  <div #commentContentEditable
       class="add-comment-box"
       contenteditable="true">
  </div>
  <button (click)="createComment()"
```

```
                class="button" >Add comment</button>
  </div>

  <ng-container *ngIf="comments.length > 0">
    <div class="title">All comments</div>
    <mac-comment *ngFor="let comment of comments; let index = index"
                 [comment]="comment"
                 [user]="user"
                 (outUpdateComment)="updateComment(index, $event)">
    </mac-comment>
  </ng-container>
```

To allow users to create new comments, we're making use of the contenteditable API by
adding a DIV element that contains the `contenteditable` attribute. We're using a local
view reference called `#commentContentEditable` on that element so that we can quickly
reference it from within our component class.

To add a new comment, we will use a button with a click event binding that calls the
`createComment` method on our component class.

Below the section where users can add new comments, we will create another section that
will list all the existing comments. If no comments exist, we just don't render the section.

We're using a particular view element called `<ng-container>` to group our **All comments**
title together with the list of comments. This container element is handy in situations where
you're using template elements, like with the use of `NgIf`, but you don't want to create an
artificial HTML element for that purpose. Using an `<ng-container>` element in
conjunction with `NgIf` allows you to show or hide a list of elements conditionally, but
without the need to have a common parent HTML element.

With the help of the `NgFor` directive, we are repeating over all existing comments and
rendering a comment component for each repetition. We are binding the comment object to
our comment component and also adding an output binding to handle updated comments.

Let's create the class of our comments component by changing the content of
the `src/app/comments/comments/comments.component.ts` file:

```
import {
  Component, ViewEncapsulation, ChangeDetectionStrategy, Input, Output,
  EventEmitter, ViewChild, ElementRef
} from '@angular/core';
import {Comment, CommentUpdate, User} from '../../model';

@Component({
  selector: 'mac-comments',
```

```
  templateUrl: './comments.component.html',
  styleUrls: ['./comments.component.css'],
  encapsulation: ViewEncapsulation.None,
  changeDetection: ChangeDetectionStrategy.OnPush
})
export class CommentsComponent {
  @Input() user: User;
  @Input() comments: Comment[];
  @Output() outUpdateComment = new EventEmitter<CommentUpdate>();
  @Output() outCreateComment = new EventEmitter<Comment>();
  @ViewChild('commentContentEditable') commentContentEditable: ElementRef;

  createComment() {
    this.outCreateComment.emit({
      user: this.user,
      time: +new Date(),
      content: this.commentContentEditable.nativeElement.textContent
    });
    this.commentContentEditable.nativeElement.textContent = '';
  }

  updateComment(index: number, comment: Comment) {
    this.outUpdateComment.next({
      index,
      comment
    });
  }
}
```

Our component class has two inputs. The user input is expected to be set to the currently logged in user. The comments input is a list of comments that is used in our component view to iterate over and render comment components.

We also have two outputs in our component. The fist one, outUpdateComment, is used to tell our parent that one of the comments has been updated. The output value is of type CommentUpdate, which holds the index of the comment that got updated and the comment object itself. Inside of the updateComment method, which is called from the binding on comment components in our view, we're constructing a comment update object and emitting it through the outUpdateComment output.

The `outCreateComment` output is used to tell our parent that a new comment should be created. The `createComment` method is used to create a new comment object and emit it through that output. Additionally, we're using a view query to get hold of the editable DOM element within our component view and store it into the member property `commentContentEditable`. When a new comment is created using the `createComment` method, after we've emitted the newly created comment object, we're using the reference to the editable item to reset its text content. This way, after creating a new comment, the editable content element will be blank again.

Integrating the commenting system into projects

So far, we've created our comments model and updated our in-memory web API database. We've created the comment and comments components along with a new view pipe called `fromNow` to format relative times in our comment view template. The only missing part is to integrate our comments component in our project. For this, we are making use of the second tab on our project component, which we've already prepared for for our commenting system. To keep our data flow tight, we're introducing a final component to fill the gap between our projects and the comments component.

Let's use Angular CLI to create the project comments container component:

```
ng generate component --spec false -ve none -cd onpush container/project-
comments-container
```

After the component files have been generated, let's open the class file located in `src/app/container/project-comments-container/project-comments-container.component.ts` and replace its content with the following code:

```
import {Component, ViewEncapsulation, ChangeDetectionStrategy} from
'@angular/core';
import {ProjectService} from '../../project/project.service';
import {UserService} from '../../user/user.service';
import {Observable} from 'rxjs';
import {Comment, CommentUpdate, Project, User} from '../../model';
import {map, take} from 'rxjs/operators';

@Component({
  selector: 'mac-project-comments-container',
  templateUrl: './project-comments-container.component.html',
  styleUrls: ['./project-comments-container.component.css'],
  encapsulation: ViewEncapsulation.None,
  changeDetection: ChangeDetectionStrategy.OnPush
})
```

```
export class ProjectCommentsContainerComponent {
  user: Observable<User>;
  selectedProject: Observable<Project>;
  projectComments: Observable<Comment[]>;

  constructor(private projectService: ProjectService, private userService:
UserService) {
    this.user = userService.getCurrentUser();
    this.selectedProject = projectService.getSelectedProject();
    this.projectComments = this.selectedProject
      .pipe(
        map((project) => project.comments)
      );
  }

  createComment(comment: Comment) {
    this.selectedProject
      .pipe(
        take(1)
      )
      .subscribe((project) => this.projectService.updateProject({
        ...project,
        comments: [...project.comments, comment]
      }));
  }

  updateComment(update: CommentUpdate) {
    this.selectedProject
      .pipe(
        take(1)
      )
      .subscribe((project) => {
        const updatedComments = project.comments.slice();
        updatedComments[update.index] = update.comment;
        this.projectService.updateProject({
          ...project,
          comments: updatedComments
        });
      });
  }
}
```

Within our project comments container, we're storing three different observables. Let's take a look at each of them and their purposes.

The `user` observable emits the currently logged in user. Within the constructor of our container component, we're calling the `getCurrentUser` method on the user service to obtain the observable.

The `selectedProject` observable is obtained by calling `getSelectedProject` on our project service. This observable will always emit the currently selected project. If we're choosing a different project in our main navigation, the newly selected project is emitted through this observable.

Finally, the `projectComments` observable is a transformed observable with the `selectedProject` observable as a source. We would like to access the project comments directly so we can use them as input to our commenting system. By using the `map` operator inside a pipe transformation, we can select the `comments` field of the selected project and create a new output observable that is always emitting the comments list of the selected project.

Finally, we're providing two methods, `createComment` and `updateComment`, to create or update comments using the project service. We're obtaining the latest value of the `selectedProject` observable by utilizing the `take` operator and updating an existing or adding a new comment using the project service, respectively.

That's it for the code of our component class. You should be reasonably familiar with the logic inside of our container component. The patterns we're using are very similar to those from our existing task list container, or the ones present in our app component.

Let's open the view template of our project comments container component located in `src/app/container/project-comments-container/project-comments-container.component.html` and change its content to the following code:

```
<mac-comments [user]="user | async"
              [comments]="projectComments | async"
              (outCreateComment)="createComment($event)"
              (outUpdateComment)="updateComment($event)">
</mac-comments>
```

There is nothing we wouldn't expect from a regular container component template. We're merely rendering a comments UI component and binding all inputs and outputs of the component to the logic and data within our container component class. Again, we're making our comments UI component highly reusable by separating the state and data concerns with the use of a container component.

Alright, we're almost finished integrating our commenting system. The last missing bit is to include our project comments container component within our project component. Let's open the view template of the project component located in `src/app/project/project/project.component.html` and apply the necessary changes to render our commenting system:

```
<header class="header">
  <h2 class="title">
    <mac-editor [content]="project.title"
                [showControls]="true"
                (outSaveEdit)="updateTitle($event)"></mac-editor>
  </h2>
  <mac-editor [content]="project.description"
              [showControls]="true"
              (outSaveEdit)="updateDescription($event)"></mac-editor>
</header>
<mac-tabs [tabs]="tabs"
          [activeTab]="activeTab"
          (outActivateTab)="activateTab($event)">
</mac-tabs>
<mac-task-list-container *ngIf="activeTab.id === 'tasks'">
</mac-task-list-container>
<mac-project-comments-container *ngIf="activeTab.id === 'comments'">
</mac-project-comments-container>
```

We're just reusing the same logic we've already used to render our task list container. We ensure that our tabbed interface within the project component activates the project comments container component by placing an `NgIf` with the respective condition.

There you go! That wasn't too complicated, was it? We've finally created and integrated a commenting system on our projects. Due to the way we've built our commenting system, we can integrate comments in any other location we want to.

Preview your changes in the browser and play around with the commenting functionality a bit to get familiar with what you've just built:

Screenshot of the commenting system that is integrated within our project component

Recap

Within this topic, we have successfully created a fully-fledged commenting system that can be placed in various areas of our application to enable commenting. Users can interact with in-place editors to edit the content in comments, which gives them a great user experience.

While writing the code for our commenting system, we learned about the following topics:

- Creating a re-usable commenting system that can be used to add commenting functionality in every area of our application
- Implementing a simple pipe using the @Pipe decorator and the Moment.js library to provide relative time formatting

- Using the `<ng-container>` element to group elements for use within a template directive
- Re-using the editor component as an in-place editor within the comment component

Summary

The main topic of this chapter was the introduction of projects. We've created the necessary model and data layer to deal with projects to group individual tasks. We've also created UI components to display project information and a tabbed user interface component that we can reuse wherever we need it. We learned about the concept of content projection, which allows us to build beautiful content-based APIs for our components.

We've further structured our main layout and introduced some navigation components that we're currently using to provide a project navigation.

We created a simple in-place editor that provides an excellent authoring experience within our application. Going forward, we can use the editor component wherever we want to make content editable for our users. They will not have to jump into disturbing dialogues or separate configuration pages, and will be able to edit directly within their current context. This is an excellent tool for enhancing the experience of our users.

Besides our shiny new editor component, we created a whole commenting system that can be easily included in areas of our application where we'd like to provide commenting capabilities. We have added the commenting system within our project and users can now comment on projects by navigating to the **Comments** tab on the project details.

The project navigation and the tabbed interface we've built are both great. However, it would be nice to think that the concern of navigation could be separated from our regular application composition. We also want to leverage the browser's location URL and the native functionality of the browser history. Within the next chapter, we're going to address this and learn everything required to integrate the Angular router into our application.

Component-Based Routing

5

Routing is an integral part of today's frontend applications. In general, a router serves three main purposes:

- It makes your application navigable so that users can use their browser's back button and store and share links within the application
- It offloads parts of the application composition so that the router takes responsibility for composing your application, based on routes and route parameters
- It stores part of your application state within the URL of your browser

The router that comes with Angular supports many different use-cases, and it comes with an easy-to-use API. It supports child routes that are similar to the Angular UI-Router nested states, Ember.js nested routes or child routers in the Durandal framework. Tied to the component tree, the router also makes use of its own tree structure to store states and to resolve requested URLs.

In this chapter, we will refactor our code to use the component-based router of Angular. We will look into the core elements of the router and how to use them to enable routing in our application.

The following topics will be covered in this chapter:

- Introducing to the Angular router
- The router, container, and pure components
- An overview of the refactoring needed to enable the router in our application
- Creating a route configuration file and look into different route configuration possibilities

- Using the `RouterOutlet` directive to create insertion points that are controlled by the router
- Using the `RouterLink` directive and the router DSL to create navigation links
- Using reactive router properties to obtain route parameters
- Using both the `RouterActive` directive as well as the programmatic router API for reacting to activated route paths
- Programmatically navigate using the router API
- Creating a route guard for the project container

An introduction to the Angular router

The router in Angular is closely coupled to our component tree. The design of the Angular router is built on the assumption that a component tree is directly related to our URL structure. This is certainly true for most of the cases. If we have a component **B**, which is nested within a component **A**, the URL to represent our location would very likely be `/a/b`.

To specify the location in our template where we'd like to enable the router to instantiate components, we can use so-called `outlets`. Simply by including a `<router-outlet>` element, we can mark the location in our template, where the Angular router will instantiate components.

Based on some route configuration that we can provide in our main module, the router then decides which components need to be instantiated and placed into the corresponding router outlets. Routes can also be parameterized, and we can access these parameters within the instantiated components.

Using our component tree and the router configuration, we can build a hierarchical routing and decouple child routes from their parent routes. Such nested routes make it possible to compose our application layout on a meta level and reuse parent components for multiple child routes. By using the router we can add another layer of composition to our application. Take a look at the following diagram:

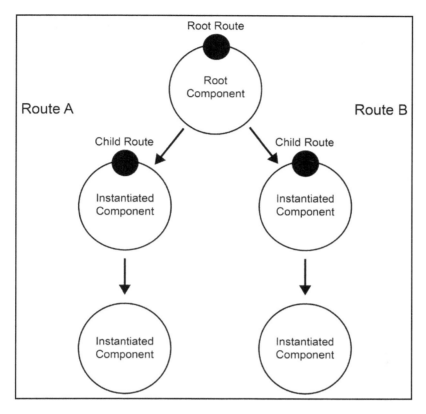

Router hierarchy established through a component tree and router outlet

Let's look at the elements of the router again in more detail:

- **Route configuration**: The route configuration is done while importing the router into our application module. By configuring child routes, we can build decoupled nested routes easily.
- **Router outlets**: Outlets are the locations of components that will be managed by the router. Instantiated components that are based on the route configuration will be placed into these outlets.
- **Router link**: These are links built with a DSL style notation that enable the developer to build complex links through the routing tree.

Within this chapter, we'll go through these different concepts of the Angular router and refactor our application to implement proper routing.

Composition using the router

So far, we have achieved composition by including subcomponents in component templates directly. However, we'd now like to give the control to the router to compose our main application layout.

The following diagram provides an overview of the component architecture of our application, which we're going to enable for the router:

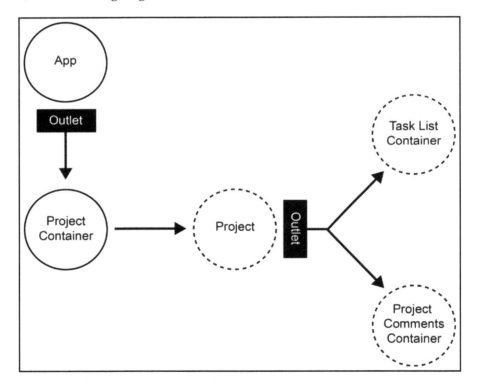

A component tree displaying routed container components (solid line) and components included via router outlets

After the changes that we're going to implement, the project container component is not directly included in our app component anymore. Instead, we use a router outlet in the template of our app component. This way, we can give control to the router and let it decide which component should be placed into the outlet. Currently, we only have the project component as a first-level route, but this will change in later chapters when we add more features to our application.

The project component will contain another router outlet, which enables us to do nested child routing. There, we'll be able to create child routings that enable us to switch between the different project detail views.

Routing with container components

The composition that we've dealt with so far was purely based on instantiation via template inclusion. We used input and output properties to decouple and encapsulate components and followed nice reusable patterns.

Using the router, which instantiates components dynamically, we can't use template bindings on routed components anymore. While we previously relied on input and output properties to connect our components together, we're losing this possibility by using the router and we can't bind to inputs or outputs any longer.

Luckily, we already know about the concept of container components. Container components connect our state and data to our user interface components. They should not have any input or output properties and act as top-level components. They are by definition the perfect candidates for routed components:

- Since container components don't rely on input or output properties, they will work out-of-the-box when instantiated by the router
- We can simply consider the router as a different source for state and pass down information from the URL state into our UI components

Router configuration

Angular uses tree data structures to represent the router state. You can imagine that every navigation in your application activates a branch in this tree. Let's look at the following example.

We have an application that consists of four possible routes:

- `/`: This is the root route of the application, which is handled in a component called **A**.
- `/b/:id`: This is the route where we can access the b detail view, which is handled in a component called **B**. In the URL, we can pass an `id` parameter (that is, `/b/100`).
- `/b/:id/c`: This is the route where the b detail view has another navigation possibility, which reveals more specific details that we call c. This is handled in a **C** component.
- `/b/:id/d`: This is the route where we can also navigate to a d view in the b detail view. This is handled by a component called **D**:

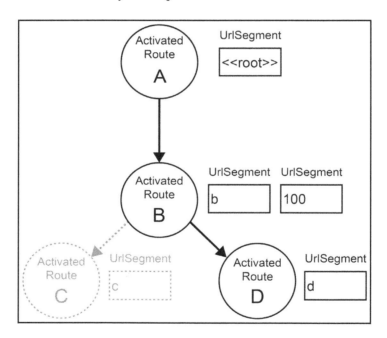

A route tree consisting of an active branch of route segments for the activated route /b/100/d

Let's assume that we activate a route in our example by navigating the URL, /b/100/d. In this case, we'd activate a route that reflects the state that is outlined in the preceding diagram. Note that the route segment **B** actually consists of two URL segments. The reason for this is that we've specified that our route **B** actually consists of the b identifier and an :id route parameter.

Using this tree data structure, we have a perfect abstraction to deal with navigation trees. We can compare trees, check whether certain segments exist in a tree, and extract parameters present on activated routes.

Within each routed component, we have the possibility to inject the activated route of that level. Let's assume we'd want to access the :id parameter from the URL within component **B**. We can inject the ActivatedRoute into the constructor of our component and extract the route parameter from there by using the following code:

```
@Component({
  selector: 'mac-b',
  templateUrl: './b.component.html'
})
export class BComponent {
  constructor(route: ActivatedRoute) {
    route.params.subscribe(params => console.log(params.id));
  }
}
```

The Angular router reuses component instances by default. This means that if the router is activating the same component again but with different parameters, Angular is not destroying the previous component instance. It re-uses the previous instance and provides the updated parameters to our component. That's the reason why the params property on the ActivatedRoute object is an observable stream. We can simply subscribe to this observable, which allows us to react on route parameter changes.

As you can see, the router API is quite flexible, and it allows us to inspect route activity on a very fine granularity. The tree structures that are used in the router make it possible to compare complex router states in our application without bothering about the underlying complexity.

Back to the routes

All right, now it's time to implement routing for our application! In the upcoming topics, we'll create the following routes for our application:

Route path	Description
`/projects/:projectId`	This route will activate the project container component in the outlet of our root application component. This consists of the `projects` URL segment as well as the `:projectId` URL segment to specify the project ID.
`/projects/:projectId/tasks`	This route will activate the `TaskListContainer` component inside of our project component. While we're currently rendering the task list directly within the template of the project component, we will make use of an other router outlet instead.
`/projects/:projectId/comments`	This route will activate the `ProjectCommentsContainer` component inside of our project component. The same router outlet within the project component is used to instantiate the project comments container component.

You can directly relate the preceding route configuration to the composition illustrated within the diagram of the previous topic, *Composition using the router*.

To use the router of Angular, the first thing that we need to do is to create a route configuration. Let's create a new file on the path `src/app/routes.ts` and add our initial route configuration, using this code:

```
import {Route} from '@angular/router';
import {ProjectContainerComponent} from './container/project-
container/project-container.component';

export const routes: Route[] = [{
  path: 'projects/:projectId',
  component: ProjectContainerComponent
}, {
  path: '',
  pathMatch: 'full',
  redirectTo: '/projects/1'
}];
```

For the moment we'll only configure the route for projects and add the child routes to project comments and tasks later.

The `path` property within our route configuration objects is used as a pattern to match against the URL in the browser. The router will observe URL changes in the browser and then try to match each path in our configuration against the new URL.

 The Angular router will always match with a "first match wins" strategy. This means that you can have configuration scenarios where more than one configuration results in a match. However, only the first matching configuration within the list will be activated.

With the component property in our route configuration, we can tell Angular which component should be instantiated when a specific route is activated.

For our project route, we're also using a parameter segment to pass the ID of the project we want to display.

The second route in our configuration is a special route that will redirect users to the first project within our project list when they enter our app on the root URL (`http://localhost:4200/` in the case of our development server).

In redirect route configurations we can omit the `component` property but specify a `redirectTo` property to tell Angular that we'd like to redirect the user to a different URL. Within redirect routes, you always need to specify how you want to match the URL path. By default, Angular matches using a prefix match strategy. However, in many situations, you want to match the whole URL and not only a prefix. You can use the `pathMatch` property and set it to the value `'full'` for this purpose.

By specifying an empty path pattern, we can tell Angular to activate a route when there's an empty path segment within the browser's URL. However, when using the default prefix match strategy, this pattern will always result in a match. It's only when we set the `pathMatch` property to `'full'`, that we can cause a match when the user navigates to the root URL.

Okay, let's move on and include the router within our application. We can use the router configuration that we've just created to initialize the Angular router. Let's open up our main module located on the path `src/app/app.module.ts` and apply the following changes. Irrelevant code parts that did not change are hidden from the code excerpt and are marked with an ellipsis character. The effective changes within the code are marked in bold:

```
...
import {RouterModule} from '@angular/router';
import {routes} from './routes';

@NgModule({
  declarations: [
    ...
  ],
  imports: [
    BrowserModule,
    HttpClientModule,
    HttpClientInMemoryWebApiModule.forRoot(Database, {
      delay: 0
    }),
    RouterModule.forRoot(routes)
  ],
  providers: [TaskService, UserService, ProjectService],
  bootstrap: [AppComponent]
})
export class AppModule {
}
```

In the preceding code's changes to our main model, we're simply importing the routes configuration we've prepared and the Angular router module from `@angular/router`. By calling the module factory function `RouterModule.forRoot` we can pass our route configuration to the router and import the resulting router module into our application.

That was easy! You've successfully created your first route configuration and included the router in your application. When you preview your changes and reload your browser, you should already see the redirect configuration kicking in. Your browser URL should be relocated to `http://localhost:4200/projects/0`. However, we don't leverage the compositional features of the router yet and our project navigation needs to be changed too.

Composing projects using the router

We've already prepared the route configuration for navigating our projects. The next step is to enable the router to handle the composition of projects correctly based on user navigation. Together, we'll execute the following three steps to achieve this:

1. Using the `<router-outlet>` element within our root component to allow the router to place instantiated components.
2. Using the router link directives to make our project navigation work with the router.
3. Getting rid of the selected project state in our project service and instead rely on the URL state, which now includes the project ID of the navigated project. We can then refactor our project container component to make use of this route parameter.

Let's start with the template of our root component. Currently, we're including the project container component within the template directly. Since we'd want to give control to the router to determine which component will be visible to the user, we need to change that and include a `<router-outlet>` in the template instead.

Let's open the template of our root component, which is located in `src/app/app.component.html`, and apply the following changes. Again, the ellipsis symbol indicates irrelevant code parts that remain the same:

```
...
<main class="main">
  <router-outlet></router-outlet>
</main>
```

We have removed the static inclusion of the project container component and added a router outlet element. This way the Angular router knows that it should instantiate activated components at this location within our template.

The next thing on our list is to use the router link directives in order to enable project navigation. Luckily we're already in the right place to perform this change. The project navigation is part of the root component template and we need to add the router link directives there. Within the template `src/app/app.component.html`, we perform the following changes:

```
...
<mac-navigation-section title="Projects">
  <mac-navigation-item *ngFor="let project of projects | async"
                       [navId]="project.id"
```

```
                               [title]="project.title"
                               routerLinkActive="active"
                               [routerLink]="['/projects', project.id]">
      </mac-navigation-item>
   </mac-navigation-section>
   ...
```

The router link directive allows us to make any element act like a link, which activates a given route. By using the router DSL, we can specify a route as individual segment elements within an array. Since we're iterating over all projects to render navigation item components, we can use the project ID to construct links that activate our previously configured route path, /projects/:projectId.

The second change is to use the routerLinkActive directive on our navigation items. This directive is a simple helper that adds a CSS class to any element where a router link directive is present. If the configured router link URL matches the URL in the browser, then the CSS class will be added. You can specify the CSS class name within the routerLinkActive attribute value. This helps us to style the active navigation item so that the user always sees which project is currently navigated.

Great! You have successfully updated the navigation within our root component to use the Angular router directives. While previewing the changes, you can already see that the URL in your browser is updated when you're navigating between the different projects within the project navigation.

While so far we've been relying on our project service to tell us which project is currently selected, we're now leveraging the URL state of the router to store this information. Let's remove the selectedProject member and the call to the project service from our root component located in src/app/app.component.ts. We can also get rid of the selectProject method since the router is now in charge of selecting projects:

```
...
@Component({
   selector: 'mac-root',
   templateUrl: './app.component.html',
   styleUrls: ['./app.component.css'],
   encapsulation: ViewEncapsulation.None
})
export class AppComponent {
   openTasksCount: Observable<number>;
   user: Observable<User>;
   projects: Observable<Project[]>;

   constructor(taskListService: TaskService,
               userService: UserService,
```

```
              private projectService: ProjectService) {
    this.openTasksCount = taskListService.getTasks()
      .pipe(
        map((tasks: Task[]) => {
          return tasks
            .filter((task) => !task.done)
            .length;
        })
      );
    this.projects = projectService.getProjects();
    this.user = userService.getCurrentUser();
  }
}
```

There's still one step missing to complete the switch to the router for our project composition. If you have been previewing the changes we've performed so far, you've noticed that we're already changing the URL and that the project navigation items get activated correctly. However, we always see the first project title and description within the project component. The project container component is currently still relying on the project service to obtain the selected project. We need to change that so that we use the state from the router.

Let's implement the changes in the container component `src/app/container/project-container/project-container.component.ts` in order to obtain the project ID parameter from the activated route and display the correct project after navigation:

```
...
import {ActivatedRoute} from '@angular/router';
import {combineLatest} from 'rxjs';
import {map} from 'rxjs/operators';

@Component({
  selector: 'mac-project-container',
  templateUrl: './project-container.component.html',
  styleUrls: ['./project-container.component.css'],
  encapsulation: ViewEncapsulation.None,
  changeDetection: ChangeDetectionStrategy.OnPush
})
export class ProjectContainerComponent {
  ...

  constructor(private projectService: ProjectService,
              private route: ActivatedRoute) {
    this.selectedProject = combineLatest(
      projectService.getProjects(),
      route.params
```

```
    ).pipe(
      map(([projects, routeParams]) =>
        projects.find((project) => project.id === +routeParams.projectId)
      )
    );
  }

  ...

}
```

We're still using a member `selectedProject` which is of type `Observable<Project>` to represent the currently selected project. However, we're no longer obtaining this observable from the project service directly. Instead, we're using the `combineLatest` RxJS helper to combine two observable streams together in order to produce an output stream that emits the selected project.

We are combining the observable route parameters from the activated route with the project list from our project service. We can then use the `map` operator to find the right project within the project list using the ID obtained from the route parameters. The resulting observable stream will emit the selected project and re-emit whenever the route parameter or the project list changes.

Now, go ahead and preview the changes in your browser again. You should now see that the router navigation using the project navigation on the left should also cause an update on our project component. It should always display the correct project information depending on what project ID is present within the browser's URL.

Child routes for project details

Within this section, we're going to use the router for navigating the detail views on our projects. We currently have two detail views on our projects:

- Project tasks view using the task list container component
- Project comments view using the project comments container component

We also need to make sure that we're able to activate the sub-views using our tabbed interface on projects. Our current solution is to store the activated tab within the project container component. Based on that, we're deciding which detail view to show within the template of our project component. There, we're using a simple `ngIf` directive in order to determine which of the two child container components to show.

Let's start with our refactoring by including child route configurations for both our detail views. Open up the router configuration file on the path `src/app/routes.ts` and perform the following changes:

```
import {Route} from '@angular/router';
import {ProjectContainerComponent} from './container/project-
container/project-container.component';
import {TaskListContainerComponent} from './container/task-list-
container/task-list-container.component';
import {ProjectCommentsContainerComponent} from './container/project-
comments-container/project-comments-container.component';

export const routes: Route[] = [{
  path: 'projects/:projectId',
  component: ProjectContainerComponent,
  children: [{
    path: 'tasks',
    component: TaskListContainerComponent
  }, {
    path: 'comments',
    component: ProjectCommentsContainerComponent
  }, {
    path: '**',
    redirectTo: 'tasks'
  }]
}, {
  path: '',
  pathMatch: 'full',
  redirectTo: '/projects/1'
}];
```

Using the `children` property on route configurations, we can configure nested routes. It allows us to tell Angular that somewhere below the routed parent component, there will be another router outlet that can be used to instantiate components activated by child routes.

Let's say a user is navigating to the path `/projects/1/tasks` with our new configuration. This would activate a path in our route configuration. The project container component is activated and instantiated into the router outlet within our root component. Additionally, the route parameter `:projectId` is set to the value 1. Since we've configured a matching child route with the path `tasks`, this child route will also be activated. The Angular router is now searching for a nested router outlet below the project container component so that it can instantiate the task list container component there.

Let's take a look at the diagram in the previous section, *Composition using the router* of this chapter again. This figure reflects our end goal in terms of composition using router outlets and instantiated components and illustrates where we need to add our nested router outlet element.

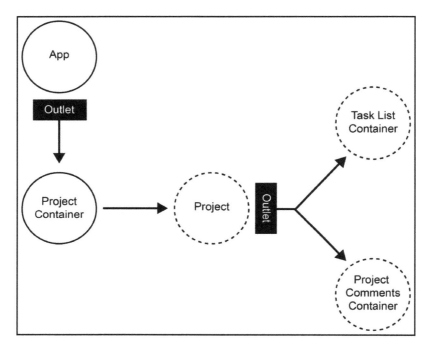

A component tree displaying routed container components (solid line) and components included via router outlets

Let's now apply some changes to our project components in order to make our child routes work. There are three changes involved:

1. Remove the static inclusion of the task view and the comments view within the project component and use a nested router outlet instead.
2. Update the project container component to obtain the active tab from the child route name. Again, we're using the router to store the state for which tab is currently active.
3. Update both the project comments container components as well as the task list container component to obtain the selected project from the router instead of the project service.

Let's start with the first step, which is quite a simple one. Let's open up the file
`src/app/project/project/project.component.ts` and replace the static inclusion of
the detail views with a router outlet:

```
<header class="header">
  <h2 class="title">
    <mac-editor [content]="project.title"
                [showControls]="true"
                (outSaveEdit)="updateTitle($event)"></mac-editor>
  </h2>
  <mac-editor [content]="project.description"
              [showControls]="true"
              (outSaveEdit)="updateDescription($event)"></mac-editor>
</header>
<mac-tabs [tabs]="tabs"
          [activeTab]="activeTab"
          (outActivateTab)="activateTab($event)">
</mac-tabs>
<router-outlet></router-outlet>
```

Okay, now the router is in control of instantiating the right project details component
within our nested router outlet.

The second change we're going to apply is concerning the tabbed interface component
within our project component. Since our tabbed component is a pure component, it relies
on the project container component to provide the active tab. Also, when we activate a tab,
the project container component is implementing what should happen on an activation.
Until now, the state for which of the tabs is currently active has been stored within the
project container component directly. Now, we want to change this behaviour so that we
use the router to store this state. An activation of a tab should then also trigger a route
change. Let's open the file `src/app/container/project-container/project-
container.component.ts` and implement the following changes:

```
...
import {ActivatedRoute, Router} from '@angular/router';
import {combineLatest} from 'rxjs';
import {map} from 'rxjs/operators';

@Component({
  selector: 'mac-project-container',
  templateUrl: './project-container.component.html',
  styleUrls: ['./project-container.component.css'],
  encapsulation: ViewEncapsulation.None,
  changeDetection: ChangeDetectionStrategy.OnPush
})
export class ProjectContainerComponent {
```

```
selectedProject: Observable<Project>;
tabs: Tab[] = [
  {id: 'tasks', title: 'Tasks'},
  {id: 'comments', title: 'Comments'},
  {id: 'activities', title: 'Activities'}
];
activeTab: Observable<Tab>;

constructor(private projectService: ProjectService,
            private route: ActivatedRoute,
            private router: Router) {
  this.selectedProject = combineLatest(
    projectService.getProjects(),
    route.params
  ).pipe(
    map(([projects, routeParams]) =>
      projects.find((project) => project.id === +routeParams.projectId)
    )
  );

  this.activeTab = combineLatest(
    this.selectedProject,
    route.url
  ).pipe(
    map(([project]) =>
      this.tabs.find((tab) =>
        router.isActive(
          `/projects/${project.id}/${tab.id}`,
          false
        )
      )
    )
  );
}

...
}
```

The tabs component is a pure component and this time we don't want to use the router link directives in order to make our project detail tabs navigable. Keeping things pure and not polluting your UI components with context-specific router link configurations can pay off when scaling your application. Instead, we want to use the router programmatically within our container component to cause navigation. We'd also like to have a way of telling which tab should be currently active according to the router state.

Within the preceding code changes, we're injecting the router instance within our component constructor. Additionally, we've changed the `activeTab` property to be of type `Observable<Tab>`. Now we need a way to react on router URL changes and figure out what of the tabs is active after the URL change. The observable behind `router.url` is exactly what we're looking for to start our reactive pipeline. On every navigation that causes the router to change the browser URL, this observable will emit an item. However, we're also going to need a reference to the currently selected project to figure out which tab is currently activated. For this purpose, we're combining the URL changes observables together with our `selectedProject` observable. Now, we have a stream that emits on URL changes and on changes of the selected project. Within a `map` operator, we're then using the `router.isActive` method in order to figure out which of the tabs is currently active. We can pass a URL string to the `isActive` method, and it tells us if that URL string is currently active within the router. We use the project ID of the selected project as well as the IDs of the individual tabs to construct this test URL string. At the end of our operator chain, the observable spits out the active tab object or null if none of the tabs is active.

Okay, we're almost there! The last change we need to apply to make our tabs work again is to refactor the `activateTab` method within the project container component class. Instead of updating a local state to represent the active tab, we now need to trigger a router navigation programmatically by using this code:

```
...
import {map, take} from 'rxjs/operators';

@Component({
  selector: 'mac-project-container',
  templateUrl: './project-container.component.html',
  styleUrls: ['./project-container.component.css'],
  encapsulation: ViewEncapsulation.None,
  changeDetection: ChangeDetectionStrategy.OnPush
})
export class ProjectContainerComponent {
  ...
  activateTab(tab: Tab) {
    this.selectedProject
      .pipe(take(1))
      .subscribe((project: Project) => {
        this.router.navigate([
          '/projects',
          project.id,
          tab.id
        ]);
      });
  }
```

```
    ...
  }
```

In order to navigate to a new URL programmatically, we can use the method `router.navigate` and use the router DSL to construct the URL segments of the desired route. Besides the ID of the activated tab, we also need the ID of the selected project to construct the target URL. Because the selected project is represented as an observable stream, we can transform using the take operator and subscribe to the output stream in order to get hold of the currently selected project object. Now, within the subscription, we have everything at hand to execute the programmatic navigation.

Since we're now using an observable to represent the active tab, we need to modify our template on the path `src/app/container/project-container/project-container.component.html` and use the async pipe to subscribe to the observable as follows:

```
<mac-project [project]="selectedProject | async"
             [tabs]="tabs"
             [activeTab]="activeTab | async"
             (outActivateTab)="activateTab($event)"
             (outUpdateProject)="updateProject($event)">
</mac-project>
```

You've successfully refactored our tabs to work with the router and our configured child routes. If you preview your changes within the browser, you should be able to navigate between tabs again, and the browser URL should be updated while doing so. You can also try to reload your browser with a specific URL that directly navigates to a specific tab—the same scenario that would apply to a user using a bookmark to a specific tab on a project. Try, for example, to navigate to `http://localhost:4200/projects/2/comments` and see whether you're ending up where you'd expect to.

The last of the three steps to complete our child route refactoring is still outstanding. Currently, both of the detail views are still relying on the project service to determine the selected project. We need to change both of them to use the router instead and extract the selected project ID from the route, similarly as we do within the project container component already. Let's start with the task list container component within the file `src/app/container/task-list-container/task-list-container.component.ts`:

```
  ...
  import {combineLatest} from 'rxjs';
  import {ActivatedRoute} from '@angular/router';

  @Component({
```

```
  selector: 'mac-task-list-container',
  templateUrl: './task-list-container.component.html',
  encapsulation: ViewEncapsulation.None,
  changeDetection: ChangeDetectionStrategy.OnPush
})
export class TaskListContainerComponent {
  ...

  constructor(private taskService: TaskService,
              private projectService: ProjectService,
              private route: ActivatedRoute) {
    this.selectedProject = combineLatest(
      projectService.getProjects(),
      route.parent.params
    ).pipe(
      map(([projects, routeParams]) =>
        projects.find((project) => project.id === +routeParams.projectId)
      )
    );

    ...
  }

  ...
}
```

Instead of obtaining the selected project observable from the project service, we're combining the project list observable, together with the route parameters, to find the selected project. This should look very familiar since we're using almost the same code as within the project container component. The only difference is that we need to access the parent route first. By calling `route.parent.params`, we can access the parent route and obtain the params from there. This is required since we're using nested routes and the task list container is a sub-view of the project container where the `:projectId` parameter is available.

Let's apply the same change to our project comments container component. Open up the file `src/app/container/project-comments-container/project-comments-container.component.ts` and update the code with the following changes:

```
...
import {combineLatest} from 'rxjs';
import {ActivatedRoute} from '@angular/router';
```

```
@Component({
  selector: 'mac-project-comments-container',
  templateUrl: './project-comments-container.component.html',
  styleUrls: ['./project-comments-container.component.css'],
  encapsulation: ViewEncapsulation.None,
  changeDetection: ChangeDetectionStrategy.OnPush
})
export class ProjectCommentsContainerComponent {
  ...

  constructor(private projectService: ProjectService,
              private userService: UserService,
              private route: ActivatedRoute) {
    this.user = userService.getCurrentUser();
    this.selectedProject = combineLatest(
      projectService.getProjects(),
      route.parent.params
    ).pipe(
      map(([projects, routeParams]) =>
        projects.find((project) => project.id === +routeParams.projectId)
      )
    );
    this.projectComments = this.selectedProject
      .pipe(
        map((project) => project.comments)
      );
  }
  ...

}
```

Congratulations! We've successfully implemented all changes necessary to provide a fully navigable project structure including child routes. We are no longer relying on the project service to store the selected project within our application. As the last step, we can remove the unnecessary code from the project service, since none of our components rely on it anymore. Let's open up the file `src/app/project/project.service.ts` and remove all code related to selecting projects:

```
import {Injectable} from '@angular/core';
import {HttpClient} from '@angular/common/http';
import {BehaviorSubject} from 'rxjs';
import {Project} from '../model';

@Injectable()
export class ProjectService {
  private projects = new BehaviorSubject<Project[]>([]);
```

```
constructor(private http: HttpClient) {
  this.loadProjects();
}

private loadProjects() {
  this.http.get<Project[]>('/api/projects')
    .subscribe((projects) => this.projects.next(projects));
}

getProjects() {
  return this.projects.asObservable();
}

updateProject(project: Project) {
  this.http.post(`/api/projects/${project.id}`, project)
    .subscribe(() => this.loadProjects());
}
}
```

Nothing feels better than removing abandoned code, right? It's like a reward for our hard work refactoring and cleaning up our code. Let's preview our changes within the browser and test our newly added router features. You should now be able to use the application the same way as before our refactoring. However, we now store the selected project and the active project detail tab within the browser's URL. Navigate across the different views and also try to use the back and forward buttons within your browser. It just feels so much better to be able to navigate like this.

Guarding our projects

Sometimes, it's a good idea to prevent certain routes from being navigated, and to provide a fallback navigation for those scenarios. This is especially true when your routes include dynamic route parameters, which can change over time, meaning users may still have outdated bookmarks to those old URLs.

Guards are the perfect helper for preventing these navigation errors. While guards help you to prevent access to certain routes and redirect accordingly, you should never rely on them to provide any kind of security for your application. Security always needs to come from a server. Using guards, you can just provide the necessary usability of a user accessing an area where he would be confronted with errors, maybe because of missing permissions to call a backend web service, or simply because a navigated detail view by an item ID no longer exists.

Within this section, we're going to create a guard to prevent navigation to a non-existing project. We haven't used the Angular CLI for a while now. Let's give it a long deserved spin and use it to create the stub of our project container guard:

```
ng generate guard --spec=false --module=app guards/project-container
```

This will generate a stub guard and include it into our main app module in the provider section. Let's open up the guard file located at src/app/guards/project-container.guard.ts and change its content to the following:

```
import {Injectable} from '@angular/core';
import {CanActivate, ActivatedRouteSnapshot, Router} from
'@angular/router';
import {ProjectService} from '../project/project.service';
import {map} from 'rxjs/operators';

@Injectable()
export class ProjectContainerGuard implements CanActivate {
  constructor(private projectService: ProjectService,
              private router: Router) {}

  canActivate(next: ActivatedRouteSnapshot) {
    return this.projectService.getProjects()
      .pipe(
        map(projects => {
          const projectExists = !!projects.find(project => project.id ===
+next.params.projectId);
          if (!projectExists) {
            this.router.navigate(['/projects', projects[0].id]);
          }
          return projectExists;
        })
      );
  }
}
```

Within this simple project guard, we're implementing the CanActivate interface, which comes from the router module. By implementing this interface we can write a guard that allows us to control if a user can navigate a certain route. As the first argument of the canActivate method, we're receiving the activated route snapshot object of the target route. The method should return an observable of type Observable<boolean>. If we'd like to prevent the navigation, we can emit false through the observable stream that is returned.

In our case, we're using the project list observable obtained from the project service as an input observable. We then map the observable in order to determine if the project with the ID, extracted from the target route snapshot params, is existing. We're using the variable `projectExists` to store this information, which we return as the result of our mapping function. Additionally, if the project with the navigated ID does not exist, we're redirecting to the first project in the project list. We can do that by using the `router.navigate` method.

Now, the only thing left to activate our guard is to include it in our router configuration. Let's open the file `src/app/routes.ts` and add the following changes:

```
...
import {ProjectContainerGuard} from './guards/project-container.guard';

export const routes: Route[] = [{
  path: 'projects/:projectId',
  component: ProjectContainerComponent,
  canActivate: [ProjectContainerGuard],
  children: [{
    path: 'tasks',
    component: TaskListContainerComponent
  }, {
    path: 'comments',
    component: ProjectCommentsContainerComponent
  }, {
    path: '**',
    redirectTo: 'tasks'
  }]
}, {
  path: '',
  pathMatch: 'full',
  redirectTo: '/projects/1'
}];
```

Every route configuration supports a `canActivate` property, which can be set to a list of guards that implement the `CanActivate` interface. All we need to do is add our guard to the project route configuration.

That's it! We have guarded our project container component and it's no longer possible to cause errors because of navigations to projects that don't exist. You can preview your changes in the browser and try to navigate to a non-existing project. Just try to navigate to `http://localhost:4200/projects/100` for example. You should be redirected to the first project overview.

Summary

In this chapter, we learned about the basic concepts of the router in Angular. We looked at how we can use the existing component tree to configure child routes in nested-router scenarios. We have learned about the router outlet element and the basic router link directive.

We have refactored our existing navigation elements, such as the project navigation and the tabbed interface on the project view. We've used router links and programmatic navigation to fulfil different navigation scenarios.

We looked into some common route configuration specifics and the basics of the router link DSL. We've also learned about route matching patterns as well as parameter placeholders and how to access these parameters in activated routes.

Last but not least, we've created a simple guard which prevents our users from accessing project details with invalid project IDs.

In the next chapter, we will learn about SVG and how to use this web standard in order to draw graphics in our Angular applications. We will visualize an activity log of our application activities using SVG and see how Angular makes this technology even greater by enabling composability.

6
Keeping up with Activities

In this chapter, we'll build an activity log in our task management system, using **Scalable Vector Graphics** (**SVG**) to build graphical components with Angular. SVG is the perfect candidate when it comes to complex graphical content, and by using Angular components, we can easily build encapsulated and reusable content.

Since we want to log all of the activities within our application, such as adding comments or renaming tasks, we are going to create a central repository for activities. We can then display these activities and render them as an activity timeline by using SVG.

To add an overview of all of the activities and to provide user input to narrow the range of activities displayed, we're going to create an interactive slider component. This component will use a projection to render timestamps, in the form of ticks and activities, directly on the slider's background. We'll also use SVG to render the elements within the component.

We'll cover the following topics in this chapter:

- A basic introduction to SVG
- Making SVG composable with Angular components
- Using namespaces in component templates
- Creating a simple pipe to format calendar times using Moment.js
- Using the `@HostListener` decorator to handle user input events, to create an interactive slider element
- Making use of Shadow DOM using `ViewEncapsulation.Native`, in order to create native style encapsulation

Creating a service for logging activities

The goal of this chapter is to provide a way to keep track of all user activities within a task management application. For that purpose, we'll need a system that will allow us to log activities within components and access previously logged activities.

Within this chapter, we'll only track activities on projects. However, the activity tracker can be used in any feature within our application. We're going to use TypeScript discriminated unions to describe our activities. Let's jump right into it and start by creating the model used within our new activities feature.

Let's open our model file, located in `src/app/model.ts`, and add the following changes:

```
...
export type ActivityAlignment = 'left' | 'right';

export interface ActivitySliderSelection {
  start: number;
  end: number;
}

export interface ActivityBase {
  kind: string;
  id?: number;
  user: User;
  time: number;
  category: string;
  title: string;
  message: string;
}

export interface ProjectActivity extends ActivityBase {
  kind: 'project';
  projectId: number;
}

export type Activity = ProjectActivity;
```

Activities, as entities, should be quite generic, and should have the following fields with their respective purposes:

- `user`: The user object of the user that is responsible for this activity.
- `time`: The timestamp of the activity. We will format this timestamp to a readable display format, but will also use it for our projection math when we draw our activity slider.

- `category`: This field provides an additional way of tagging the activity. For projects, we will currently use two categories; **comments** and **tasks**.
- `title`: This refers to the title of the activity, which will provide a very brief summary of what the activity is about. This could be something such as *New task was added* or *Comment was added*.
- `message`: This is the field where the real beef of the activity goes. It should contain enough information to provide good traceability of what happened during the activity.

Additionally, we're creating an interface, `ActivitySliderSelection`, which we're going to use when communicating selection changes within our custom slider UI component.

The custom type, `ActivityAlignment`, will be used to store information about the positioning of activities on a timeline.

Let's also update our in-memory database with some initial data, so that we have something to work with when creating our UI components for the activities view. Open up the file located in `src/app/database.ts`, and apply the following changes:

```
import {InMemoryDbService} from 'angular-in-memory-web-api';
import {Activity, Project, Task, User} from './model';

export class Database implements InMemoryDbService {
  createDb() {
    ...

    const now = +new Date();

    const activities: Activity[] = [{
      id: 1,
      kind: 'project',
      user: users[0],
      time: now - 1000 * 60 * 60 * 8,
      projectId: 1,
      category: 'tasks',
      title: 'A task was updated',
      message: 'The task \'Task 1\' was updated on #project-1.'
    }, {
      id: 2,
      kind: 'project',
      user: users[0],
      time: now - 1000 * 60 * 60 * 5,
      projectId: 2,
      category: 'tasks',
      title: 'A task was updated',
```

```
      message: 'The task \'Task 1\' was updated on #project-2.'
    }, {
      id: 3,
      kind: 'project',
      user: users[0],
      time: now - 1000 * 60 * 60 * 2,
      projectId: 2,
      category: 'tasks',
      title: 'A task was updated',
      message: 'The task \'Task 2\' was updated on #project-2.'
    }];

    return {users, projects, tasks, activities};
  }
}
```

Now, we can go ahead and create a service to load activities and log new activities. Let's use the Angular CLI to create the stub of our service:

```
ng generate service --spec false activities/activities
```

This will generate a new service class on the path `src/app/activities/activities.service.ts`. Let's open that file and add the necessary code to implement our service:

```
import {Injectable} from '@angular/core';
import {HttpClient} from '@angular/common/http';
import {BehaviorSubject} from 'rxjs';
import {Activity, ProjectActivity, User} from '../model';
import {UserService} from '../user/user.service';
import {map, mergeMap, take} from 'rxjs/operators';

@Injectable()
export class ActivitiesService {
  private activities = new BehaviorSubject<Activity[]>([]);

  constructor(private http: HttpClient, private userService: UserService) {
    this.loadActivities();
  }

  private loadActivities() {
    this.http.get<Activity[]>('/api/activities')
      .subscribe((activities) => this.activities.next(activities));
  }

  getActivities() {
    return this.activities
```

```
      .asObservable().pipe(
        map(activities => activities.sort((a, b) => b.time - a.time))
      );
  }

  logProjectActivity(projectId: number, category: string, title: string,
message: string) {
    this.userService.getCurrentUser()
      .pipe(
        take(1),
        mergeMap((user: User) => this.http
          .post('/api/activities', <ProjectActivity>{
            kind: 'project',
            time: +new Date(),
            projectId,
            user,
            category,
            title,
            message
          })
        )
      ).subscribe(() => this.loadActivities());
  }
}
```

There's not much that we need to discuss here. Our service is very similar to the task list or project service that we already created. Additionally, when obtaining an observable of our activities behavior subject, we're performing a sort on the emitted activity list. We always want to emit the activity list sorted by activity time.

Since activities can't be edited or deleted, we only need to be concerned with newly added activities.

In the `logProjectActivity` method, we're simply posting a new activity into our in-memory web database, using the Angular HTTP client. The user service will provide us with information on the currently logged-in user.

That's it on the data front. We have created a simple platform that will help us keep track of activities within our application. Later in this book, we can use the activities service to track all sorts of activities. For now, we're just concerned with project-related activities.

Logging activities

We have created a nice system to log activities. Now, let's go ahead and use it within our components, to keep an audit of all of the activities happening within the context of projects.

First, let's use our activities service to log activities when project tasks get updated and created. Logging activities can be viewed as an application side effect, and we don't want to cause side effects within our pure UI components. Instead, the container components are the perfect places to perform these kinds of operations.

Let's open the container component for our task list on the path `src/app/container/task-list-container/task-list-container.component.ts`, and apply the following changes:

```
...
import {ActivitiesService} from '../../activities/activities.service';
import {limitWithEllipsis} from '../../utilities/string-utilities';

@Component({
  selector: 'mac-task-list-container',
  templateUrl: './task-list-container.component.html',
  encapsulation: ViewEncapsulation.None,
  changeDetection: ChangeDetectionStrategy.OnPush
})
export class TaskListContainerComponent {
  ...

  constructor(private taskService: TaskService,
              private projectService: ProjectService,
              private route: ActivatedRoute,
              private activitiesService: ActivitiesService) {
    ...
  }

  activateFilterType(type: TaskListFilterType) {
    this.activeTaskFilterType.next(type);
  }

  addTask(title: string) {
    this.selectedProject
      .pipe(
        take(1)
      )
      .subscribe((project) => {
        const task: Task = {
```

```
          projectId: project.id, title, done: false
        };
        this.taskService.addTask(task);
        this.activitiesService.logProjectActivity(
          project.id,
          'tasks',
          'A task was added',
          `A new task "${limitWithEllipsis(title, 30)}" was added to
#project-${project.id}.`
        );
      });
  }

  updateTask(task: Task) {
    this.taskService.updateTask(task);
    this.activitiesService.logProjectActivity(
      task.projectId,
      'tasks',
      'A task was updated',
      `The task "${limitWithEllipsis(task.title, 30)}" was updated on
#project-${task.projectId}.`
    );
  }
}
```

Using the `logProjectActivity` method of our activities service, we can easily log an activity for creating and updating tasks.

In the message body of our activities, we've used a new utility function, `limitWithEllipsis`, which we're importing from a new module, called `string-utilities`. This function truncates an input string and cuts it off at a position specified with a second parameter. In addition, it appends an ellipsis character (...) at the end of the truncated string. This is a nice utility for when we want to create a preview of text that might be lengthy.

Let's quickly craft this little helper function and create a new file on the path `src/app/utilities/string-utilities.ts`. Open up the file and add the following code:

```
export function limitWithEllipsis(str: string, limit: number): string {
  if (str.length > limit) {
    return str.slice(0, limit - 1) + '...';
  } else {
    return str;
  }
}
```

That's it for now. We're successfully logging activities upon task creation and updates. We're also going to use the activity service within the project comments container component to create logs for added and edited comments. Since the steps involved are very similar to what we've just done for the task list container component, we're going to skip over this. You can always take a look at the final code base for this chapter to add activity logs for the project comments container component.

Leveraging the power of SVG

SVG has been a part of the Open web platform standards since 1999, and was first recommended in 2001, under the SVG 1.0 standard. SVG is a consolidation of two independent proposals for an XML-based vector image format. **Precision Graphics Markup Language** (**PGML**), mainly developed by Adobe and Netscape, and **Vector Markup Language** (**VML**), which was mainly represented by Microsoft and Macromedia, were both different XML formats that served the same purpose. The W3C consortium declined both of the proposals in favor of the newly developed SVG standard, which unified the best of both worlds into a single standard:

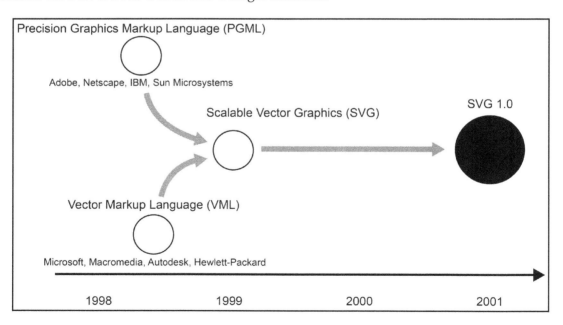

Timeline showing the development of the SVG standard

All three standards had a common goal, which was to provide a format for the web to display vector graphics in the browser. SVG is a declarative language that specifies graphical objects using XML elements and attributes.

Let's look at a simple example of how to create an SVG image with a black circle, using SVG:

```
<?xml version="1.0" encoding="utf-8"?>
<svg version="1.1" xmlns="http://www.w3.org/2000/svg"
      width="20px" height="20px">
   <circle cx="10" cy="10" r="10" fill="black" />
</svg>
```

This rather simple example represents an SVG image with a black circle, whose center is located at `cx="10"` px and `cy="10"` px. The radius of the circle is `10` px, which makes this circle `20` px in width and height.

The origin of the coordinate system in SVG sits on the top-left corner, where the *y*-axis faces the south direction and the *x*-axis eastward:

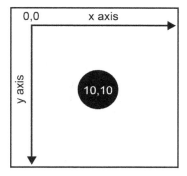

The coordinate system within SVG

Using not only primitive shapes, such as circles, lines, and rectangles, but also complex polygons, the possibilities for creating graphical content are nearly unlimited.

SVG is not only used within the web, but has also become a very important intermediate format for exchanging vector graphics between different applications. Almost any application that supports vector graphics also supports the import and export of SVG files.

The real power of SVG comes to the surface when we do not include an SVG file as an HTML image element, but rather, include the SVG content directly within our DOM. Since HTML5 directly supports the SVG namespace within an HTML document and will render the graphics that we define within our HTML, a whole bunch of new possibilities spring up. We can now style our SVG with CSS, manipulate the DOM with JavaScript, and easily make our SVG interactive.

Taking the previous example of our circle image to the next level, we could make it interactive by changing the circle color (by clicking on it). First, let's create a minimal HTML document and include our SVG elements directly within the DOM:

```
<!doctype html>
<title>Minimalistic Circle</title>
<svg width="20px" height="20px">
  <circle id="circle" cx="10" cy="10" r="10" fill="black">
</svg>
<script>
  document
    .getElementById('circle')
    .addEventListener('click', function(event) {
      event.target.setAttribute('fill', 'red');
    });
</script>
```

As you can see, we can get rid of the version and the XML namespace declaration when we use SVG directly within the DOM of our HTML document. What's interesting here is that we can treat SVG very much like regular HTML. We can assign an ID, and even classes, to SVG elements, and access them from JavaScript.

Within the `script` tag of our HTML document, we can directly access our `circle` element using the ID we've previously assigned to it. We can add event listeners to SVG elements the same way as with regular HTML elements. In this example, we added a `click` event listener and changed the color of our circle to red.

For the sake of simplicity, we used an inline `script` tag in this example. It would, of course, be much cleaner to have a separate JavaScript file to do the scripting.

Styling SVG

I'm a purist when it comes to the separation of concerns within the web. I still strongly believe in the separation of structure (HTML), appearance (CSS), and behavior (JavaScript), as well as producing the most maintainable applications when following this practice.

First, it seems weird to have SVG in your HTML, and you might think that this breaks the contract of a clean separation. Why is this graphical content, consisting of only appearance-relevant data, sitting in my HTML, which is supposed to contain only raw information? After dealing with a lot of SVGs within a DOM, I have come to the conclusion that we can establish a clean separation when using SVG by dividing our appearance responsibilities into the two following subgroups:

- **Graphical structure**: This subgroup deals with the process of defining the basic structure of your graphical content. This is about shapes and layout.
- **Visual appearance**: This subgroup deals with the process of defining the look and feel of our graphical structures, such as colors, line widths, line styles, and text alignment.

If we separate the concerns of SVG into these groups, we can actually gain great maintainability. The graphical structure is defined by the SVG shapes themselves. They are directly written within our HTML, but don't have a particular look and feel. We only store the basic structural information within HTML.

Luckily, instead of using attributes on SVG elements, all the properties for visual appearance, such as color, can also be specified with corresponding CSS properties. That allows us to offload all of the look-and-feel relevant aspects of the structure to CSS.

Let's go back to the example where we drew a black circle; we'll tweak this a bit, to fit our demands of separation of concerns, so that we can distinguish graphical structure from graphical appearance:

```
<!doctype html>
<title>Minimalistic Circle</title>
<svg width="20px" height="20px">
  <circle class="circle" cx="10" cy="10" r="10">
</svg>
```

Styling our graphical structures can now be achieved by using CSS, including a style sheet with the following content:

```
.circle {
  fill: black;
}
```

This is fantastic, as we can not only reuse some graphical structures, but can also apply different visual appearance parameters using CSS, similar to those enlightening moments when we managed to reuse some semantic HTML by only changing some CSS.

Let's look at the most important CSS properties that we can use to style SVG shapes:

- `fill`: When working with solid SVG shapes, there's always a shape fill and stroke option available; the `fill` property specifies the color of the shape fill.
- `stroke`: This property specifies the color of the SVG shape's outline.
- `stroke-width`: This property specifies the width of the SVG shape's outline on solid shapes. For non-solid shapes, such as lines, this can be thought of as the line width.
- `stroke-dasharray`: This specifies a dash pattern for strokes. Dash patterns are space-separated values that define a pattern.
- `stroke-dashoffset`: This specifies an offset for the dash pattern, which is specified with the `stroke-dasharray` property.
- `stroke-linecap`: This property defines how line caps should be rendered. They can be rendered as square, butt, or rounded caps.
- `stroke-linejoin`: This property specifies how lines are joined together within a path.
- `shape-rendering`: Using this property, you can override the shape-rendering algorithm that, as the name suggests, is used to render shapes. This is particularly useful if you need crispy edges on your shapes.

For a complete reference of the available appearance-relevant SVG attributes, visit the Mozilla Developer website at
`https://developer.mozilla.org/en-US/docs/Web/SVG/Attribute`.

I hope that this brief introduction gave you a better feeling about SVG and the great power it comes with. In this chapter, we're going to use some of that power to create nice, interactive graphical components. If you would like to learn more about SVG, I strongly recommend that you go through the great articles by Sara Soueidan.

Building SVG components

When building Angular components with SVG templates, there are a couple of things that you need to be aware of. The first and most obvious one is XML namespaces. Modern browsers are very intelligent when parsing HTML. Besides being probably the most fault-tolerant parsers in the history of computer science, DOM parsers are very smart in recognizing markup, and then deciding how to treat it. They will automatically decide the correct namespaces for us, based on element names, so we don't need to deal with them when writing HTML.

If you've messed around with the DOM API a bit, you've probably recognized that there are two methods for creating new elements. In the document object, for example, there's a `createElement` function, but there's also `createElementNS`, which accepts an additional namespace URI parameter. Also, every element created has a `namespaceURI` property that tells you the namespace of the specific element. That is important, since HTML5 is a standard that consists of at least three namespaces:

- **HTML**: This is the standard HTML namespace, with the `http://www.w3.org/1999/xhtml` URI.
- **SVG**: This embraces all SVG elements and attributes and uses the `http://www.w3.org/2000/svg` URI. You can sometimes see this namespace URI in an `xmlns` attribute of the `svg` elements. In fact, this is not really required, as the browser is smart enough to decide on the correct namespace itself.
- **MathML**: This is an XML-based format to describe mathematical formulas, and it is supported in most modern browsers. It uses the `http://www.w3.org/1998/Math/MathML` namespace URI.

We can mix all of these elements from different standards and namespaces within a single document, and our browser will figure out the correct namespace itself, when it creates elements within the DOM.

 If you want more information on namespaces, I recommend that you go through the *Namespaces Crash Course* article on the Mozilla Developer Network
at https://developer.mozilla.org/en/docs/Web/SVG/Namespaces_Crash _Course.

As Angular will compile templates for us and render elements into the DOM using the DOM API, it needs to be aware of the namespaces when doing so. Similar to the browser, Angular provides some intelligence for deciding the correct namespace when creating elements. However, there will be some situations where you will need to help Angular recognize the correct namespace.

To illustrate some of this behavior, let's transform the circle example that we've been working on into an Angular component:

```
@Component({
  selector: 'awesome-circle',
  template: `
    <svg [attr.width]="size" [attr.height]="size">
      <circle [attr.cx]="size/2" [attr.cy]="size/2"
              [attr.r]="size/2" fill="black" />
    </svg>
  `
})
export class AwesomeCircle {
  @Input() size;
}
```

We've wrapped our circle SVG graphics into a simple Angular component. The `size` input parameter determines the actual width and height of the circle by controlling the SVG's width and height attributes and the circle's cx, cy, and r attributes.

To use our circle component, simply use the following template within another component:

```
<awesome-circle [size]="20"></awesome-circle>
```

It's important to note that we need to use attribute bindings on SVG elements, and we can't set DOM element properties directly. This is due to the nature of SVG elements that have special property types (for example, SVGAnimatedLength) that can be animated with **Synchronized Multimedia Integration Language** (**SMIL**). Instead of interfering with these rather complex element properties, we can simply use attribute bindings to set the attribute values of the DOM element.

Let's go back to our namespace discussion. Angular will know that it needs to use the SVG namespace to create the elements within this template. It will function in this way simply because we're using the svg element as a root element within our component, and it can switch the namespace within the template parser for any child elements automatically.

However, there are certain situations where we need to help Angular determine the correct namespace for the elements we'd like to create. This strikes us if we're creating nested SVG components that don't contain a root svg element:

```
@Component({
  selector: '[awesomeCircle]',
  template: `
      <svg:circle [attr.cx]="size/2" [attr.cy]="size/2"
                  [attr.r]="size/2" fill="black" />
  `
})
export class AwesomeCircle {
  @Input('awesomeCircle') size;
}

@Component({
  selector: 'app'
  template: `
    <svg width="20" height="20">
      <g [awesomeCircle]="20"></g>
    </svg>
  `,
  directives: [AwesomeCircle]
})
export class App {}
```

In this example, we're nesting SVG components, and our awesome circle component does not have an svg root element to tell Angular to switch the namespace. That is why we've created the svg element within our app component, and then included the awesome circle component in an SVG group.

We need to explicitly tell Angular to switch to the SVG namespace within our circle component, and we can do this by including the namespace name as a prefix separated by a colon, as you can see in the highlighted section of the preceding code excerpt.

If you have multiple elements that need to be created explicitly within the SVG namespace, you can rely on the fact that Angular does apply the namespace for child elements, too, and groups all of your elements with an SVG group element. So, you only need to prefix the group element with `<svg:g>` ... `</svg:g>`, but none of the contained SVG elements.

That is enough to know about Angular internals when dealing with SVG. Let's move on and create some real components!

Building an interactive activity slider component

In the previous topics, we covered the basics of working with SVG and dealing with SVG in Angular components. Now, it's time to apply our knowledge to the task management application and create some awesome components using SVG.

The first component we'll be creating in this context is an interactive slider that allows the user to select the time range of activities that he or she is interested in checking out. Displaying a simple HTML5 range input could be a solution, but since we've gained some SVG superpower, we can do better! We'll use SVG to render our own slider that will show existing activities as ticks on the slider. Let's look at a mock-up of the slider component that we're going to create:

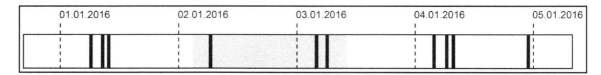

A mock-up of the activity slider component

Our slider component will actually serve two purposes. It should be a user control, and should provide a way to select a time range for filtering activities. However, it should also provide an overview of all of the activities, so that a user can filter the range more intuitively. By drawing vertical bars that represent activities, we can already give the user a feeling of the range he or she is interested in.

Let's create our new activity slider component using the Angular CLI tool:

```
ng generate component --spec false -ve none -cd onpush activities/activity-
slider
```

Open the generated component class on the path `src/app/activities/activity-slider/activity-slider.component.ts`, and add the following code:

```
import {
  ChangeDetectionStrategy, Component, ElementRef, EventEmitter,
HostListener,
  Input, OnChanges, Output, SimpleChanges, ViewEncapsulation
} from '@angular/core';
import {Activity, ActivitySliderSelection} from '../../model';

@Component({
  selector: 'mac-activity-slider',
  templateUrl: './activity-slider.component.html',
  styleUrls: ['./activity-slider.component.css'],
  changeDetection: ChangeDetectionStrategy.OnPush,
  encapsulation: ViewEncapsulation.Native
})
export class ActivitySliderComponent {
  @Input() activities: Activity[];
  @Output() outSelectionChange = new
EventEmitter<ActivitySliderSelection>();
  constructor(private elementRef: ElementRef) {}
}
```

The first thing we should mention, which differs from all of the other components we've written about so far, is that we're using `ViewEncapsulation.Native` for this component. As we learned from the *Creating our application component* section in `Chapter 2`, *Ready, Set, Go!*, when we use `ViewEncapsulation.Native` for our component encapsulation, Angular actually uses Shadow DOM to create the component. We briefly looked at this in the *Shadow DOM* section in `Chapter 1`, *Component-Based User Interfaces*, as well.

Using Shadow DOM for our component will give us this advantage: Our component will be fully encapsulated, from the CSS side of things. This not only means that none of the global CSS will leak into our component; it also means that we'll need to create local styles, in order to style our component.

So far, we've used styles coming from a global style sheet, which has been prepared for the book. We're using a component CSS naming convention within that file, in order to avoid name clashes with CSS classes. However, when using Shadow DOM, we can forego prefixes and other naming conventions to avoid name clashes, since we're only applying styles locally, within the component.

 Chrome supports Shadow DOM natively, from Version 35. Within Firefox, Shadow DOM can be enabled by visiting the about:config page and turning on the dom.webcomponents.enabled flag. IE, Edge, and Safari don't support this standard at all; however, we can set things up in a way that they can deal with Shadow DOM, by including a polyfill named webcomponents.js. You can find more information on this polyfill at https://github.com/webcomponents/webcomponentsjs.

Now, let's add the local CSS styles that we're going to use within our activity slider component. Open the file src/app/activities/activity-slider/activity-slider.component.css, and add the following code:

```css
:host {
  display: block;
}

.slide {
  fill:#f9f9f9;
}

.activity {
  fill:#3699cb;
}

.time {
  fill:#bbb;
  font-size:14px;
}

.tick {
  stroke:#bbb;
  stroke-width:2px;
  stroke-dasharray:3px;
}

.selection-overlay {
  fill:#d9d9d9;
}
```

Usually, such short class names would probably lead to name clashes within our project, but since the styles will be local to the Shadow DOM of our component, we don't need to worry about name clashes anymore.

You can see that we're using a special pseudo-selector, `:host`, within our styles. This selector is part of the Shadow DOM specification for CSS, and it allows us to style the host element of a shadow root. This becomes very handy, since we can treat the host element as a part of our component internals when styling.

Let's go back to the rest of the code inside of our activity slider component. As an input parameter, we define the list of activities that will be used, not only to determine the available range in the slider, but also to render activities on the background of the slider.

Once a selection is made by the user, our component will use the `outSelectionChange` output to notify the outside world about the change.

Within the constructor, we're injecting the host element for later use. We will need that to access the native DOM elements of our slider, in order to do some width calculations.

Projection of time

Our slider component needs to be able to project timestamps into the coordinate system of SVG. Also, when a user clicks on the timeline to select a range, we'll need to be able to project coordinates back into timestamps. For this purpose, we need to create two projection functions within our component, which will use a few helper functions and states to calculate the values, from coordinates to time, and vice-versa:

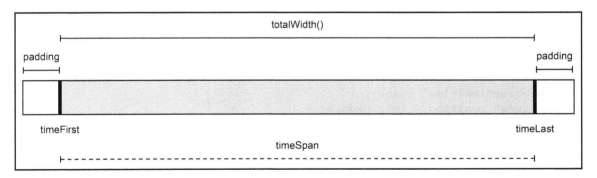

Visualization of important variables and functions for our calculations

While we will use percentages to position our SVG elements on the slider component, the padding on the sides will need to be specified in pixels. The `totalWidth` function will return the total width of the area in pixels; this is where we'll draw the activity indicators. The `timeFirst`, `timeLast`, and `timeSpan` variables will also be used by the calculations, and are specified in milliseconds.

Let's add some code to our slider to deal with the projection of our activities on the slider:

```
import {
  ChangeDetectionStrategy, Component, ElementRef, EventEmitter, Input,
Output, ViewEncapsulation
} from '@angular/core';
import {Activity, ActivitySliderSelection} from '../../model';

@Component({
  selector: 'mac-activity-slider',
  templateUrl: './activity-slider.component.html',
  styleUrls: ['./activity-slider.component.css'],
  changeDetection: ChangeDetectionStrategy.OnPush,
  encapsulation: ViewEncapsulation.Native
})
export class ActivitySliderComponent {
  @Input() activities: Activity[];
  @Output() outSelectionChange = new
EventEmitter<ActivitySliderSelection>();
  padding = 20;
  timeFirst: number;
  timeLast: number;
  timeSpan: number;

  constructor(private elementRef: ElementRef) {}

  totalWidth() {
    return this.elementRef.nativeElement.clientWidth - this.padding * 2;
  }

  projectTime(time: number) {
    const position = this.padding +
      (time - this.timeFirst) / this.timeSpan * this.totalWidth();
    return position / this.elementRef.nativeElement.clientWidth * 100;
  }

  projectLength(length: number) {
    return this.timeFirst + (length - this.padding) / this.totalWidth() *
this.timeSpan;
  }
}
```

Since we have put aside the reference to the host element, we can use its `clientWidth` property to get the full width of the component and subtract the padding. This will give us the full width of the area where we'd like to draw activity indicators, in pixels.

In the `projectTime` function, we will first transform the timestamp into a position by a simple rule of three. Because we have access to the timestamp of the first activity, as well as the total time span, this will be a quite simple task. Once we do this, we can convert our position value, which is of unit pixels, into a percentage, by dividing it by the total component width and then multiplying it by 100.

To project a pixel value back to a timestamp, we can more or less perform the reverse of `projectTime`, except that we're not dealing with percentages here, but assuming that the length parameter of the `projectLength` function is in a pixel unit.

We've used some member variables (`timeFirst`, `timeLast`, and `timeSpan`) within our projection code, but how do we set these member variables? Since we have an `activities` component input, which is expected to be a list of relevant activities, we can observe the input for changes and set the values based on the input. To observe that component input for changes, we can use the `OnChanges` life cycle hook:

```
import {
  ChangeDetectionStrategy, Component, ElementRef, EventEmitter,
HostListener,
  Input, Output, OnChanges, SimpleChanges, ViewEncapsulation
} from '@angular/core';
import {Activity, ActivitySliderSelection} from '../../model';

@Component({
  selector: 'mac-activity-slider',
  templateUrl: './activity-slider.component.html',
  styleUrls: ['./activity-slider.component.css'],
  changeDetection: ChangeDetectionStrategy.OnPush,
  encapsulation: ViewEncapsulation.Native
})
export class ActivitySliderComponent implements OnChanges {
  @Input() activities: Activity[];
  @Output() outSelectionChange = new
EventEmitter<ActivitySliderSelection>();
  padding = 20;
  timeFirst: number;
  timeLast: number;
  timeSpan: number;

  constructor(private elementRef: ElementRef) {}
```

```
ngOnChanges(changes: SimpleChanges) {
  if (changes.activities && this.activities) {
    if (this.activities.length === 1) {
      this.timeFirst = this.timeLast = this.activities[0].time;
    } else if (this.activities.length > 1) {
      this.timeFirst = this.activities[this.activities.length - 1].time;
      this.timeLast = this.activities[0].time;
    } else {
      this.timeFirst = this.timeLast = new Date().getTime();
    }

    this.timeSpan = Math.max(1, this.timeLast - this.timeFirst);
  }
}

...
}
```

First, we need to check whether the changes include changes to the `activities` input and that the current value of the input is valid. After checking for the input value, we can determine our member variables, namely `timeFirst`, `timeLast`, and `timeSpan`. We limit the `timeSpan` variable to at least 1, as our projection calculations would be messed up otherwise.

The preceding code will ensure that we will always recalculate our member variables when the `activities` input changes, and that we'll be using the most recent data-rendering activities.

Rendering activity indicators

We've already implemented the basics of the component and laid the groundwork for drawing time information into the coordinate system of our component. It's time to use our projection functions and draw our activities as indicators on the slider using SVG.

Let's open the template of our activity slider in `src/app/activities/activity-slider/activity-slider.component.html`, and add the following code:

```
<svg width="100%" height="70px">
  <rect x="0" y="30" width="100%" height="40" class="slide"></rect>
  <rect *ngFor="let activity of activities"
        [attr.x]="projectTime(activity.time) + '%'"
        height="40" width="2px" y="30" class="activity"></rect>
</svg>
```

Since we need to create an indicator for every activity within our activities list, we can simply use the ngFor directive to repeat the rectangle that represents our activity indicator.

As we know from building our activity service class in a previous topic, *Creating a service for logging activities*, activities always contain a time field with the timestamp of the activity. Within our component, we have already created a projection function that converts time into a percentage, relative to our component width. We can simply use the projectTime function within our attribute binding for the x attribute of the rect element, to position our activity indicators at the correct positions.

By only using an SVG template and our backing function to project time, we have created a nice little chart that displays activity indicators on a timeline.

You can imagine that if we have a lot of activities, our slider will actually look pretty stuffed, and it will be hard to get a feeling for when those activities may have occurred. We need to have some sort of a grid that will help us associate the chart with a timeline.

As already shown in the mock-up of our slider component, now, we're going to introduce some ticks on the slider background that will divide the slider into sections. We'll also label each tick with a calendar time. This will give our users a rough sense of time, when looking at the activity indicators on the slider.

Let's look at the code changes within our activity slider class that will enable the rendering of our ticks:

```
import {
  ChangeDetectionStrategy, Component, ElementRef, EventEmitter,
  Input, OnChanges, Output, SimpleChanges, ViewEncapsulation
} from '@angular/core';
import {Activity, ActivitySliderSelection} from '../../model';

@Component({
  selector: 'mac-activity-slider',
  templateUrl: './activity-slider.component.html',
  styleUrls: ['./activity-slider.component.css'],
  changeDetection: ChangeDetectionStrategy.OnPush,
  encapsulation: ViewEncapsulation.Native
})
export class ActivitySliderComponent implements OnChanges {
  @Input() activities: Activity[];
  @Output() outSelectionChange = new
EventEmitter<ActivitySliderSelection>();
  padding = 20;
  timeFirst: number;
  timeLast: number;
```

```
timeSpan: number;
ticks: number[];

constructor(private elementRef: ElementRef) {}

ngOnChanges(changes: SimpleChanges) {
  if (changes.activities && this.activities) {
    if (this.activities.length === 1) {
      this.timeFirst = this.timeLast = this.activities[0].time;
    } else if (this.activities.length > 1) {
      this.timeFirst = this.activities[this.activities.length - 1].time;
      this.timeLast = this.activities[0].time;
    } else {
      this.timeFirst = this.timeLast = new Date().getTime();
    }

    this.timeSpan = Math.max(1, this.timeLast - this.timeFirst);
    this.computeTicks();
  }
}

computeTicks() {
  const count = 5;
  const timeSpanTick = this.timeSpan / count;
  this.ticks = Array.from({length: count}).map((element, index) => {
    return this.timeFirst + timeSpanTick * index;
  });
}

...
}
```

First of all, we need to create a function that computes some ticks for us, which we can place onto the timeline. For this purpose, we need to create the computeTicks method, which will divide the whole timeline into five equal segments and generate timestamps that represent the positions in time for individual ticks. We will store these ticks in a new ticks member variable. With the help of these timestamps, we can easily render the ticks within our view.

 We use the Array.from ES6 function to create a new array with the desired length, and use the functional array extra function map to generate tick model objects from this array. Using Array.from is a nice trick to create an initial array of a given length, which can be used to establish a functional style.

Let's look at the template of our activity slider component, and how we can use our array of timestamps to render ticks on our slider component:

```
<svg width="100%" height="70px">
  <rect x="0" y="30" width="100%" height="40" class="slide"></rect>
  <g *ngFor="let tick of ticks">
    <text [attr.x]="projectTime(tick) + '%'" y="14" class="time">
      {{tick | calendarTime}}
    </text>
    <line [attr.x1]="projectTime(tick) + '%'" [attr.x2]="projectTime(tick)
+ '%'"
          y1="30" y2="70" class="tick"></line>
  </g>
  <rect *ngFor="let activity of activities"
        [attr.x]="projectTime(activity.time) + '%'"
        height="40" width="2px" y="30" class="activity"></rect>
</svg>
```

To render our ticks, we've used an SVG group element to place our `ngFor` directive that repeats the tick timestamps we've stored in the `ticks` member variable.

For each tick, we need to place a label, as well as a line, that spans over the slider background. We can use the SVG text element to render our label with the timestamp on top of the slider. Within the attribute binding for the x attribute of our `text` element, we've used our `projectTime` projection function to receive the projected percentage value from our timestamp. The y coordinate of our `text` element is fixed at a position where the labels will just sit on top of our slider.

SVG lines consist of four coordinates: x1, x2, y1, and y2. Together, they define two coordinate points, where a line will be drawn from one point to the other.

Now, we are getting closer to the final slider that we specified in the mock-up at the beginning of this topic. The last missing piece of the puzzle is to make our slider interactive, so a user can select a range of activities.

Bringing it to life

So far, we've covered the rendering of the slider background, as well as the rendering of the activity indicators. We've also generated ticks and displayed them with a grid line and a label, to display the calendar time of each tick.

Well, that does not really make a slider, does it? Of course, we also need to handle user input, and make the slider interactive, so that users can select a time range that they want to display the activities for.

To do this, add the following changes to the component class:

```
import {
  ChangeDetectionStrategy, Component, ElementRef, EventEmitter,
HostListener,
  Input, OnChanges, Output, SimpleChanges, ViewEncapsulation
} from '@angular/core';
import {Activity, ActivitySliderSelection} from '../../model';

@Component({
  selector: 'mac-activity-slider',
  templateUrl: './activity-slider.component.html',
  styleUrls: ['./activity-slider.component.css'],
  changeDetection: ChangeDetectionStrategy.OnPush,
  encapsulation: ViewEncapsulation.Native
})
export class ActivitySliderComponent implements OnChanges {
  @Input() activities: Activity[];
  @Output() outSelectionChange = new
EventEmitter<ActivitySliderSelection>();
  padding = 20;
  timeFirst: number;
  timeLast: number;
  timeSpan: number;
  ticks: number[];
  selection: ActivitySliderSelection;

  constructor(private elementRef: ElementRef) {}

  ngOnChanges(changes: SimpleChanges) {
    if (changes.activities && this.activities) {
      if (this.activities.length === 1) {
        this.timeFirst = this.timeLast = this.activities[0].time;
      } else if (this.activities.length > 1) {
        this.timeFirst = this.activities[this.activities.length - 1].time;
        this.timeLast = this.activities[0].time;
      } else {
        this.timeFirst = this.timeLast = new Date().getTime();
      }

      this.timeSpan = Math.max(1, this.timeLast - this.timeFirst);
      this.computeTicks();
```

```
    this.selection = {
      start: this.timeFirst,
      end: this.timeLast
    };
    this.outSelectionChange.next(this.selection);
  }
}
  ...
}
```

When we detect a change in the `activities` input property within the `OnChanges` life cycle hook, we initialize a `ActivitySliderSelection` object for the user selection in our slider component. It consists of a `start` and `end` property, both containing timestamps that represent the selected range on our activity slider.

Once we've set our initial selection, we need to use the `outSelectionChange` output property to emit an event. That way, we can let our parent component know that the selection within the slider has changed.

To display the selected range, we use an overlay rectangle within our template, which will be placed above the slider background. If you look at the mock-up image of the slider again, you'll notice that this overlay is painted in grey:

```
<svg width="100%" height="70px">
  <rect x="0" y="30" width="100%" height="40" class="slide"></rect>
  <rect *ngIf="selection"
        [attr.x]="projectTime(selection.start) + '%'"
        [attr.width]="projectTime(selection.end) -
projectTime(selection.start) + '%'"
        y="30" height="40" class="selection-overlay"></rect>
  <g *ngFor="let tick of ticks">
    <text [attr.x]="projectTime(tick) + '%'" y="14" class="time">
      {{tick | calendarTime}}
    </text>
    <line [attr.x1]="projectTime(tick) + '%'" [attr.x2]="projectTime(tick)
+ '%'"
          y1="30" y2="70" class="tick"></line>
  </g>
  <rect *ngFor="let activity of activities"
        [attr.x]="projectTime(activity.time) + '%'"
        height="40" width="2px" y="30" class="activity"></rect>
</svg>
```

This rectangle will be placed just above our slider background, and will use our projection function to calculate the `x` and `width` attributes. As we need to wait for change detection to initialize our selection within the `OnChanges` life cycle hook, we'll just check for a valid selection object by making use of the `ngIf` directive.

Now, we need to start tackling user input in our activity slider component. The mechanics for storing the state and rendering our selection are already in place, so we can implement the required host listeners to handle user input. Since we've applied quite a few changes progressively, let's look at the final, full version of the component class. The missing changes to add user interactions are marked in bold:

```
import {
  ChangeDetectionStrategy, Component, ElementRef, EventEmitter,
  HostListener,
  Input, OnChanges, Output, SimpleChanges, ViewEncapsulation
} from '@angular/core';
import {Activity, ActivitySliderSelection} from '../../model';

@Component({
  selector: 'mac-activity-slider',
  templateUrl: './activity-slider.component.html',
  styleUrls: ['./activity-slider.component.css'],
  changeDetection: ChangeDetectionStrategy.OnPush,
  encapsulation: ViewEncapsulation.Native
})
export class ActivitySliderComponent implements OnChanges {
  @Input() activities: Activity[];
  @Output() outSelectionChange = new
EventEmitter<ActivitySliderSelection>();
  padding = 20;
  timeFirst: number;
  timeLast: number;
  timeSpan: number;
  ticks: number[];
  selection: ActivitySliderSelection;
  modifySelection: boolean;

  constructor(private elementRef: ElementRef) {}

  ngOnChanges(changes: SimpleChanges) {
    if (changes.activities && this.activities) {
      if (this.activities.length === 1) {
        this.timeFirst = this.timeLast = this.activities[0].time;
      } else if (this.activities.length > 1) {
        this.timeFirst = this.activities[this.activities.length - 1].time;
        this.timeLast = this.activities[0].time;
```

```
    } else {
      this.timeFirst = this.timeLast = new Date().getTime();
    }

    this.timeSpan = Math.max(1, this.timeLast - this.timeFirst);
    this.computeTicks();

    this.selection = {
      start: this.timeFirst,
      end: this.timeLast
    };
    this.outSelectionChange.next(this.selection);
  }
}

computeTicks() {
  const count = 5;
  const timeSpanTick = this.timeSpan / count;
  this.ticks = Array.from({length: count}).map((element, index) => {
    return this.timeFirst + timeSpanTick * index;
  });
}

totalWidth() {
  return this.elementRef.nativeElement.clientWidth - this.padding * 2;
}

projectTime(time: number) {
  const position = this.padding +
    (time - this.timeFirst) / this.timeSpan * this.totalWidth();
  return position / this.elementRef.nativeElement.clientWidth * 100;
}

projectLength(length: number) {
  return this.timeFirst + (length - this.padding) / this.totalWidth() *
this.timeSpan;
}

@HostListener('mousedown', ['$event'])
onMouseDown(event) {
  this.selection.start = this.selection.end =
this.projectLength(event.offsetX);
  this.outSelectionChange.next(this.selection);
  this.modifySelection = true;
  event.stopPropagation();
  event.preventDefault();
}
```

```
    @HostListener('mousemove', ['$event'])
    onMouseMove(event) {
      if (this.modifySelection) {
        this.selection.end = Math.max(this.selection.start,
  this.projectLength(event.offsetX));
        this.outSelectionChange.next(this.selection);
        event.stopPropagation();
        event.preventDefault();
      }
    }

    @HostListener('mouseup')
    onMouseUp() {
      this.modifySelection = false;
    }

    @HostListener('mouseleave')
    onMouseLeave() {
      this.modifySelection = false;
    }
}
```

In the preceding code excerpt, we handled a total of four events on the slider host element:

- onMouseDown: We set our selection model's start and end properties with the same value. Since we're using timestamps for these properties, we projected the mouse position into the timespace first. The mouse position comes in pixels, relative to the slider component's origin. Since we know the slider's width and the total time duration displayed, we can easily convert this into timestamps. We're using the projectLength method for this purpose. By passing a second argument to the @HostListener decorator, we specified that we'd like to pass the DOM event to our onMouseDown method. We also set a state flag, modifySelection, in our component, to indicate that a selection is in progress.

- onMouseMove: If the component is in selection mode (the modifySelection flag is true), you can adjust the end property of the selection object. Here, we also made sure that we ruled out the possibility of creating a negative selection, by using Math.max and limiting the end of the selection to not be smaller than the start.

- onMouseUp: When the user releases the mouse button, the component exits the selection mode. This can be done by setting the modifySelection flag to false.

- onMouseLeave: This is the same as the onMouseUp event; the difference is that here, the component will just exit the selection mode.

Using the `@HostListener` decorator, we were able to handle all of the necessary user input to complete our component with the interactive elements that were still missing.

Recap

In this topic, we learned how to use SVG in order to create graphical and interactive components with Angular. By creating attribute bindings on our SVG elements and controlling the instantiation of graphical elements using the `ngFor` and `ngIf` directives, we built a custom slider component that provides a nice overview of our activities. At the same time, we also learned how to handle user input using the `@HostListener` decorator, in order to make our component interactive:

A screenshot of the finished activity slider component

To sum things up, we learned about the following concepts:

- Encapsulating component views using `ViewEncapsulation.Native` and importing local styles
- Covering some basic projections of timestamps onto screen coordinates, to be used with SVG elements
- Handling user input and creating a custom selection mechanism using the `@HostListener` decorator

Building the activity timeline

So far, we've built a service to log activities and a slider component to select a time range and provide an overview using activity indicators. Since we needed to perform a lot of drawing tasks within the slider component, SVG was a perfect fit for this use case. To complete our activities component tree, we still need to render the activities that were selected using the activity slider component.

Let's continue to work on our activities component tree. We will create a new component that is responsible for rendering an individual activity within an activity timeline. Let's use the Angular CLI to create our activity component:

```
ng generate component --spec false -ve none -cd onpush activities/activity
```

Now, let's start with the component template. Open the file src/app/activities/activity/activity.component.html, and add the following code:

```
<img [attr.src]="activity.user.pictureUrl"
     [attr.alt]="activity.user.name"
     class="user-image">
<div class="info" [class.info-align-right]="isAlignedRight()">
  <h3 class="title">{{activity.title}}</h3>
  <p class="author">by {{activity.user.name}} {{activity.time |
fromNow}}</p>
  <p>{{activity.message}}</p>
</div>
```

Each activity will consist of a user image, as well as an information box that will contain the activity title, message, and authoring details.

Our activity will use an input to determine its alignment. This allows us to align the activity from outside of the component. The isAlignedRight method helps us set an additional CSS class, info-align-right, on the activity information box.

Let's create our component class within the file src/app/activities/activity/activity.component.ts:

```
import {Component, Input, HostBinding, ChangeDetectionStrategy} from
'@angular/core';
import {Activity, ActivityAlignment} from '../../model';

@Component({
  selector: 'mac-activity',
  templateUrl: './activity.component.html',
  styleUrls: ['./activity.component.css'],
  changeDetection: ChangeDetectionStrategy.OnPush
})
export class ActivityComponent {
  @Input() activity: Activity;
  @Input() alignment: ActivityAlignment;
  @Input() @HostBinding('class.start-mark') startMark;
  @Input() @HostBinding('class.end-mark') endMark;
```

```
isAlignedRight() {
    return this.alignment === 'right';
}
}
```

Our activity component expects four inputs:

- `activity`: This property takes the data model of the activity that needs to be rendered with the component. This is the activity that we created using the activity service.
- `alignment`: This input property should be set to a string containing the word `left` or `right`. We used this to determine whether we needed to add an additional CSS class to our template, in order to align the activity information box to the right.
- `startMark`: This input property acts as an input and a host binding at the same time. If this input is set to `true`, the activity will get an additional CSS class, `start-mark`, which will cause a small mark on top of the timeline, to indicate the timeline termination.
- `endMark`: In the same way as `startMark`, this input uses a host binding to set an additional CSS class, `end-mark`, which will cause a small mark on the bottom of the timeline, to indicate the timeline termination.

The `isAlignedRight` method is used within the template, to determine whether we need to add an additional CSS class to the information box, in order to align it to the right.

We formatted the timestamp of the activity using the `FromNow` pipe, which we created in `Chapter 4`, *Thinking in Projects*.

We now have almost all of the components to display our activities. Still, there's something missing, which is the glue to combine the activity slider with our activity components. For this, we'll create a new component, called `activities`:

```
ng generate component --spec false -ve none -cd onpush
activities/activities
```

After the Angular CLI has generated the component files, let's open the component class in `src/app/activities/activities/activities.component.ts`, and add the following code:

```
import {Component, Input, ChangeDetectionStrategy, EventEmitter, Output}
from '@angular/core';
import {Activity, ActivitySliderSelection} from '../model';
```

```
@Component({
  selector: 'mac-activities',
  templateUrl: './activities.component.html',
  styleUrls: ['./activities.component.css'],
  changeDetection: ChangeDetectionStrategy.OnPush
})
export class ActivitiesComponent {
  @Input() activities: Activity[];
  @Input() selectedActivities: Activity[];
  @Output() outSelectionChange = new
EventEmitter<ActivitySliderSelection>();

  selectionChange(selection: ActivitySliderSelection) {
    this.outSelectionChange.emit(selection);
  }
}
```

Since this component will just act as a compositional component for arranging the slider and rendering all activities, we don't have a lot of logic in it. This is a pure component, and it relies on a parent container component to determine which of the activities should be displayed/selected. We're also re-emitting the outSelectionChange event originated at the activity slider.

Let's also take a look at the template located in src/app/activities/activities/activities.component.ts:

```
<mac-activity-slider [activities]="activities"
                     (outSelectionChange)="selectionChange($event)">
</mac-activity-slider>
<div class="l-container">
  <mac-activity *ngFor="let activity of selectedActivities, let odd = odd;
let first = first; let last =
                     last"
             [activity]="activity"
             [alignment]="odd ? 'left' : 'right'"
             [startMark]="first"
             [endMark]="last">
  </mac-activity>
</div>
```

Again, that's just simple composition. We're rendering our activity slider, and we use the ngFor directive to render our activity timeline. With the help of the local view variables odd, first, and last, we can set all of the necessary formatting inputs required on our activity component.

Alright! We are almost there. We have all of our activity UI components ready. However, we still need to create a container component for our activities and add the necessary route configuration, so that the user can navigate to the project activities tab.

Let's use the Angular CLI tool again, to create the files for our activities container component:

```
ng generate component --spec false -ve none -cd onpush container/project-
activities-container
```

Open the component class file located in src/app/container/project-activities-container/project-activities-container.component.ts, and apply the following code:

```
import {Component, ViewEncapsulation, ChangeDetectionStrategy} from
'@angular/core';
import {ProjectService} from '../../project/project.service';
import {Observable, combineLatest, BehaviorSubject} from 'rxjs';
import {Activity, ActivitySliderSelection} from '../../model';
import {map} from 'rxjs/operators';
import {ActivatedRoute} from '@angular/router';
import {ActivitiesService} from '../../activities/activities.service';

@Component({
  selector: 'mac-project-activities-container',
  templateUrl: './project-activities-container.component.html',
  styleUrls: ['./project-activities-container.component.css'],
  encapsulation: ViewEncapsulation.None,
  changeDetection: ChangeDetectionStrategy.OnPush
})
export class ProjectActivitiesContainerComponent {
  activities: Observable<Activity[]>;
  selection = new BehaviorSubject<ActivitySliderSelection | null>(null);
  selectedActivities: Observable<Activity[]>;

  constructor(private projectService: ProjectService,
              private activitiesService: ActivitiesService,
              private route: ActivatedRoute) {
    this.activities = combineLatest(
      this.activitiesService.getActivities(),
      route.parent.params
```

```
    ).pipe(
      map(([activities, routeParams]) =>
        activities
          .filter(activity => activity.kind === 'project' &&
            activity.projectId === +routeParams.projectId)
      )
    );

    this.selectedActivities = combineLatest(
      this.activities,
      this.selection
    ).pipe(
      map(([activities, selection]) => {
        if (selection) {
          return activities.filter(
            (activity) => activity.time >= selection.start && activity.time
  <= selection.end
          );
        } else {
          return activities;
        }
      })
    );
  }

  selectionChange(selection: ActivitySliderSelection) {
    this.selection.next(selection);
  }
}
```

Although this looks like a lot of code, it should actually look very familiar. Our other container components look almost the same as this. We're accessing the activities observable from our activities service and combining the observable with the parent route parameter to obtain the selected project ID.

What's special about this container is that we're storing a behavior subject, `selection`, which is used to emit the latest selection that we receive from our activity slider component. Within the `selectedActivities` observable, we're then using this selection together with a mapping function, in order to filter for only the activities that are within the range of our selection.

As is usual with container components, the template for this one is really simple. We're just rendering our activities component and create bindings using the async pipe on our container observables. Open the file `src/app/container/project-activities-container/project-activities-container.component.html`, and apply the following changes:

```html
<mac-activities [activities]="activities | async"
                [selectedActivities]="selectedActivities | async"
                (outSelectionChange)="selectionChange($event)">
</mac-activities>
```

Okay; that's it for our container. Now, we only need to add our newly created activities container component into the route configuration. Let's open our router configuration file, `src/app/routes.ts`, and apply the following changes:

```typescript
import {Route} from '@angular/router';
import {ProjectContainerComponent} from './container/project-container/project-container.component';
import {TaskListContainerComponent} from './container/task-list-container/task-list-container.component';
import {ProjectCommentsContainerComponent} from './container/project-comments-container/project-comments-container.component';
import {ProjectContainerGuard} from './guards/project-container.guard';
import {ProjectActivitiesContainerComponent} from './container/project-activities-container/project-activities-container.component';

export const routes: Route[] = [{
  path: 'projects/:projectId',
  component: ProjectContainerComponent,
  canActivate: [ProjectContainerGuard],
  children: [{
    path: 'tasks',
    component: TaskListContainerComponent
  }, {
    path: 'comments',
    component: ProjectCommentsContainerComponent
  }, {
    path: 'activities',
    component: ProjectActivitiesContainerComponent
  }, {
    path: '**',
    redirectTo: 'tasks'
  }]
}, {
  path: '',
  pathMatch: 'full',
```

```
    redirectTo: '/projects/1'
}];
```

That's it for our activities page! We've created three components that are composed together and display an activity stream, which provides a slider to filter activities for dates. Preview your changes in the browser, and you should now be able to navigate to the **ACTIVITIES** tab on your projects. Also, try to cause some activities to be logged, by adding new tasks or updating them. Click and drag on the activity slider to change your selections:

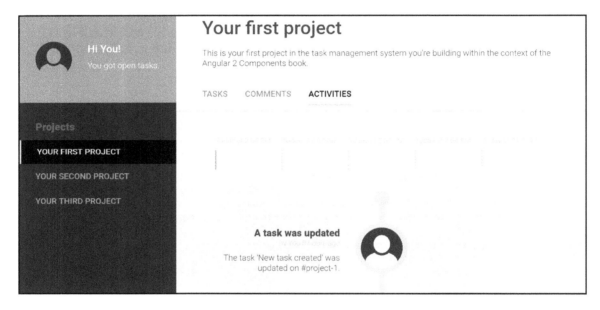

A screenshot of the finished activities view

Summary

In this chapter, we created an interactive slider component using SVG. While doing this, we learned about some SVG basics and the power of SVG within the DOM. Using Angular, we were able to make SVG composable, which it isn't by nature. We learned about namespaces, how Angular handles them, and how we can tell Angular that we'd like to use namespaces explicitly.

Besides using SVG for our slider component, we also learned how to use Shadow DOM to create native view encapsulation. As a result of this, we were able to use local styles for our component. We don't need to worry about CSS name clashes, specificity, and global CSS side effects when using local styles.

In the next chapter, we're going to enhance what we've built so far. We will create some components to enrich the user experience within our application.

7
Components for User Experience

User experience should be a core concern for developers building today's applications. We are no longer living in a world where users are content with an application that simply works. The expectations are now much higher. An application needs to be highly usable, and should provide an efficient workflow; users even expect it to bring them pleasure when performing tasks.

In this chapter, we're going to look at building some components that will increase the overall usability of our task management system. These features will enrich the current functionality and provide more efficient workflows.

We will develop the following two technical features and embed them into our current application, wherever applicable:

- **Tag management**: We'll enable the use of tags within generated content, such as comments, activities, and other areas where they can be of use. Tags will help users build links between content and navigation shortcuts.
- **Drag and drop**: We'll build generic components that will make the using drag and drop features a breeze. By enabling drag and drop features, we'll allow users to fulfill certain tasks with much higher efficiency.

We'll cover the following topics in this chapter:

- Creating a tag management system to enter and display tags
- Creating a stateful pipe to render tags using a service
- Creating a component to autocomplete tags during user input
- Using the `read` property on a `ViewChild` decorator to query for directive instances
- Going through the basics of the HTML5 drag and drop API
- Creating directives for draggable elements and drop targets
- Using `dataTransfer` objects and a custom attribute to enable selective drop targets

Tag management

The classic form of tagging enables you to establish a taxonomy within a system. It helps you to organize your content. It allows you to have a many-to-many association that can be managed quickly, and you can use it later to filter relevant information.

In our task management system, we're going to use a slightly different version of tags. Our goal is to provide a way to allow semantic shortcuts within the application. With the help of tags, a user should be able to cross-reference information between different parts of the data, providing a summary of the referenced entity, as well as a navigation shortcut.

For example, we can include a project tag within a user comment. A user can enter the tag by simply typing in the project ID. When a comment is displayed, we will see the title of the project, and when we click on the tag, we can directly navigate to the project detail page where the task is located.

In this section, we'll develop the required system of components to provide a way to use project tags to cross-reference other projects within comments. We'll also use tag management in our activities, which we created in the previous chapter, *Keeping up with Activities*.

A model for our tags

Let's start with a tag model to represent tags within our system. Open up our model module file, located in `src/app/model.ts`, and add the following interface:

```
export interface Tag {
  type: string;
  hashTag: string;
  title: string;
  link: string;
}
```

This interface represents tags; whenever we store tag information, we'll use this interface. Let's look at the individual fields and elaborate on their use:

- `hashTag`: This is the text representation of a tag. All of our tags need to be identified uniquely, using this text representation. We can define the text representation of tags as follows:
  - Hashtags always start with a hash symbol (#).
  - Hashtags only contain word characters or the minus symbol (–).
  - All other details of a tag, defined by the properties `title`, `link`, and `type`, can be somehow derived from the `hashTag` property. The hashtag can, therefore, be considered a unique identifier.

- `title`: This is a comparatively longer text representation of a tag. It should contain as much detail about the subject as possible. In the case of project tags, this could mean the project title, open tags count, assignee, and other important information. Since this is the field that will be rendered if a tag is presented to the user, it'll be beneficial if the content stays relatively condensed.

- `link`: A valid URL, which will be used when the tag is rendered. This URL will make links clickable and enable shortcut navigation. In the case of the project tags we're going to create, this will be a URL that will link to the given project view.

- `type`: This is used to distinguish between different tags and provide us with a way to organize tags at a higher granularity level.

So far, so good. We now have a data model that we can use to transfer information about tags.

Creating a tags service

The next step for implementing our tagging system is to write a tags service. The service will be responsible for gathering all possible tags within our application. The list of available tags can then be shown to the user within our editor component. That way, the user can add tags to comments and other editable fields within our application. The tags service should also be used to convert text that contains simple hashtags into HTML. That way, tags can be rendered to links, which allow us to navigate to detail views within our application. The responsibilities of our tags service can be divided into two main areas. Let's look at these responsibilities in detail:

- **Providing a list of tags**: For the moment, we only want to enable projects within our tagging system. Therefore, our tagging service needs to create one project tag for every project within our project service. This system will be extensible, and other sources for tags can easily be implemented.

- **Parsing and rendering tags**: The parsing functionality of the tags service is responsible for finding hashtags within an input string. While parsing the input string, the service will check for matching tags, and then use the `title` and `link` fields of the tag objects to render their HTML representations.

Let's use the Angular CLI tool to create the stubs of our new service:

```
ng generate service --spec false tags/tags
```

Now, let's add the following code as a starting point for our service:

```
import {Injectable} from '@angular/core';
import {ProjectService} from '../project/project.service';
import {Project, Tag} from '../model';
import {Observable} from 'rxjs';
import {map} from 'rxjs/operators';
import {limitWithEllipsis} from '../utilities/string-utilities';

@Injectable()
export class TagsService {
  tags: Observable<Tag[]>;

  constructor(private projectService: ProjectService) {
    this.tags = this.projectService.getProjects().pipe(
      map((projects: Project[]) => projects.map(project => ({
        type: 'project',
        hashTag: `#project-${project.id}`,
        title: limitWithEllipsis(project.title, 20),
        link: `/projects/${project.id}/tasks`
      }))))
```

```
        );
    }
}
```

The `tags` member of our tags service class is an observable, with the generic type `Tag[]`. This observable will always emit the most recent list of available tags within our application. Within our constructor, we're using the project list observable from the project service as a base to convert all projects to project tags.

In the case of projects, we set the type of our tag object to `'project'`. In a later stage of our project, we can also use sources other than projects to generate tags, but for the moment, we're only concerned about projects.

For the `hashTag` property, we're using the prefix `'#project-` and appending the ID of the project. That way, our hashtags can be identified as project tags, and by using the appended ID, we can also identify exactly which project is referenced. For the `title` field, we used a helper function, `limitWithEllipsis`, which truncates project titles that are longer than 20 characters. For the `link` field of the tag object, we specify the URL that will navigate to the project details view.

Rendering tags

We now have a service that uses a reactive approach to generate tags from the available projects. This already addresses the first concern of our service. Let's look at its other responsibility, which is parsing text content for tags and rendering HTML.

Before we start writing our parse method in the tags service, we need to create a small utility function for string replacement. Open the file `src/app/utilities/string-utilities.ts`, where we have already created our `limitWithEllipsis` function, and add the following code:

```
export function replaceAll(
  target: string,
  search: string,
  replacement: string): string {
  return target.split(search).join(replacement);
}
```

The preceding method uses a small JavaScript trick to replace all occurrences of a string with another string. Unfortunately, that's not possible with the default `replace` function on strings.

Let's move on with our tags service. Rendering tags is not a big deal, since we have already abstracted the data model of tags in a clean way. Since tags have URLs that point to a location, we're going to use anchor HTML elements to represent our tags. These elements also have classes that will help us style tags differently than regular content. Let's create another method within the tags service that can be used to parse text, recognize tags within the text content, and render them into HTML. Open up the tags service file located in `src/app/tags/tags.service.ts`, and apply the following changes:

```
import {Injectable} from '@angular/core';
import {ProjectService} from '../project/project.service';
import {Project, Tag} from '../model';
import {Observable, of} from 'rxjs';
import {map} from 'rxjs/operators';
import {limitWithEllipsis, replaceAll} from '../utilities/string-
utilities';

@Injectable()
export class TagsService {
  tags: Observable<Tag[]>;

  constructor(private projectService: ProjectService) {
    this.tags = this.projectService.getProjects().pipe(
      map((projects: Project[]) => projects.map(project => ({
        type: 'project',
        hashTag: `#project-${project.id}`,
        title: limitWithEllipsis(project.title, 20),
        link: `/projects/${project.id}/tasks`
      }))
    );
  }

  parse(textContent: string): Observable<string> {
    const hashTags: string[] = textContent.match(/#[\w\/-]+/g);
    if (!hashTags) {
      return of(textContent);
    }

    return this.tags.pipe(
      map((tags: Tag[]) => {
        hashTags.forEach(hashTag => {
          const tag = tags.find(t => t.hashTag === hashTag);
          if (tag) {
            textContent = replaceAll(
              textContent,
              hashTag,
              `<a class="tag tag-${tag.type}"
```

```
                href="${tag.link}">${tag.title}</a>`
            );
        }
    });
    return textContent;
   })
  );
 }
}
```

Let's quickly recap the preceding changes and look at the `parse` method step by step:

1. First, we're searching the text content that was passed into the `parse` method for hashtags and storing the list of discovered hashtags into a variable called `hashTags`.

2. If no hashtags have been discovered, we immediately return a new observable stream with the original text content that was passed into the method. We're using the RxJS `of` helper to do so.

3. The next step is to render all discovered hashtags with the corresponding tag objects within our service. We don't store tags directly within our service, but rather, we use an observable stream to convert different sources into tags. We use a `map` operator to obtain the list of tags, and then render all discovered hashtags into HTML.

4. We are using `Array.prototype.forEach` to iterate through all discovered hashtags within the initial text content. We are then trying to find a matching tag object within the list of available project tags. We do that by simply comparing the hashtag found within the text to the `hashTag` property on our tag objects.

5. If a matching tag was found, we use our newly created `replaceAll` helper function to replace all occurrences of a given hashtag with a rendered HTML version of that tag. We're using the tag object's `type`, `link`, and `title` fields to render an anchor HTML element.

6. After all hashtags have been replaced with the HTML versions of those tags, we're returning the rendered HTML content from the observable mapping function.

That's it for our tags service. As a next step, we will create a pipe that will use our service to render tags directly within the view of components.

Integrating tags using a pipe

All of the concerns of our task service have now been taken care of, and it is already storing tags for available projects. We can now go ahead and integrate our service into the application.

Since our tags service turns text with simple hashtags into HTML with links, a pipe would be a perfect helper to integrate the functionality within our components.

Let's create a new pipe by using the Angular CLI tool:

```
ng generate pipe --spec false pipes/tags
```

Open up the generated file, located in `src/app/pipes/tags.pipe.ts`, and add the following code:

```typescript
import {Pipe, PipeTransform} from '@angular/core';
import {TagsService} from '../tags/tags.service';
import {DomSanitizer} from '@angular/platform-browser';
import {map} from 'rxjs/operators';

@Pipe({
  name: 'tags',
  pure: false
})
export class TagsPipe implements PipeTransform {
  constructor(private tagsService: TagsService,
              private sanitizer: DomSanitizer) {}

  transform(value) {
    if (typeof value !== 'string') {
      return value;
    }
    return this.tagsService.parse(value).pipe(
      map(parsed => this.sanitizer.bypassSecurityTrustHtml(parsed))
    );
  }
}
```

We have already created a few pipes. However, this pipe is a bit different, in that it isn't a pure pipe. Pipes are considered pure if their `transform` function always returns the same output for a given input. This implies that the `transform` function should not be dependent on any other external source that can influence the outcome of the transform, and the only dependencies are the input values. This is not true for our tags pipe, though. It depends on the tags service to transform the input, and new tags can be stored in the tags service at any time. Successive transformations can successfully render tags that were non-existent just a moment ago.

By telling Angular that our pipe is not pure, we can disable the optimization it performs on pure pipes. This also means that Angular will need to re-validate the output of the pipe on every change detection. This can lead to performance issues; therefore, the pure flag should be used with caution.

Within our pipe, we're injecting the tags service, which helps us to convert simple text into rendered HTML. However, Angular has some security mechanisms preventing us from using this HTML string directly within our template. To ensure Angular that we know what we're doing here, we can use the DOM sanitizer instance to create trusted HTML, which we can then render within `innerHTML` bindings. By calling `bypassSecurityTrustHtml` on the sanitizer, passing our generated HTML string, we can tell Angular to put aside any security concerns for that instance, and we can go ahead and render the HTML within our view.

Alright; as far as rendering tags is concerned, we are all set. Let's integrate our tags functionality into our editor component so we can make use of them within the commenting system.

All that we really need to do is include the tags pipe within our editor component template. Let's open the editor template located in `src/app/ui/editor/editor.component.html`, and apply the following change:

```
<div #editableContentElement
    class="editable-content"
    contenteditable="true"></div>
<div class="output" [innerHTML]="content ? (content | tags | async) : '-
'"></div>
<div *ngIf="showControls && !editMode"
    class="controls">
  <button (click)="beginEdit()" class="icon-edit"></button>
</div>
<div *ngIf="showControls && editMode"
    class="controls">
  <button (click)="saveEdit()" class="icon-save"></button>
  <button (click)="cancelEdit()" class="icon-cancel"></button>
```

```
</div>
```

The only change that we've made in the template is where we display the editor content. We are using a property binding to the `innerHTML` property of our editor's output HTML element. This allows us to render the HTML content generated by our tags service. Since the tags pipe is returning an observable, we need to chain in an async pipe, as well.

Congratulations! Your tagging system is already halfway done! We've created a tags service that collects available tags within the application, and, together with our newly created pipe, renders tags within our editor component. Preview your changes within the browser, and try to add hashtags to some comments on the comments tab of projects. Currently, we only have two projects within our application. Try to add the following hashtag to a comment—`#project-2`—and save the changes in the editor. You should now be able to see the rendered tag in the comment. If you're editing the comment again, you'll see the hashtag text representation.

Let's digress for a moment. We've already created a tagging system, and we just integrated it into our editor component by using the tags pipe. If a user writes project tags in any comment, they will now be rendered by the tags service. This is fantastic! Users can now establish cross-links to other projects within comments, which will be automatically rendered as links and show a truncated project title. All a user needs to do is add the text representation of a project tag to a comment.

The following two screenshots illustrate an example of the commenting system. The first screenshot is an example of an editor in edit mode, under the commenting system, where a text tag is entered:

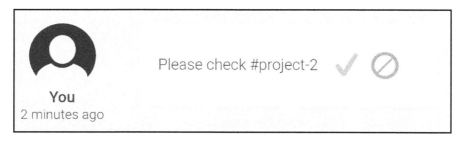

An example of when a text tag is entered

The second screenshot is an example of a rendered tag enabled in the commenting system through our editor integration:

An example of a rendered tag through editor integration

In this section, we looked at the following concepts:

- We built a tags service that generates, caches, and renders tags
- We built a stateful pipe using the `pure` flag
- We used the `[innerHTML]` property binding to render HTML content into an element
- We used the DOM sanitizer to bypass security checks when using `innerHTML` bindings

We're not done yet, when it comes to entering tags. We cannot expect our users to know all of the available tags within the system and then enter them manually within comments. Let's look at how we can improve this in the next section.

Supporting tag input

Here, we're going to build a component (and its supporting structures) to make the process of entering tags a smooth experience for our users. So far, they can write project tags, but it requires them to know the project IDs, which makes our tag management quite useless. What we'd like to do is provide the user with some choices when they are about to write a tag. Ideally, we will show them the available tags as soon as they start writing a tag by typing the hash (#) symbol.

What sounds simple at first is actually a quite tricky thing to implement. Our tag input needs to deal with the following challenges:

- Handling input events to monitor tag creation. Somehow, we need to know when a user starts writing a tag, and we need to know when the typed tag name is updated or cancelled by using an invalid tag character.
- Calculating the position of the input caret of the user. Yeah, I know this sounds pretty simple, but it actually isn't. Calculating the viewport offset position of a user's input caret requires the use of the browser's Selection API, which is quite low-level and needs some abstraction.

In order to tackle these challenges, we are going to introduce a utility directive that we can use to handle those rather complicated low-level user input events.

Creating a tag input directive

Since recognizing hashtags within user input is not such a simple task, we're going to create a directive that helps us with that. This is actually our first directive that we're creating together! If you remember from Chapter 1, *Component-Based User Interfaces*, directives are there to create custom behaviors without the need for an own view. Our tags input directive will collect and recognize hashtags from user input, but it does not actually render its own view.

Let's add two more interfaces to our model file in src/app/model.ts, to help us communicate hashtag user input:

```
export interface InputPosition {
  top: number;
  left: number;
  caretOffset: number;
}

export interface HashTagInput {
  hashTag: string;
  position: InputPosition;
}
```

For every user input that is recognized as hashtag input by our directive, we will communicate using hashtag input objects. Besides the actual text content of the hashtag, we're also sending an input position that consists of the following properties:

- `top` and `left`: Represent the top and left screen, offset in pixels of the caret position where the actual input happened.
- `caretOffset`: Describes the character offset of the hashtag within the text content of the editable element. This will be useful when we want to replace the hashtag within the editable element and achieve a feeling of autocomplete.

From the `top` and `left` properties of the `InputPosition` interface, you can see that we want to compute the coordinates where the actual user input happened. This sounds very trivial, but it actually isn't. To help us with that computation, we're going to introduce a new helper function, which we're creating within a new file, on the path `src/app/utilities/dom-utilities.ts`. Create that new file and add the following content:

```
import {InputPosition} from '../model';

export function getRangeBoundingClientRect(): InputPosition | null {
  if (window.getSelection) {
    const selection = window.getSelection();
    if (!selection.rangeCount) {
      return null;
    }

    const range = selection.getRangeAt(0);
    const rect = range.getBoundingClientRect();

    if (!range.collapsed) {
      return {
        top: rect.top,
        left: rect.left,
        caretOffset: range.startOffset
      };
    }

    const dummy = document.createElement('span');
    range.insertNode(dummy);
    const pos: InputPosition = {
      top: rect.top,
      left: rect.left,
      caretOffset: range.startOffset
    };
    dummy.parentNode.removeChild(dummy);
```

```
      return pos;
    }

  if (document['selection']) {
    return document['selection']
      .createRange()
      .getBoundingClientRect();
  }
}
```

Let's not get into too much detail here. What this code basically does is try to find the bounding box DOMRect object, which describes the top, right, bottom, and left offsets of the caret position, relative to the viewport. The problem is that the Selection API does not allow us to get the position of the caret directly; it only allows us to get the position of the current selection. If the caret is not placed correctly, we will need to insert a dummy element at the location of the caret and return the bounding box DOMRect object of the dummy element. Of course, we'll need to remove the dummy element again, before we return the DOMRect object.

So, that's all that we need to write our tags input directive. Let's use the Angular CLI to create our first directive. The command to create directives is very similar to that to create components:

ng generate directive --spec false tags/tags-input

That generated the stub for our new directive. Let's open the file src/app/tags/tags-input.directive.ts, and add the following code:

```
import {Directive, HostListener} from '@angular/core';
import {getRangeBoundingClientRect} from '../utilities/dom-utilities';
import {HashTagInput} from '../model';
import {BehaviorSubject} from 'rxjs';

@Directive({
  selector: '[macTagsInput]'
})
export class TagsInputDirective {
  private hashTagInput: HashTagInput | null = null;
  private hashTagSubject = new
BehaviorSubject<HashTagInput>(this.hashTagInput);
  hashTagChange = this.hashTagSubject.asObservable();
}
```

The private `hashTagInput` property is an internal state to store the current hashtag input information. The `hashTagSubject` member is a behavior subject, which we're using internally to publish hashtag input changes. We're using the `asObservable` method on the subject to expose an observable stream that emits hashtag input objects on every change. We're storing this derived observable stream in the member `hashTagChange`, which has public visibility. Other components can access this property and subscribe to get notified when there are hashtag input events.

Let's now add more parts to our directive, piece by piece. Let's first add a reset method, which we can call when the hashtag input should be reset. This method will be used internally, when an input is aborted, but can also be called from outside, from another component, to abort tag entry:

```
reset() {
  this.hashTagInput = null;
  this.hashTagSubject.next(this.hashTagInput);
}
```

The next method is used to update the internal hashtag input object, based on user input:

```
private updateHashTag(hashTag, position = this.hashTagInput.position) {
  this.hashTagInput = {hashTag, position};
  this.hashTagSubject.next(this.hashTagInput);
}
```

Now, let's add the two main methods to our tags input directive, to collect user input. We're using the `HostListener` decorator to create event bindings on the host element for `keydown` and `keypress` events:

```
updateTextTag(textTag, position = this.position) {
  this.textTag = textTag;
  this.position = position;
}
```

The `keyDown` method will be called by the host event binding to `keydown` events. We are concerned about the backspace, which should also remove the last character of the tag that is currently entered. If we can detect a backspace (char code 8), we're calling our `updateHashTag` method, and updating the current hashtag by removing the last character, using the `Array.prototype.slice` function:

```
@HostListener('keydown', ['$event'])
keyDown(event: KeyboardEvent) {
  if (this.hashTagInput && event.which === 8) {
    this.updateHashTag(this.hashTagInput.hashTag.slice(0, -1));
  }
}
```

The `keyPress` method is called from the host element event binding on `keypress` events. This is where the main logic of this supporting directive lies. Here, we handle two different cases:

- If the pressed key is a hash symbol, we will start over with a new tag
- If the pressed key is not a valid word character or a hash symbol, we will reset it to its initial state, which will cancel the tag entry
- Any other valid character, we'll add to the current text tag string

Add the following code to the tags input directive:

```
@HostListener('keypress', ['$event'])
keyPress(event: KeyboardEvent) {
  const char = String.fromCharCode(event.which);
  if (char === '#') {
    this.updateHashTag('#', getRangeBoundingClientRect());
  } else if (!/[\w-]/i.test(char)) {
    this.reset();
  } else if (this.hashTagInput) {
    this.updateHashTag(this.hashTagInput.hashTag + char);
  }
}
```

When a new hashtag is entered (if a user inserts the hash symbol), we will update the internal hashtag input object and use our utility function, `getRangeBoundingClientRect`, to set the input object's position to the current caret position.

Okay; now we have all of the support we need to handle tag input. However, we still need a way to show the available tags in the tags service to the user. For this purpose, we'll create a new tags select component. It will show a list of available tags to the user, and will make use of the tag input changes emitted by our support directive in order to filter and position the list.

Creating a tags select component

To support the user in finding the right tag, we'll provide them with a drop-down menu with the available tags. To do this, we need to use the hashtag input objects emitted by our tags input directive. Let's briefly look at the requirements of this component:

- It should display the available tags gathered from our tags service in a tooltip/callout box
- It should support a limitation of displayed tags
- It should receive a hashtag input object to filter the available tags and to position itself using the positional data on the hashtag input object
- It should emit an event once the user clicks on a tag in the listed tags
- The component should hide if the filter is invalid, or if there are no elements matching the filter:

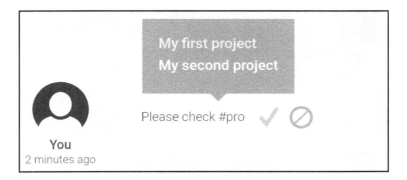

Finished tags select component, filtered with user input

Let's start by updating our application model, located in `src/app/model.ts`, to include a new interface to be used to communicate tag selection. Add the following code to the file:

```
export interface TagSelection {
  tag: Tag;
  hashTagInput: HashTagInput;
}
```

If a tag gets selected, we want to know which tag object was selected, but also, the corresponding hashtag input object should be passed along. This data is required so that we can properly react to the selected tag and correctly update the editable element.

Let's move on with our component, and create the component class. First, let's scaffold a new component using the Angular CLI:

```
ng generate component --spec false -cd onpush tags/tags-select
```

This will generate a new component, where we'll opening the component class file, located in src/app/tags/tags-select/tags-select.component.ts, and add the following code:

```
import {ChangeDetectionStrategy, Component, EventEmitter, HostBinding,
Input, OnChanges, Output} from '@angular/core';
import {HashTagInput, Tag, TagSelection} from '../../model';

const tagListLimit = 4;

@Component({
  selector: 'mac-tags-select',
  templateUrl: './tags-select.component.html',
  styleUrls: ['./tags-select.component.css'],
  changeDetection: ChangeDetectionStrategy.OnPush
})
export class TagsSelectComponent implements OnChanges {
  @Input() tags: Tag[];
  @Input() hashTagInput: HashTagInput | null;
  @Output() outSelectTag = new EventEmitter<TagSelection>();

  filteredTags: Tag[];

  filterTags() {
    const filter = this.hashTagInput.hashTag.slice(1).toLowerCase();
    this.filteredTags = this.tags
      .filter(tag =>
        tag.hashTag.toLowerCase().includes(filter) ||
        tag.title.toLowerCase().includes(filter)
      )
      .slice(0, tagListLimit);
  }

  selectTag(tag: Tag) {
    this.outSelectTag.next({
      tag,
      hashTagInput: this.hashTagInput
    });
```

```
  }

  ngOnChanges(changes) {
    if ((changes.hashTagInput || changes.tags) && this.hashTagInput) {
      this.filterTags();
    }
  }
}
```

Our component has two input elements. The `tags` input is used to pass all available tags into the tags select component. This is the list of tags that will be presented to the user when selecting available tags. The `hashTagInput` input is the hashtag input object that we obtain from the tags input directive we create previously. We will extract the current user input from that object in order to filter the displayed tags. We will also use the position data from that object to position the component onto the screen coordinates of the caret position where the user started to write the hashtag input.

The output `outSelectTag` is used to emit an event when a user selects a tag from the list of tags. The `filteredTags` property is used for the computed filtered list of tags. We're calling the `filterTags` method when there's a change in the `hashTagInput` or `tags` input objects. Here, we're filtering the list of all tags with the current hashtag input data that we have. Since this is only a computed state, our component is still a pure component, and we can still use the `OnPush` change detection strategy.

The `selectTag` method is called from the view when the user selects a tag from the list of filtered tags. There, we're emitting a new tag selection object that consists of the selected tag, as well as the hashtag input object.

Let's move on and add a few accessor properties to our component, which we're using to create host element style bindings. The following accessor property—`hasFilteredTags`—is bound to the host element's display style property. It will control whether the component is displayed or hidden. We will only display the component if the filter is valid and the filtered tags contain at least one tag:

```
  @HostBinding('style.display')
  get hasFilteredTags() {
    return this.filteredTags && this.filteredTags.length > 0 ? 'block' :
'none';
  }
```

The following two accessor properties use host bindings to set the `top` and `left` styles of our host element, based on the `hashTagInput` input of the component:

```
@HostBinding('style.top')
get topPosition() {
  return this.hashTagInput && this.hashTagInput.position ?
    `${this.hashTagInput.position.top}px` : 0;
}

@HostBinding('style.left')
get leftPosition() {
  return this.hashTagInput && this.hashTagInput.position ?
    `${this.hashTagInput.position.left}px` : 0;
}
```

The template for our component is rather simple. Let's open the view template that is stored in `src/app/tags/tags-select/tags-select.component.html`, and apply the following changes:

```
<ul class="list">
  <li *ngFor="let tag of filteredTags"
      (click)="selectTag(tag)"
      class="item">{{tag.title}}</li>
</ul>
```

We used the `NgFor` directive to iterate over all of the tags within the `filteredTags` member. If a tag is clicked, we will need to execute the `selectTag` method and pass the tag of the current iteration. In the listing, we'll only display the tag title that should help the user identify the tag that they would like to use.

Now, we have built all of the pieces that we need to enable smooth tag entering for our users. However, we still need to wire everything together. The next step is to enable tag selection within our project comments.

Integrating tag selection within the editor component

As the first step, we should amend our editor component to utilize the tags input directive in conjunction with the tags select component that we just created.

Before we start changing our editor, let's look at a new string helper function, `splice`, which allows us to pass a specific location within the text, where we want to replace the partial hashtag entered by the user with the final hashtag from the selected tag object.

The `splice` method works similar to the `Array.prototype.splice` function, and allows us to remove a certain part within a string and add a new part to that string, at the same location. This allows us to replace certain areas in strings very specifically, which is exactly what we need in this situation. Let's implement this little helper function within our string utility module, located in `src/app/utilities/string-utilities.ts`:

```
...
export function splice(
  target: string,
  index: number,
  deleteCount: number,
  content: string): string {
  return target.slice(0, index) +
    content +
    target.slice(index + deleteCount);
}
```

Let's go back to our editor component and look at the changes to be made inside of the component template, located in `src/app/ui/editor/editor.component.html`. Effective changes in the template are marked in bold:

```
<div #editableContentElement
     class="editable-content"
     contenteditable="true"
     macTagsInput></div>
<mac-tags-select
  *ngIf="tags && tagsInput.hashTagChange | async"
  [hashTagInput]="tagsInput.hashTagChange | async"
  [tags]="tags"
  (outSelectTag)="selectTag($event)">
</mac-tags-select>
<div class="output" [innerHTML]="content ? (content | tags | async) : '-'"></div>
<div *ngIf="showControls && !editMode"
     class="controls">
  <button (click)="beginEdit()" class="icon-edit"></button>
</div>
<div *ngIf="showControls && editMode"
     class="controls">
  <button (click)="saveEdit()" class="icon-save"></button>
  <button (click)="cancelEdit()" class="icon-cancel"></button>
</div>
```

The first thing that we need to add is our tags input directive, which will help us to collect input data when a user enters a hashtag within our editable content field.

Just below the editable content element, we're adding our new tags select component. We're only rendering the tags select component if a list of tags was provided to the editor component as input. We're using the extracted hashtag input object from our tags input directive and passing it into the tags select `hashTagInput` input. If the tags select component emits a `outSelectTag` event, we're calling a new `selectTag` method, which we're going to implement on our editor component.

Now, let's apply the necessary changes to our component class, located in `src/app/ui/editor/editor.component.html`. The ellipsis character (...) indicates code parts that have not changed. Effective changes are marked in bold:

```
...
import {TagsInputDirective} from '../../tags/tags-input.directive';
import {Tag, TagSelection} from '../../model';
import {splice} from '../../utilities/string-utilities';

@Component({
  selector: 'mac-editor',
  templateUrl: './editor.component.html',
  styleUrls: ['./editor.component.css'],
  encapsulation: ViewEncapsulation.None,
  changeDetection: ChangeDetectionStrategy.OnPush
})
export class EditorComponent implements OnChanges, AfterViewInit {
  @ViewChild('editableContentElement') editableContentElement: ElementRef;
  @ViewChild('editableContentElement', {
    read: TagsInputDirective
  }) tagsInput: TagsInputDirective;
  ...

  saveEdit() {
    this.editMode = false;
    this.tagsInput.reset();
    this.outSaveEdit.emit(this.getEditableContent());
  }

  cancelEdit() {
    this.editMode = false;
    this.tagsInput.reset();
    this.setEditableContent(this.content);
    this.outCancelEdit.emit();
  }
  ...
```

```
  selectTag(tagSelection: TagSelection) {
    this.setEditableContent(
      splice(
        this.getEditableContent(),
        tagSelection.hashTagInput.position.caretOffset,
        tagSelection.hashTagInput.hashTag.length,
        tagSelection.tag.hashTag
      ));
    this.tagsInput.reset();
  }
}
```

First, we're adding another view query for our editable content element, using the view reference `editableContentElement`. However, this time, we're using an additional configuration object within the view query decorator. The `read` property in the view query option allows us to specify that we don't want to select the default `ElementRef` object, but a reference to a component instance or a directive instance that is present on the element. In our case, we want to get a handle on the tags input directive, which we've placed onto the editable content element.

Within the `saveEdit` and the `cancelEdit` methods of our editor, we can now additionally call the reset method on our tags input directive. This will ensure that we're not persisting any previous tag entry when a user saves or cancels an edit.

Finally, we're adding a new method: `selectTag`. This method is called from the editor view, as a reaction to the `outSelectTag` event from the tags select component. All we're doing here is replacing the part of the hashtag in our editable content element that was entered by the user with the hashtag that is emitted in the tag selection object.

Great stuff! We have completed our work on the tags select component and integrated it, with our tags input directive, into the editor component.

Integrating tag selection in project comments

Since the editor component now relies on a list of available tags to be passed as input, we need to apply some changes to our project comment components.

Let's start with the project comments container component, located in `src/app/container/project-comments-container/project-comments-container.component.ts`. The ellipsis character is hiding irrelevant code parts, while effective changes are in bold:

```
...
import {Comment, CommentUpdate, Project, Tag, User} from '../../model';
...
import {TagsService} from '../../tags/tags.service';

@Component({
  ...
})
export class ProjectCommentsContainerComponent {
  ...
  tags: Observable<Tag[]>;

  constructor(private projectService: ProjectService,
              private userService: UserService,
              private route: ActivatedRoute,
              private activitiesService: ActivitiesService,
              private tagsService: TagsService) {
    ...
    this.tags = this.tagsService.tags;
  }
  ...
}
```

Now, let's look at the view template changes within the container component located in `src/app/container/project-comments-container/project-comments-container.component.ts`:

```
<mac-comments [user]="user | async"
              [comments]="projectComments | async"
              [tags]="tags | async"
              (outCreateComment)="createComment($event)"
              (outUpdateComment)="updateComment($event)">
</mac-comments>
```

That was easy! All we did was get the tags observable from our tags service, subscribe in the view, and pass the resulting tags list down into our comments component.

Let's change our comments component to accept that list of tags as input. Open the file `src/app/comments/comments/comments.component.ts`, and add the following changes:

```
...
import {Comment, CommentUpdate, Tag, TagSelection, User} from
'../../model';
import {TagsInputDirective} from '../../tags/tags-input.directive';
import {splice} from '../../utilities/string-utilities';

@Component({
  ...
})
export class CommentsComponent {
  ...
  @Input() tags: Tag[];
  @ViewChild('commentContentEditable', {
    read: TagsInputDirective
  }) tagsInput: TagsInputDirective;
  ...

  selectTag(tagSelection: TagSelection) {
    this.commentContentEditable.nativeElement.textContent =
      splice(
        this.commentContentEditable.nativeElement.textContent,
        tagSelection.hashTagInput.position.caretOffset,
        tagSelection.hashTagInput.hashTag.length,
        tagSelection.tag.hashTag
      );
    this.tagsInput.reset();
  }
}
```

Using the same mechanism that we use within our editor, we're also enabling tag selection within the comment editable element. Let's look at the changes within the view template of our comments component, located in `src/app/comments/comments/comments.component.html`:

```
<div class="title">Add new comment</div>
<div class="add-comment-section">
  <div #commentContentEditable
       class="add-comment-box"
       contenteditable="true"
       macTagsInput>
  </div>
  <mac-tags-select
```

```
      *ngIf="tags && tagsInput.hashTagChange | async"
      [hashTagInput]="tagsInput.hashTagChange | async"
      [tags]="tags"
      (outSelectTag)="selectTag($event)">
  </mac-tags-select>
  <button (click)="createComment()"
          class="button" >Add comment</button>
</div>

<ng-container *ngIf="comments.length > 0">
  <div class="title">All comments</div>
  <mac-comment *ngFor="let comment of comments; let index = index"
               [comment]="comment"
               [user]="user"
               [tags]="tags"
               (outUpdateComment)="updateComment(index, $event)">
  </mac-comment>
</ng-container>
```

Besides implementing our own tag selection for the comments editable content element, we're also passing the tags, which we've received from our parent container component, down into each comment component as input.

Let's continue and complete the integration of our tagging system. Open up the comment component class, located in `src/app/comments/comment/comment.component.ts`, and apply the following changes:

```
...
import {Comment, Tag, User} from '../../model';

@Component({
  ...
})
export class CommentComponent {
  ...
  @Input() tags: Tag[];
  ...
}
```

All we needed to add was an additional input, to receive our tag list. Let's also reflect the necessary changes to our comment component view template, located in `src/app/comments/comment/comment.component.html`:

```
...
<div class="main">
  <div class="content">
    <mac-editor [content]="comment.content"
                [showControls]="comment.user.id === user.id"
                [tags]="tags"
                (outSaveEdit)="updateComment($event)">
    </mac-editor>
  </div>
</div>
```

Alright! There were quite a few changes for integration. However, they were pretty simple changes, and now we're ready to use our tagging system!

Finishing up our tagging system

Congratulations! You've now successfully implemented the first of the three usability components.

With the help of a tag input directive, we have hidden the low-level programming of user input and the processing of the user caret position. Then, we created a component to display the available tags to the user, and provided a way for them to select a tag by clicking on it. In our editor component, we used the tags input directive, together with the tags select component, to enable the smooth entering of tags when editing comments.

We've covered the following concepts in this section:

- We processed complex user input within a designated directive, to offload logic from our components
- We used host bindings to set positional style attributes
- We used the read property on a ViewChild decorator, to query for directive instances
- We implemented fully reactive components that rely on observables and don't create side effects during change detection

In the next section, we're going to look at how we can integrate drag and drop functionality within our application. We will build Angular directives, which will help us to easily integrate drag and drop capabilities into any area of our task management application.

Drag and drop

We have learned to use our computer mouse and keyboard with great efficiency. Using keyboard shortcuts, different click actions, and contextual mouse menus, can provide us with support for performing tasks. However, there is one pattern that has gained more attention in applications lately, given the current mobile and touch device hype. Drag and drop actions are a very intuitive and logical way to express actions, such as moving or copying items. One particular task, performed on user interfaces, benefits from drag and drop: ordering items within a list. If we need to order items via action menus, it gets very confusing. Moving items step-by-step, using the up and down buttons, works great, but it takes a lot of time. If you can drag items around and drop them in a place where you'd like them to be reordered, you can sort a list of items extremely quickly.

In this topic, we will build the required elements to enable drag and drop within our application. We will use the drag and drop feature to enable users to reorder their task lists. By developing reusable directives to provide this functionality, we can later enable the feature at any spot within our application.

To implement our directives, we will make use of the HTML5 drag and drop API, which is supported in all of the major browsers at the time of writing this book.

Since we would like to reuse our drag and drop behavior on multiple components, we will use directives for the implementation. We are going to create two directives in this section:

- **Draggable directive**: This directive should be attached to components, which should be enabled for dragging
- **Draggable drop zone directive**: This directive should be attached to components that will act as drop targets

We'll also implement a feature wherein we can be selective about what can be dragged where. For this, we will use a type attribute on our draggable directives, as well as an accepted type attribute on our drop zones.

Updating our model for ordering tasks

As a first step, we should enable our task model for ordering. By introducing an `order` field on our task object, we can then use that field to sort tasks accordingly. Let's make the following changes to our model file, located in `src/app/model.ts`:

```
export interface Task {
  readonly id?: number;
```

```
    readonly projectId?: number;
    readonly title: string;
    readonly done: boolean;
    readonly order: number;
}
...

    export type DraggableType = 'task';
```

We have also added a new type alias, DraggableType, which we're using to identify things that can be dragged within our application. We will use this type to make sure that we can only drag and drop to locations that support the given type.

Since we have changed the model for our tasks to include an order property, we will need to make some changes to our existing application state management, in order to work with the order property.

Let's first change our in-memory database, and open the file src/app/database.ts to apply the following changes:

```
...

export class Database implements InMemoryDbService {
  createDb() {
    ...

    const tasks: Task[] = [
      {id: 1, projectId: 1, title: 'Task 1', done: false, order: 1},
      {id: 2, projectId: 1, title: 'Task 2', done: false, order: 2},
      {id: 3, projectId: 1, title: 'Task 3', done: true, order: 3},
      {id: 4, projectId: 1, title: 'Task 4', done: false, order: 4}
    ];

    ...
  }
}
```

Now, all of our initial tasks contain an order property. Now, we need to take care of two additional things:

- When new tasks get created, we need to compute the next available order value and use it to create a new task
- We need to change our task list to use the order property for sorting

We can implement both of these changes within our task list container component. Let's open the file `src/app/container/task-list-container/task-list-container.component.ts`, and apply some changes. Irrelevant code parts are hidden using the ellipsis character, while the effective changes are marked in bold:

```
...

@Component({
  selector: 'mac-task-list-container',
  templateUrl: './task-list-container.component.html',
  encapsulation: ViewEncapsulation.None,
  changeDetection: ChangeDetectionStrategy.OnPush
})
export class TaskListContainerComponent {
  ...

  constructor(private taskService: TaskService,
              private projectService: ProjectService,
              private route: ActivatedRoute,
              private activitiesService: ActivitiesService) {
    ...

    this.tasks = this.selectedProject.pipe(
      switchMap((project) => this.taskService.getProjectTasks(project.id)),
      map(tasks => tasks.sort((a: Task, b: Task) => b.order - a.order))
    );

    ...
  }

  ...

  addTask(title: string) {
    combineLatest(this.selectedProject, this.tasks)
      .pipe(
        take(1)
      )
      .subscribe(([project, tasks]) => {
        const position = tasks.reduce(
          (max, t: Task) => t.order > max ? t.order : max, 0
        ) + 1;
        const task: Task = {
          projectId: project.id, title, done: false, order: position
        };
        this.taskService.addTask(task);
        this.activitiesService.logProjectActivity(
          project.id,
```

```
                'tasks',
                'A task was added',
                `A new task "${limitWithEllipsis(title, 30)}" was added to
                #project-${project.id}.`
              );
          });
      }

      ...

    }
```

Alright; that's it, for now. We've successfully introduced a new `order` property, which is now used to sort our task list. This order becomes very important when we want to use our drag and drop feature to sort the task list.

Implementing the draggable directive

The `draggable` directive will be attached to the elements that we want to enable for drag and drop. Let's get started by creating a new directive using the Angular CLI tool:

ng generate directive --spec false draggable/draggable

Let's open the directive class file, located in `src/app/draggable/draggable.directive.ts`, and add the following code:

```
import {Directive, HostBinding, HostListener, Input} from '@angular/core';
import {DraggableType} from '../model';

@Directive({
  selector: '[macDraggable]'
})
export class DraggableDirective {
  @HostBinding('draggable') draggable = 'true';
  @Input() draggableData: any;
  @Input() draggableType: DraggableType;
  @HostBinding('class.dragging') dragging = false;
}
```

By setting the HTML attribute `draggable` to `true`, using a host binding, we tell the browser that we're considering this element a draggable element. This HTML attribute is already part of the drag and drop API of the browser.

The `draggableData` input is used to specify the data that represents the element that can be dragged. This data will be serialized to JSON and transferred to our drop zones once a drag action is completed.

By specifying a draggable type using the `draggableType` input, which we have introduced to our model, we can be more selective when the element is dragged over a drop zone. Within the drop zone, we can include a counterpart that controls what types are acceptable to be dropped.

Additionally, we can use a host binding to set a class, called `dragging`, which will apply some special styles that will make it easy to recognize that an element is dragged.

Now, we need to handle two events within our directive, to implement the behavior of a draggable element. The following DOM events are triggered by the drag and drop DOM API:

- `dragstart`: This event is emitted on elements that are grabbed and moved across the screen
- `dragend`: If the previously initiated dragging of the element is ended, because of a successful drop or a release outside of a valid drop target, this DOM event will be triggered

Let's use the `HostListener` decorator to implement the logic for the `dragstart` event:

```
import {Directive, HostBinding, HostListener, Input} from '@angular/core';
import {DraggableType} from '../model';

@Directive({
  selector: '[macDraggable]'
})
export class DraggableDirective {
  @HostBinding('draggable') draggable = 'true';
  @Input() draggableData: any;
  @Input() draggableType: DraggableType;
  @HostBinding('class.dragging') dragging = false;

  @HostListener('dragstart', ['$event'])
  dragStart(event) {
    event.dataTransfer.effectAllowed = 'move';
    event.dataTransfer.setData('application/json',
JSON.stringify(this.draggableData));
    event.dataTransfer.setData(`draggable-type:${this.draggableType}`, '');
    this.dragging = true;
  }
}
```

Now, let's discuss the different actions that we can perform in the implementation of our host listener.

We will need to access the DOM event object in our host listener. If we were to create this binding within the template, we would probably need to write something similar to this: `(dragstart)="dragStart($event)"`. Within event bindings, we can make use of the synthetic variable `$event`, which is a reference to the event that would have triggered the event binding. If we are creating an event binding on our host element using the `HostListener` decorator, we need to construct the parameter list for the binding by using the second argument of the decorator.

The first action in our event listener is to set the desired `effectAllowed` property on the data transfer object. Currently, we only support the `move` effect, as our main concern is to reorder tasks within the task list using drag and drop. The drag and drop API is very system-specific, but usually, there are different drag effects if a user holds a modifier key (such as *Ctrl* or *Shift*) while initiating the dragging. Within our `draggable` directive, we can force the `move` effect for all drag actions.

In the next code snippet, we set the data that should be transferred by dragging. It's important to understand the core purpose of the drag and drop API. It not only provides a way to implement drag and drop for elements in your DOM, but it also supports the dragging of files and other objects into your browser. Because of this, the API undergoes some constraints, one of which is making it impossible to transfer data, other than simple string values. In order for us to transfer complex objects, we will serialize the data from the `draggableData` input, using `JSON.stringify`.

Another limitation caused by some security constraints within the API is that data can only be read after a successful drop. This means that we cannot inspect the data if the user is just hovering over an element. However, we need to know some facts about the data when hovering over drop zones. We need to know the type of draggable element when entering a drop zone. This way we can control that certain draggable elements can only be dropped in specific drop zones. We're using a small workaround for this issue. The drag and drop API hides the data when we drag data over a drop target. However, it tells us what type of data it is. Knowing this fact, we can use the `setData` function to encode our draggable type. Accessing the data keys only is considered secure, and can therefore be done in all drop zone events.

Finally, we'll set the dragging flag to `true`, which will cause the class binding to re-validate and add the `dragging` class to the element.

After dealing with the `dragstart` event, we now need to handle the `dragend` event, to complete our draggable directive. The only thing we do within the `dragEnd` method that is bound to the `dragend` event is set the dragging member to false. This will cause the `dragging` class to be removed from the host element:

```
import {Directive, HostBinding, HostListener, Input} from '@angular/core';
import {DraggableType} from '../model';

@Directive({
  selector: '[macDraggable]'
})
export class DraggableDirective {
  ...

  @HostListener('dragend')
  onDragEnd() {
    this.dragging = false;
  }
}
```

That's it for the behavior of our draggable directive. Now, we need to create its counterpart directive, to provide the behavior of a drop zone.

Implementing a drop target directive

Drop zones will act as containers where draggable elements can be dropped. For this, we'll create a new draggable drop zone directive. Let's use the Angular CLI to create the directive:

```
ng generate directive --spec false draggable/draggable-drop-zone
```

Let's open the directive file, located in `src/app/draggable/draggable-drop-zone.directive.ts`, and add the following code:

```
import {Directive, EventEmitter, HostBinding, HostListener, Input, Output}
from '@angular/core';
import {DraggableType} from '../model';

@Directive({
  selector: '[macDraggableDropZone]'
})
export class DraggableDropZoneDirective {
  @Input() dropAcceptType: DraggableType;
  @Output() outDropDraggable = new EventEmitter<any>();
  @HostBinding('class.over') over = false;
```

```
    dragEnterCount = 0;
  }
```

Using the `dropAcceptType` input, we can specify what types of draggable elements we accept in this drop zone. This will help the users identify whether they are able to drop off the draggable elements, when approaching the drop zone.

Upon successful drops into the drop zone, we will need to emit an event, so that the components using our drag and drop functionality can react accordingly. For that purpose, we will use the `dropDraggable` output property.

The `over` member field will store the state if an accepted element is in the process of being dragged over the drop zone. We are using a host binding to set the class `over` on our host element. That way, a drop zone element can be styled differently when we are about to drop an item onto it.

Now, let's add a method to check whether our drop zone should accept any given drag and drop event by checking against our `dropAcceptType` member. Remember the security problems that we needed to work around when creating the draggable directive? Now, we're implementing the counterpart, to extract the draggable type from the drag event and check whether the dragged item is supported by this drop zone:

```
import {Directive, EventEmitter, HostBinding, HostListener, Input, Output}
from '@angular/core';
import {DraggableType} from '../model';

@Directive({
  selector: '[macDraggableDropZone]'
})
export class DraggableDropZoneDirective {
  @Input() dropAcceptType: DraggableType;
  @Output() outDropDraggable = new EventEmitter<any>();
  @HostBinding('class.over') over = false;

  dragEnterCount = 0;

  private typeIsAccepted(event: DragEvent) {
    const draggableType = Array.from(event.dataTransfer.types).find((key)
=>
      key.indexOf('draggable-type') === 0);
    return draggableType && draggableType.split(':')[1] ===
this.dropAcceptType;
  }
}
```

We can only read the keys of the data within data transfer objects for drag events, where the data itself is hidden until a successful `drop` event has occurred. To bypass this security limitation, we've encoded the draggable type information into a data key itself. Since we can list all of the data keys safely by using the `types` field on data transfer objects, it's not too hard to extract the encoded draggable type information. We search for a data type key that starts with `'draggable-type'`, and then split it by the column character. The value after the column character is our type information, which we can then compare against the `dropAcceptType` directive input property.

We will use two events to determine whether a draggable element is moved to our drop zone:

- `dragenter`: This event is fired by an element if another element is dragged over it
- `dragleave`: This event is fired by an element if the previously entered element has left again

There's one problem with the preceding events, which is that they actually bubble, and we will receive a `dragleave` event if the dragged element is moved to a child element within our drop zone. Because of the bubbling, we will then also receive `dragenter` and `dragleave` events from the child elements. This is not desired, in our case, and we need to build some functionality to improve this behavior. We make use of a counter member field, `dragEnterCount`, which counts up on all `dragenter` events and counts down on `dragleave` events. This way, we can now say that only on `dragleave` events, where the counter becomes zero, the users' mouse cursor will leave the drop zone. Let's look at the following diagram, which illustrates the problem:

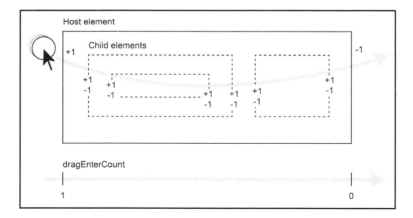

Visualization of important variables and functions for our calculations

```
import {Directive, EventEmitter, HostBinding, HostListener, Input, Output}
from '@angular/core';
import {DraggableType} from '../model';

@Directive({
  selector: '[macDraggableDropZone]'
})
export class DraggableDropZoneDirective {
  @Input() dropAcceptType: DraggableType;
  @Output() outDropDraggable = new EventEmitter<any>();
  @HostBinding('class.over') over = false;

  dragEnterCount = 0;

  private typeIsAccepted(event: DragEvent) {
    const draggableType = Array.from(event.dataTransfer.types).find((key)
=>
      key.indexOf('draggable-type') === 0);
    return draggableType && draggableType.split(':')[1] ===
this.dropAcceptType;
  }

  @HostListener('dragenter', ['$event'])
  dragEnter(event: DragEvent) {
    if (this.typeIsAccepted(event)) {
      this.over = true;
      this.dragEnterCount++;
    }
  }

  @HostListener('dragleave', ['$event'])
  dragLeave(event: DragEvent) {
    if (this.typeIsAccepted(event) && --this.dragEnterCount === 0) {
      this.over = false;
    }
  }
}
```

Within both of the events, we first check whether the event is carrying a data transfer object, of which we accept the type. After validating the type using our `typeIsAccepted` method, we deal with the counter, and set the `over` member field, if required.

We need to handle another event, which is important for drag and drop functionality. The dragover event helps us to set the accepted dropEffect of the current dragging action. This will tell our browser that the initiated dragging action from our draggable is suitable for this drop zone. It's also important that we prevent the default browser behavior, so that there's no default browser behavior in the way of our custom drag and drop implementation. Let's add another host listener to cover those concerns:

```
import {Directive, EventEmitter, HostBinding, HostListener, Input, Output}
from '@angular/core';
import {DraggableType} from '../model';

@Directive({
  selector: '[macDraggableDropZone]'
})
export class DraggableDropZoneDirective {
  ...

  @HostListener('dragover', ['$event'])
  dragOver(event: DragEvent) {
    if (this.typeIsAccepted(event)) {
      event.preventDefault();
      event.dataTransfer.dropEffect = 'move';
    }
  }
}
```

Finally, we need to handle the most important event in the drop zone, which is the drop event that is triggered if a user drops a draggable item into our drop zone:

```
import {Directive, EventEmitter, HostBinding, HostListener, Input, Output}
from '@angular/core';
import {DraggableType} from '../model';

@Directive({
  selector: '[macDraggableDropZone]'
})
export class DraggableDropZoneDirective {
  ...

  @HostListener('dragover', ['$event'])
  dragOver(event: DragEvent) {
    if (this.typeIsAccepted(event)) {
      event.preventDefault();
      event.dataTransfer.dropEffect = 'move';
    }
  }
```

```
    @HostListener('drop', ['$event'])
    drop(event: DragEvent) {
      if (this.typeIsAccepted(event)) {
        const data =
  JSON.parse(event.dataTransfer.getData('application/json'));
        this.over = false;
        this.dragEnterCount = 0;
        this.outDropDraggable.next(data);
      }
    }
  }
```

After checking whether the dropped element is of an accepted type, we can go ahead and read the data transfer object data from the event. This data was previously set by the draggable directive, and needs to be deserialized, using JSON.parse.

Since the drop was successful, we can reset our dragEnterCount member and set the over flag to false.

Finally, we will emit the deserialized data from the draggable element using our outDropDraggable output property.

That's all we need to build a highly reusable drag and drop behavior. We can now attach the draggable and the draggable drop zone to any components within our application where we feel the need to enable drag and drop.

In the next section, we're going to integrate the drag and drop functionality within our application.

Integrating drag and drop

We can now use the draggable and draggable drop zone directives in our task list component, so that we can enable the reordering of tasks using drag and drop.

We can do this by attaching both of the directives to the task elements within the task list component template. Yeah, that's right! We want to make our task components draggable, but also a drop zone at the same time. That way, we can drop tasks onto other tasks, and that gives us the foundation for reordering. What we will do is reorder the list on a drop, so that the dropped task will be squeezed into the position right before the task where it was dropped.

First, let's apply the drag and drop directives to the task host elements in the task list component template. Open the file `src/app/tasks/task-list/task-list.component.html`, and apply the following changes:

```
<mac-toggle [buttonList]="taskFilterTypes"
            [activeButton]="activeTaskFilterType"
            (outActivate)="activateFilterType($event)">
</mac-toggle>
<mac-enter-task (outEnterTask)="addTask($event)"></mac-enter-task>
<div class="tasks">
  <mac-task *ngFor="let task of tasks"
            [task]="task"
            (outUpdateTask)="updateTask($event)"
            macDraggable
            draggableType="task"
            [draggableData]="task"
            macDraggableDropZone
            dropAcceptType="task"
            (outDropDraggable)="dropTask(task, $event)"></mac-task>
</div>
```

Alright; using the preceding attributes, we made our tasks not only draggable, but also drop zones at the same time. By specifying both `draggableType` and `dropAcceptType` to the `'task'` string, we are telling our drag and drop behavior that these task elements can be dropped into other task elements. Our draggable drop zone directive is set to emit an `outDropDraggable` event whenever a valid draggable is dropped off. On a successful drop, we will call a new method within our task list component `dropTask`, to which we will pass the current task and the drop zone event object. The draggable drop zone directive will emit the data that was previously set using the `draggableData` input of the draggable directive. In other words, the `dropTask` method is called with the target task as the first parameter and the source task as the second parameter.

Let's implement the `dropTask` method within our component class, located in `src/app/tasks/task-list/task-list.component.ts`:

```
...

@Component({
  selector: 'mac-task-list',
  templateUrl: './task-list.component.html',
  encapsulation: ViewEncapsulation.None,
  changeDetection: ChangeDetectionStrategy.OnPush
})
export class TaskListComponent {
  ...
```

```
dropTask(target: Task, source: Task) {
  if (target.id === source.id) {
    return;
  }

  this.outUpdateTask.emit({
    ...target,
    order: source.order
  });
  this.outUpdateTask.emit({
    ...source,
    order: target.order
  });
}
}
```

Let's elaborate on the implementation within our task list component:

1. If you check the template again, you will see that we bound to the `dropTask` method with the following expression: `(outDropDraggable)="dropTask(task, $event)"`. Since the drop zone emitted an event with deserialized data that was bound using the draggable input property `draggableData`, we can safely assume that we will receive a copy of the task that was dropped into the drop zone. As the first parameter to our binding, we added the local view variable `task`, which is actually the task that acts as the drop zone. Therefore, we can say that the first parameter of our `dropTask` method represents the target, while the second represents the source task.

2. As a first check in our method, we compare the source ID with the target ID, and if they match, we can assume that the task was dropped to itself, and we don't need to perform any further actions.

3. Now, all we do is emit two update task events from our task list component, to reorder both the source and target task. We do that by switching the order property between the source and target. This is just one way to reorder, and we can also implement this differently.

How great is that? We have successfully implemented drag and drop on our task list, to provide a very useful feature to reorder tasks.

Recapitulate on drag and drop

With the use of the low-level drag and drop API, using events and data transfer objects, we have implemented two directives that can now be used to execute smooth drag and drop functionality within our application, wherever we desire.

With almost no effort, we have implemented our drag and drop behavior on the task list, to provide a nice feature to reorder the tasks within the list. The only thing that we needed to do, besides hooking up the directives, was implement a method where we could reorder the tasks based on the information from the draggable drop zone directive output.

We worked with the following concepts in this section:

- We learned the basics of the HTML5 drag and drop API
- We used the data transfer object to securely transfer data within drag and drop events
- We built reusable behavior patterns, using directives
- We enriched the standard drag and drop API by providing our own custom selection mechanisms, using a custom data type that encodes draggable type information

Summary

In this chapter, we built two features to enhance the usability of our application. Users can now make use of tags, to easily annotate comments with navigable items that provide summaries to the subject. They can also use drag and drop, to reorder tasks within the task list component.

Usability is a key asset in today's applications, and, by providing highly encapsulated and reusable components to address usability concerns, we can make our lives a lot easier when building those applications. When dealing with usability, thinking in terms of components is a very good thing, not only for easing development, but for establishing consistency. Consistency itself plays a major role in making an application usable.

In the next chapter, we're going to create some nifty components to manage time within our task management system. This will also include some new user input components, to enable simple work time-entry fields.

8
Time Will Tell

Our task-management system is shaping up. However, we have not been concerned about one crucial aspect of managing our projects so far. Time plays a major role in all projects, and it's probably the aspect that is often the most complicated to manage.

In this chapter, we will add a few features to our task management system that will help our users to manage time more efficiently. Reusing some components that we created earlier, we will be able to provide a consistent user experience to manage time.

On a higher level, we will develop the following features to enable time management in our application:

- **Task details**: So far, we did not include a details page of tasks because all the necessary information about tasks could be displayed on the task list of our project page. As our time management will increase the complexity of our tasks quite a bit, we will create a new detail view of project tasks that will also be accessible through routing.
- **Efforts management**: We will include some new data on our tasks to manage efforts on tasks. Efforts are always represented by an estimated duration of time and an effective duration of spent time. We will make both properties of efforts optional so that they can exist independently. We will create new components to enable users to provide time duration input easily.

The following topics will be covered in this chapter:

- Creating a project task detail component to edit task details and enable a new route
- Modifying our tag management system to include task tags
- Creating new pipes to deal with formatting time durations
- Creating task information components to display task overview information on the existing task components

- Creating a time duration component that enables users to easily input time durations using a no-UI user interaction approach
- Implementing time effort tracking on tasks
- Creating an SVG component to display progress on tasks

Task details

So far, our task list was sufficient enough to display all details of tasks directly in the listing. However, as we will add more details to tasks in this chapter, it's time to provide a detailed view where users can edit the task.

We already laid the groundwork for project navigation using the router in Chapter 5, *Component-Based Routing*. Adding a new routable component that we'll use in the context of our projects will be a breeze.

Before we start creating a new task details component, let's introduce a new state within our task model. Users should have the additional option to provide a task description in addition to the task title. This description will be editable on the task details view.

Let's open our model file, located in src/app/model.ts, and add an optional description field to our task interface:

```
...

export interface Task {
  readonly id?: number;
  readonly projectId?: number;
  readonly title: string;
  readonly description?: string;
  readonly done: boolean;
  readonly order: number;
}

...
```

Okay, so now we can store a description with each of our tasks. When new tasks are created on the task list, however, we will still only store the title of the task. A user needs to access the new detail view in order to update the description of a task.

Alright, let's create a new component for our task detail view using the Angular CLI:

```
ng generate component --spec false -cd onpush tasks/task-details
```

Let's open the generated component class file in `src/app/tasks/task-details/task-details.component.ts` and add the following code:

```
import {
  ChangeDetectionStrategy, Component, EventEmitter, Input, Output,
  ViewEncapsulation
} from '@angular/core';
import {Tag, Task} from '../../model';

@Component({
  selector: 'mac-task-details',
  templateUrl: './task-details.component.html',
  styleUrls: ['./task-details.component.css'],
  encapsulation: ViewEncapsulation.None,
  changeDetection: ChangeDetectionStrategy.OnPush
})
export class TaskDetailsComponent {
  @Input() task: Task;
  @Input() tags: Tag[];
  @Output() outUpdateTask = new EventEmitter<Task>();

  updateTitle(title: string) {
    this.outUpdateTask.emit({
      ...this.task,
      title
    });
  }

  updateDescription(description: string) {
    this.outUpdateTask.emit({
      ...this.task,
      description
    });
  }
}
```

Within the task details, we're enabling the user to edit both the title and description of tasks. We're working on a simple UI component to represent the task details view. Therefore, we're expecting the task object to be set as a component input. The `outUpdateTask` output is used to communicate task updates to our parent component. We've also added two methods to be used within our view in order to update the task title and description.

We'd also like to support tag selection when a user edits the description of a task. For this purpose, we're adding a `tags` input, which can be provided by the parent component.

Alright, let's now take a look at the template of our component, and see how we'll deal with the task data to provide an interface to edit the details. Open the template file located in `src/app/tasks/task-details/task-details.component.html` and add the following content:

```
<h3 class="title">Task Details of task #{{task.id}}</h3>
<div class="content">
  <div class="label">Title</div>
  <mac-editor [content]="task.title"
              [showControls]="true"
              (outSaveEdit)="updateTitle($event)"></mac-editor>
  <div class="label">Description</div>
  <mac-editor [content]="task.description"
              [showControls]="true"
              [tags]="tags"
              (outSaveEdit)="updateDescription($event)"></mac-editor>
</div>
```

By reusing the editor component that we created in Chapter 4, *Thinking in Projects*, we can rely on simple UI composition to make the title and description of our tasks editable.

As we stored the task data into the `task` member variable on our component, we can reference the `title` and `description` fields to create a binding to the `content` input property of our editor components.

While the title should only consist of plaintext, we can support the tagging functionality that we created in Chapter 7, *Components for User Experience*, on the description field of the task. For this, we simply pass the list of available tags into the editor component.

We are using the editor components' `outSaveEdit` output property to call our update functions for updating the title or description, respectively.

So far, so good. We created a task details component that makes it easy to edit the title and description of tasks using our editor UI component. Now, we need to create a container component for our task details view and enable it as a child route within our application.

Let's use the Angular CLI to create a task details container component:

```
ng generate component --spec false -cd onpush container/task-details-
container
```

As always, the view of our container components is dead simple. We're simply rendering a UI component and passing down the required data. Let's do that by editing the template of our task details container component, which is located in `src/app/container/task-details-container/task-details-container.component.html`:

```
<mac-task-details [task]="task | async"
                  [tags]="tags | async"
                  (outUpdateTask)="updateTask($event)">
</mac-task-details>
```

The task details UI component required a task object to be passed as input as well as the list of tags supported by our application. We'll obtain this data using the observables provided from the respective services. When a task is updated we'll receive the `outUpdateTask` output event and call a method `updateTask` on our container component. Let's open the component class located in `src/app/container/task-details-container/task-details-container.component.ts` and add the following code:

```
import {ChangeDetectionStrategy, Component, ViewEncapsulation} from
'@angular/core';
import {ActivatedRoute} from '@angular/router';
import {TaskService} from '../../tasks/task.service';
import {Observable, combineLatest} from 'rxjs';
import {Tag, Task} from '../../model';
import {map} from 'rxjs/operators';
import {TagsService} from '../../tags/tags.service';

@Component({
  selector: 'mac-task-details-container',
  templateUrl: './task-details-container.component.html',
  styleUrls: ['./task-details-container.component.css'],
  encapsulation: ViewEncapsulation.None,
  changeDetection: ChangeDetectionStrategy.OnPush
})
export class TaskDetailsContainerComponent {
  task: Observable<Task>;
  tags: Observable<Tag[]>;

  constructor(private taskService: TaskService,
              private route: ActivatedRoute,
              private tagsService: TagsService) {
    this.task = combineLatest(
      this.taskService.getTasks(),
      route.params
    ).pipe(
      map(([tasks, routeParams]) =>
        tasks.find((task) => task.id === +routeParams.taskId)
```

```
      )
    );
    this.tags = this.tagsService.tags;
  }

  updateTask(task: Task) {
    this.taskService.updateTask(task);
  }
}
```

There's nothing new here. We're using a route parameter called taskId to obtain a specific task from the task list coming from our task service.

The only thing left to enable our new task details view is to create a child route within our route configuration. Let's open our route configuration, located in src/app/routes.ts, to make the necessary modifications:

```
...
import {TaskDetailsContainerComponent} from './container/task-details-
container/task-details-container.component';

export const routes: Route[] = [{
  path: 'projects/:projectId',
  component: ProjectContainerComponent,
  canActivate: [ProjectContainerGuard],
  children: [{
    path: 'tasks',
    component: TaskListContainerComponent
  }, {
    path: 'tasks/:taskId',
    component: TaskDetailsContainerComponent
  }, {
    path: 'comments',
    component: ProjectCommentsContainerComponent
  }, {
    path: 'activities',
    component: ProjectActivitiesContainerComponent
  }, {
    path: '**',
    redirectTo: 'tasks'
  }]
}, {
  path: '',
  pathMatch: 'full',
  redirectTo: '/projects/1'
}];
```

We added a new child route on our project view, which is now accessible with the URL /projects/:projectId/tasks/:taskId. By including the parameter :taskId in the route configuration, we can pass the concerned task ID into the task details container component.

Fantastic! We've created a new task details view and enabled it within our router. You can preview your changes within the browser and access the details view of a task by entering the following URL into your browser: http://localhost:4200/projects/1/tasks/1. You should now see the details view of the first task within our first project. Try editing the title and description before we move on with the integration of our task details view.

Navigating to task details

In order to make our task details route navigable, we need to modify our task component within the task list. We would like to add a small button to our task component that will navigate to the details view. Let's start with the template changes; open our task component template, located in src/app/tasks/task/task.component.html, and apply the following changes:

```html
<mac-checkbox [checked]="task.done"
              (outCheck)="updateTask($event)"></mac-checkbox>
<div class="content">
  <div class="title">
    <mac-editor [content]="task.title"
                [showControls]="true"
                (outSaveEdit)="updateTitle($event)"></mac-editor>
  </div>
  <button class="button button-small"
(click)="showDetails()">Details</button>
  <button class="delete" (click)="deleteTask()"></button>
</div>
```

Let's move right into our component class and implement the new showDetails method. Open the file src/app/tasks/task/task.component.html and apply the following changes:

```
...

@Component({
  selector: 'mac-task',
  templateUrl: './task.component.html',
  encapsulation: ViewEncapsulation.None,
  changeDetection: ChangeDetectionStrategy.OnPush
```

```
})
export class TaskComponent {
  ...
  @Output() outShowDetails = new EventEmitter<Task>();

  ...

  showDetails() {
    this.outShowDetails.emit(this.task);
  }
}
```

Alright, now we need to make sure that we're carrying the event to show task details all the way up to the task list container component. Our next step is the task list UI component, where we need to delegate the `outShowDetails` output of our task component.

Let's start with the template changes in `src/app/tasks/task-list/task-list.component.html` and apply the following change:

```
...
<div class="tasks">
  <mac-task *ngFor="let task of tasks"
            [task]="task"
            (outUpdateTask)="updateTask($event)"
            (outDeleteTask)="deleteTask($event)"
            (outShowDetails)="showDetails($event)"
            macDraggable
            draggableType="task"
            [draggableData]="task"
            macDraggableDropZone
            dropAcceptType="task"
            (outDropDraggable)="dropTask(task, $event)"></mac-task>
</div>
```

That was easy! Now, let's add the changes to the task list component class located in `src/app/tasks/task-list/task-list.component.ts`:

```
...

@Component({
  selector: 'mac-task-list',
  templateUrl: './task-list.component.html',
  encapsulation: ViewEncapsulation.None,
  changeDetection: ChangeDetectionStrategy.OnPush
})
export class TaskListComponent {
  ...
```

```
@Output() outShowDetails = new EventEmitter<Task>();

...

showDetails(task: Task) {
  this.outShowDetails.emit(task);
}
}
```

Great, the next stop in our component tree is the task list container, which is where we'll implement the logic to navigate to the details view. Let's open the template of the task list container, located in `src/app/container/task-list-container/task-list-container.component.html`, and create the necessary binding:

```
<mac-task-list
  [tasks]="filteredTasks | async"
  [taskFilterTypes]="taskFilterTypes"
  [activeTaskFilterType]="activeTaskFilterType | async"
  (outUpdateTask)="updateTask($event)"
  (outDeleteTask)="deleteTask($event)"
  (outShowDetails)="showDetails($event)"
  (outActivateFilterType)="activateFilterType($event)"
  (outAddTask)="addTask($event)">
</mac-task-list>
```

Finally, we need to implement the `showDetails` method within the container component class located in `src/app/container/task-list-container/task-list-container.component.ts`:

```
...

@Component({
  selector: 'mac-task-list-container',
  templateUrl: './task-list-container.component.html',
  encapsulation: ViewEncapsulation.None,
  changeDetection: ChangeDetectionStrategy.OnPush
})
export class TaskListContainerComponent {
  ...

  showDetails(task: Task) {
    this.selectedProject
      .pipe(take(1))
      .subscribe(selectedProject => {
        this.router.navigate(['/projects', selectedProject.id, 'tasks',
task.id]);
      });
```

```
    }
  }
```

Hurray! We have finally made our task details view navigable using a new navigation button on our task component!

Now, you might ask yourself, why have we implemented such a crazy output delegation path, just to trigger a navigation? Wouldn't it be much easier to just use a `routerLink` directive within the task UI component and be done?

Of course, that would be much easier. However, there's a slight problem with using router links within simple UI components. By doing so, we rely on a specific route configuration being present in our system. Using router links directly within UI components restricts them to a very specific context. We'd like to avoid this, so we can reuse our components in many different contexts. The only meaningful way to solve this issue is to use output delegation and control your navigation within container components programmatically:

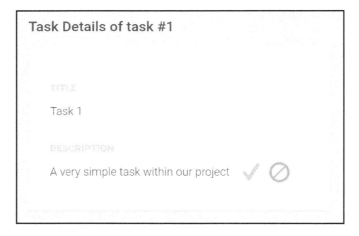

Newly created task detail view with editable title and description

Enabling tags for tasks

So far, the tag-management system that we created in Chapter 7, *Components for User Experience*, only supports project tags. As we have now created a detail view for tasks, it would be nice to also support task tags directly in our tagging system. Our tagging system is quite flexible, and we can implement new tags with very little effort.

Let's modify our tags service, located in `src/app/tags/tags.service.ts`, in order to enable tags for our tasks:

```
import {Injectable} from '@angular/core';
import {ProjectService} from '../project/project.service';
import {Project, Tag, Task} from '../model';
import {Observable, of, combineLatest} from 'rxjs/Observable';
import {map} from 'rxjs/operators';
import {limitWithEllipsis, replaceAll} from '../utilities/string-utilities';
import {TaskService} from '../tasks/task.service';

@Injectable()
export class TagsService {
  tags: Observable<Tag[]>;

  constructor(private projectService: ProjectService,
              private taskService: TaskService) {
    this.tags = combineLatest(
      this.projectService.getProjects().pipe(
        map((projects: Project[]) => projects.map(project => ({
          type: 'project',
          hashTag: `#project-${project.id}`,
          title: limitWithEllipsis(project.title, 20),
          link: `/projects/${project.id}/tasks`
        })))
      ),
      this.taskService.getTasks().pipe(
        map((tasks: Task[]) => tasks.map(task => ({
          type: 'task',
          hashTag: `#task-${task.id}`,
          title: `${limitWithEllipsis(task.title, 20)} (${task.done ?
'done' : 'open'})`,
          link: `/projects/${task.projectId}/tasks/${task.id}`
        })))
      )
    ).pipe(
      map(([projectTags, taskTags]) => [...projectTags, ...taskTags])
    );
  }

  ...
}
```

In addition to the project service, we're also injecting the task service within the constructor of our tags service. Very similar to what we already do for projects, we need to create a tag object for every single task within our application. We're using the observable provided by the task service and use the `map` operator to convert all tasks to tags.

Finally, we're using the `combineLatest` observable helper to merge both project tags and task tags into a single observable stream. Within a final map operator, we're concatenating those two tag lists into a single array.

This wasn't too complicated, right? This relatively simple change results in a huge improvement for our users. They can now reference individual tasks everywhere in our system where we have enabled tags. By clicking a task tag, we are navigating to our newly created task details view:

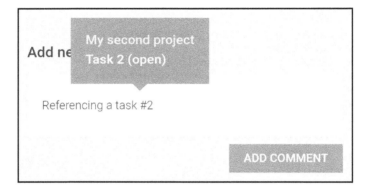

The editor component of the project comments tab displaying the newly added task tags

Managing efforts

In this section, we will create some components that help us keep track of work efforts. Primarily, we will use this to manage efforts on tasks, but this could be applied to any part of our application where we need to keep track of time.

Efforts in our context always consist of two things:

- **Estimated duration**: This is the duration that is initially estimated for the task
- **Effective duration**: This is the duration of time that is spent on a given task

For time durations, we assume some time units and rules that will simplify the processing of time and align to some working standards. The goal here is not to provide razor sharp time management but something that is accurate enough to bring value. For this purpose, we define the following working time units:

- **Minute**: One minute is a regular 60 seconds
- **Hour**: One hour always represents 60 minutes
- **Day**: One day represents a regular workday of eight hours
- **Week**: One week is equivalent to five working days (5 * 8 hours)

When working with durations and efforts we would like to have some type safety, and for this reason, we're introducing a few new interfaces to our model. Let's open our model, located in `src/app/model.ts`, and add the following two interfaces:

```
...

export interface TimeUnit {
  short: string;
  milliseconds: number;
}

export interface TimeEfforts {
  estimated: number;
  effective: number;
}
```

The `short` property on the `TimeUnit` interface will be used to recognize time entry by the user. We will use the letters m, h, d, and w for the different time units and store how many milliseconds each time frame contains.

Since we'd like to keep track of the time and efforts spent on tasks, let's also modify our task model. Find the `Task` interface within our model file and add the following property:

```
export interface Task {
  readonly id?: number;
  readonly projectId?: number;
  readonly title: string;
  readonly description?: string;
  readonly done: boolean;
  readonly order: number;
  readonly efforts?: TimeEfforts;
}

...
```

We have added a new optional `efforts` property to our task interface, which is storing the efforts spent working on our tasks.

Alright, we have prepared our model for the upcoming time tracking features. In the next section, we're going to implement our first UI component to enter time durations.

No-UI time duration input

We could now start to write a complex user interface component, where users can enter individual time units in different input elements. However, I believe it's much more convenient to treat time duration input with a no-UI approach.

Put very simply, no-UI means that we use regular text input to provide user interactions. Well, that's nothing new right? Text input is where it all started. However, there's a significant trend in providing no-UI interactions lately. By combining intelligence in how we process the text input of users, no-UI interactions can actually be surprisingly efficient, and outperform complex user interfaces by far.

Instead of building a complex user interface to enter time duration, we can simply agree on a textual short form to write durations. We can let the user write something, such as `1.5d` or `5h 30m`, in order to provide input. Sticking to the convention that we established at the beginning of this section, *Managing Efforts*, we can build a simple parser that can handle this sort of input.

This approach has several advantages. Besides that, this is one of the most efficient ways to enter time durations, and it's also easy for us to implement. We can simply reuse our editor component to gather text input from the user. Then, we use a conversion process to parse the entered time duration.

Let's spin up a new utility module that helps us deal with these conversions. Let's start by creating a new empty file on the path `src/app/utilities/time-utilities.ts`.

First, we need to have a constant that defines all the units we need for the conversion process. Add this first code excerpt to our newly created file:

```
import {TimeUnit} from '../model';

export const UNITS: TimeUnit[] = [{
  short: 'w',
  milliseconds: 5 * 8 * 60 * 60 * 1000
}, {
```

```
    short: 'd',
    milliseconds: 8 * 60 * 60 * 1000
}, {
    short: 'h',
    milliseconds: 60 * 60 * 1000
}, {
    short: 'm',
    milliseconds: 60 * 1000
}];
```

We make use of the `TimeUnit` interface which we've created in our model.

These are all the units that we need to deal with for now. You can see the milliseconds being calculated at run-time. We can also write the milliseconds as number literals, but calculating them in place provides us with some transparency on how we get to these values and we can spear on some comments.

Let's look at our parsing function, which we can use to parse text input into time durations. Append the following code to our file:

```
export function parseDuration(formattedDuration: string): number {
  const pattern = /[\d\.]+\s*[wdhm]/g;
  let timeSpan = 0;
  let result;
  while (result = pattern.exec(formattedDuration)) {
    const chunk = result[0].replace(/\s/g, '');
    const amount = Number(chunk.slice(0, -1));
    const unitShortName = chunk.slice(-1);
    timeSpan += amount * UNITS.find((unit) => unit.short ===
unitShortName).milliseconds;
  }
  return timeSpan || null;
}
```

Let's analyze the preceding code briefly to explain what we do here:

1. First, we define a regular expression that helps us dissect the text representation of a duration. This pattern will extract chunks from the text input that are important to calculate the duration behind the text representation. These chunks always consist of a number, followed by either w, d, h, or m. Therefore, the text 10w 3d 2h 30m will be split into the chunks 10w, 3d, 2h, and 30m.

2. We initialize a `timeSpan` variable with 0, so we can add all the milliseconds from discovered chunks together and later return this sum.

3. For each of the previously-extracted chunks, we now extract the number component into a variable called `amount`, and the unit (w, d, h, or m) into a variable called `unitShortName`.

4. Now, we can look up the data in the `UNITS` constant for the unit of the chunk that we will process, multiply the amount of milliseconds of the unit by the amount we extract from the chunk, and then add that result to our `timeSpan` variable.

Well, this is quite a neat function we have built here. It accepts a formatted time duration string and converts it into milliseconds. This is already half of what we need to deal with the textual representation of time durations. The second piece is the opposite of what just built. We need a function to convert a duration in milliseconds into a formatted duration string. Let's append another piece of code to our file:

```
export function formatDuration(timeSpan: number): string {
  return UNITS.reduce((str, unit) => {
    const amount = timeSpan / unit.milliseconds;
    if (amount >= 1) {
      const fullUnits = Math.floor(amount);
      const formatted = `${str} ${fullUnits}${unit.short}`;
      timeSpan -= fullUnits * unit.milliseconds;
      return formatted;
    } else {
      return str;
    }
  }, '').trim();
}
```

Let's also explain briefly what the `formatDuration` function does:

- We use the `Array.prototype.reduce` function to format a string that contains all time units and their amount. We iterate over all available time units in the `UNITS` constant, starting with the largest unit for weeks.
- We then divide the `timeSpan` variable, which is in milliseconds, by the milliseconds of the unit, which gives us the amount of the given unit.
- If the amount is greater than or equal to 1, we can add the unit with the given amount and unit short name to our formatted string.
- As we could be left with some fractions after the comma in the amount, which we will need to encode in smaller units, we subtract the floored version of our amount from the `timeSpan` before we return to the `reduce` function again.
- This process is repeated for every unit, where each unit will only provide a formatted output if the amount is greater than or equal to 1.

This is all we need to convert back and forth between formatted time duration and time duration represented in milliseconds.

We'll do one more thing before we create the actual component to enter time durations. We will create a simple pipe that basically just wraps our formatTime function. For this, we will create a new pipe using the Angular CLI:

```
ng generate pipe --spec false pipes/format-duration
```

Let's open the generated file src/app/pipes/format-duration.pipe.ts and add the following content:

```
import {Pipe, PipeTransform} from '@angular/core';
import {formatDuration} from '../utilities/time-utilities';

@Pipe({
  name: 'formatDuration'
})
export class FormatDurationPipe implements PipeTransform {
  transform(value) {
    if (value == null || typeof value !== 'number') {
      return value;
    }

    return formatDuration(value);
  }
}
```

Using the formatTime function of our new time utility module, we now have the ability to format durations in milliseconds directly in our component templates.

Components to manage efforts

Okay, this is enough time-math for the moment. Let's now use the elements that we've created to shape some components that will help us gather user input.

In this section, we will create two components to manage efforts:

- **Duration component**: The duration component is a simple UI component, enabling user input of time durations using the formatted time strings we dealt with in the previous topics. It uses an editor component to enable user input and makes use of the time formatting pipe as well as the parseDuration utility function.

- **Efforts component**: The efforts component is just a composition of two duration components that represent the estimated effort and the effective effort spent on a given task. Following a strict rule of composition, this component is important for us so that we don't repeat ourselves and instead compose a larger component.

Let's start with the duration component and use the Angular CLI to scaffold our initial component structure:

```
ng generate component --spec false -cd onpush ui/duration
```

Alright, let's now open the component class located in `src/app/ui/duration/duration.component.ts` and apply the following changes:

```
import {ChangeDetectionStrategy, Component, EventEmitter, Input, Output,
ViewEncapsulation} from '@angular/core';
import {parseDuration} from '../../utilities/time-utilities';

@Component({
  selector: 'mac-duration',
  templateUrl: './duration.component.html',
  styleUrls: ['./duration.component.css'],
  encapsulation: ViewEncapsulation.None,
  changeDetection: ChangeDetectionStrategy.OnPush
})
export class DurationComponent {
  @Input() duration: number;
  @Output() outDurationChange = new EventEmitter<number>();

  editSaved(formattedDuration: string) {
    this.outDurationChange.emit(parseDuration(formattedDuration));
  }
}
```

There's nothing fancy about this component really, because we created the bulk of the logic already and we simply compose a higher component.

For the `duration` input, we expect a time duration in milliseconds, while the `outDurationChange` output property will emit the updated duration in milliseconds when the user provides some input.

The `editSaved` method serves in the binding to the underlying editor component. Whenever the user saves his edits on the editor component, we'll take this input, convert the formatted time duration into milliseconds using the `parseDuration` function, and re-emit the converted value using the `outDurationChange` output property.

Let's look at the template of our component in
`src/app/ui/duration/duration.component.ts`:

```
<mac-editor [content]="duration | formatDuration"
            [showControls]="true"
            (outSaveEdit)="editSaved($event)"></mac-editor>
```

Surprised with how simple our template is? Well, this is exactly what we should achieve with higher order components, once we establish a good foundation of base components. Well-organized composition radically simplifies our code. The only thing that we deal with here is our good old editor component.

We bind the `duration` input property of our duration component to the `content` input property of the editor component. As we'd like to pass the formatted time duration and not the duration in milliseconds, we use the `formatDuration` pipe to convert within the binding expression.

If the editor component notifies us about a saved edit, we call the `editSaved` method on our duration component, which will parse the entered duration and re-emit the resulting value a s milliseconds.

As we initially defined all efforts to consist of an estimated and an effective duration, we would now like to create another component that combines these two durations within a single component.

Let's create a new efforts component by using the Angular CLI tool:

```
ng generate component --spec false -cd onpush efforts/efforts
```

Open up the template file of the generated component, located in `src/app/efforts/efforts/efforts.component.html`, and add the following content:

```
<div class="label">Estimated:</div>
<mac-duration [duration]="efforts?.estimated"
              (outDurationChange)="estimatedChange($event)"></mac-duration>
<div class="label">Effective:</div>
<mac-duration [duration]="efforts?.effective"
              (outDurationChange)="effectiveChange($event)"></mac-duration>
<button class="button small" (click)="addEffectiveHours(1)">+1h</button>
<button class="button small" (click)="addEffectiveHours(4)">+4h</button>
<button class="button small" (click)="addEffectiveHours(8)">+1d</button>
```

First, we add two duration components, where the first one is used to gather input for the estimated time and the later one for effective time.

In addition to this, we provide three small buttons to increase the effective duration by a simple click. In this way, the user can quickly add one or four hours (half a working day) or a complete working day (which we defined as eight hours).

Let's open the file `src/app/efforts/efforts/efforts.component.ts` and implement the component class:

```
import {Component, ViewEncapsulation, Input, Output, EventEmitter,
ChangeDetectionStrategy} from '@angular/core';
import {UNITS} from '../../utilities/time-utilities';
import {TimeEffort} from '../../model';

@Component({
  selector: 'mac-efforts',
  templateUrl: './efforts.component.html',
  styleUrls: ['./efforts.component.css'],
  encapsulation: ViewEncapsulation.None,
  changeDetection: ChangeDetectionStrategy.OnPush
})
export class EffortsComponent {
  @Input() efforts: TimeEffort;
  @Output() outEffortsChange = new EventEmitter<TimeEffort>();

  estimatedChange(estimated: number) {
    this.outEffortsChange.emit({
      ...this.efforts,
      estimated
    });
  }

  effectiveChange(effective: number) {
    this.outEffortsChange.emit({
      ...this.efforts,
      effective
    });
  }

  addEffectiveHours(hours: number) {
    const hourMilliseconds = UNITS.find((unit) => unit.short ===
'h').milliseconds;
    let effective = this.efforts && this.efforts.effective ?
this.efforts.effective : 0;
    effective += hours * hourMilliseconds;

    this.outEffortsChange.emit({
      ...this.efforts,
      effective
```

```
        });
    }
  }
}
```

The component provides an input named `efforts` to provide a `TimeEfforts` object. If you take a look at the component template again, the `estimated` and `effective` properties of the efforts object are directly bound to the input properties of the duration components.

The `estimatedChange` and `effectiveChange` methods are used to create bindings to the `outDurationChange` output properties of the respective duration components. All we do here is emit an aggregated data object that contains the effective and estimated time in milliseconds using the `outEffortsChange` output property.

The `addEffectiveHours` method is used for our quick buttons within the template of our efforts component. We calculate the effective property by multiplying the number of milliseconds for a working hour with the number of hours passed to the function. We use our `UNITS` constant from the time utility module in order to get the number of milliseconds for an hour. After we've calculated the new effective duration, we're using the `outEffortsChange` output to propagate the update.

That's all we need in order to provide a user input to manage efforts on our tasks. To complete this topic, we will add our newly-created efforts component to the task details component in order to manage efforts on tasks.

Let's first look at the code changes in the task details component template located in `src/app/tasks/task-details/task-details.component.html`:

```html
<h3 class="title">Task Details of task #{{task.id}}</h3>
<div class="content">
  <div class="label">Title</div>
  <mac-editor [content]="task.title"
              [showControls]="true"
              (outSaveEdit)="updateTitle($event)"></mac-editor>
  <div class="label">Description</div>
  <mac-editor [content]="task.description"
              [showControls]="true"
              [tags]="tags"
              (outSaveEdit)="updateDescription($event)"></mac-editor>
  <div class="label">Efforts</div>
  <mac-efforts [efforts]="task.efforts"
               (outEffortsChange)="updateEfforts($event)">
  </mac-efforts>
</div>
```

We're simply including our new efforts component in the task details template. Since we have the efforts object already present on our task objects, we can create the necessary binding without additional changes in the component class. However, for updating the efforts when a user changes the estimated or effective durations, we will need to implement a new method `updateEfforts`.

Let's open our component class, located in `src/app/tasks/task-details/task-details.component.html`, and implement the new method:

```
import {
  ChangeDetectionStrategy, Component, EventEmitter, Input, Output,
  ViewEncapsulation
} from '@angular/core';
import {Tag, Task, TimeEfforts} from '../../model';

@Component({
  selector: 'mac-task-details',
  templateUrl: './task-details.component.html',
  styleUrls: ['./task-details.component.css'],
  encapsulation: ViewEncapsulation.None,
  changeDetection: ChangeDetectionStrategy.OnPush
})
export class TaskDetailsComponent {
  ...

  updateEfforts(efforts: TimeEfforts) {
    this.outUpdateTask.emit({
      ...this.task,
      efforts
    });
  }
}
```

We added a new `updateEfforts` method that deals with the output provided by the efforts component. Because the efforts property is part of the task object, we can simply reuse the `outUpdateTask` output to delegate the update. Our container component is already prepared to deal with task updates.

Awesome stuff! We have successfully implemented a no-UI component and used the concept of composition to it's best. You should now be able to preview the changes in your browser and manage efforts on the task details view:

Our new Efforts component that consists of two duration input components

The visual efforts timeline

Although the components that we have created so far to manage efforts provide a good way to edit and display effort and time durations, we can still improve this with some visual indication.

In this section, we will create a visual efforts timeline using SVG. This timeline should display the following information:

- The total estimated duration as a grey background bar
- The total effective duration as a green bar that overlays on the total estimated duration bar
- A yellow bar that shows any overtime (if the effective duration is greater than the estimated duration)

The following two figures illustrate the different visual states of our efforts timeline component:

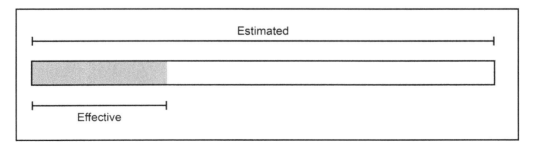

The visual state if the estimated duration is greater than the effective duration

If a task's effective time will be more than the originally estimated time, we can show that overtime in a different colour:

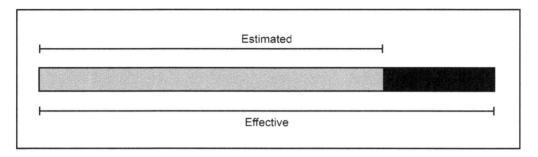

The visual state if the effective duration exceeds the estimated duration (the overtime is displayed as a yellow bar)

Let's start fleshing out our visual timeline component by using Angular CLI to create our component stubs:

```
ng generate component --spec false -cd onpush efforts/efforts-timeline
```

Alright, let's first look at the component class located in src/app/efforts/efforts-timeline/efforts-timeline.component.ts and implement the necessary logic to render our SVG timeline:

```
import {Component, Input, ViewEncapsulation, ChangeDetectionStrategy,
OnChanges, SimpleChanges} from '@angular/core';
import {TimeEfforts} from '../../model';

@Component({
  selector: 'mac-efforts-timeline',
  templateUrl: './efforts-timeline.component.html',
  styleUrls: ['./efforts-timeline.component.css'],
  encapsulation: ViewEncapsulation.None,
  changeDetection: ChangeDetectionStrategy.OnPush
})
export class EffortsTimelineComponent implements OnChanges {
  @Input() efforts: TimeEfforts;

  done: number;
  overtime: number;

  ngOnChanges(changes: SimpleChanges) {
    this.done = 0;
    this.overtime = 0;
```

```
    if (
      !this.efforts.estimated && this.efforts.effective ||
      (this.efforts.estimated && this.efforts.estimated ===
this.efforts.effective)
    ) {
      this.done = 100;
    } else if (this.efforts.estimated < this.efforts.effective) {
      this.done = this.efforts.estimated / this.efforts.effective * 100;
      this.overtime = 100 - this.done;
    } else {
      this.done = this.efforts.effective / this.efforts.estimated * 100;
    }
  }
}
```

Our component has only one input. The `efforts` input is a `TimeEfforts` object which we're supposed to render on a graphical timeline. All the other properties that we need to render our timeline are derived from this efforts object.

In the `OnChanges` lifecycle hook, we set two component member fields, which are based on the estimated and effective time:

- **done**: This contains the width of the green bar in percent, which displays the effective duration without overtime that exceeds the estimated duration
- **overtime**: This contains the width of the yellow bar in percent that displays any overtime, which is any time duration that exceeds the estimated duration

Let's look at the template of the efforts timeline component and see how we can now use the `done` and `overtime` member fields to draw our timeline.

Open the template file located in `src/app/efforts/efforts-timeline/efforts-timeline.component.ts` and apply the following changes:

```
<svg width="100%" height="10">
  <rect height="10"
        x="0" y="0" width="100%"
        class="remaining"></rect>
  <rect *ngIf="done" x="0" y="0" [attr.width]="done + '%'" height="10"
        class="done"></rect>
  <rect *ngIf="overtime" [attr.x]="done + '%'" y="0"
        [attr.width]="overtime + '%'" height="10"
        class="overtime"></rect>
</svg>
```

Our template is SVG-based, and it contains three rectangles for each of the bars that we want to display. The background bar of our efforts timeline will always be displayed.

Above the remaining bar, we conditionally display the done and the overtime bar using the calculated widths from our component class.

That's all we need for representing our efforts timeline. We can now go ahead and include the efforts timeline component in our efforts component. This way, our users will have visual feedback when they edit the estimated or effective duration, and it provides them with a sense of overview.

Let's open the template of the efforts component, located in `src/app/efforts/efforts/efforts.component.html`, and apply the following changes:

```
<div class="label">Estimated:</div>
<mac-duration [duration]="efforts?.estimated"
              (outDurationChange)="estimatedChange($event)"></mac-duration>
<div class="label">Effective:</div>
<mac-duration [duration]="efforts?.effective"
              (outDurationChange)="effectiveChange($event)"></mac-duration>
<button class="button small" (click)="addEffectiveHours(1)">+1h</button>
<button class="button small" (click)="addEffectiveHours(4)">+4h</button>
<button class="button small" (click)="addEffectiveHours(8)">+1d</button>
<mac-efforts-timeline *ngIf="efforts"
                      [efforts]="efforts">
</mac-efforts-timeline>
```

As we have the efforts object readily available in our component, we can simply create a binding to the efforts timeline component `efforts` input property.

Congratulations! You've just put the cherry on the cake with this last change. Our users can now not only enter estimations and effective working hours using our efforts component, they also have a visual feedback of time available, spent, and overtime. Spin up the application in your browser and mess around with the new efforts component a bit. I'm sure you'll enjoy the text-based no-UI input elements we've just created. Let's take a look at a screenshot of our efforts timeline in action:

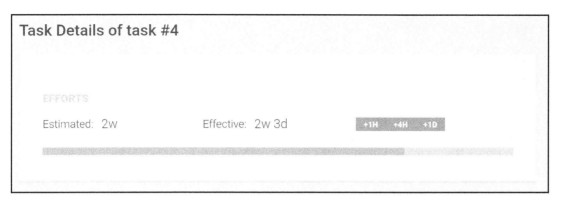

The Efforts component displaying our newly-created efforts timeline component (the overtime of six hours is visualized with the yellow bar)

Recapitulating on efforts management

In this section, we have created components that allow users to manage efforts easily and add a simple but powerful time tracking to our tasks. We've done the following to achieve this:

- We implemented some utility functions to deal with the time math in order to convert time durations in milliseconds into formatted time durations and vice versa
- We created a pipe to format time durations in milliseconds using our utility functions
- We created a duration UI component, which wraps an editor component and uses our time utilities to provide a no-UI kind of input element to enter durations
- We created an efforts component that acts as a composition of two duration components for estimated and effective time, and provides additional buttons to add effective spent time quickly
- We integrated the efforts component into the task details component in order to manage efforts on tasks
- We created a visual efforts timeline component using SVG, which displays the overall progress on a task

Summary

In this chapter, we implemented some components that help our users keep track of time. They can now log efforts on tasks and manage milestones on projects. We created a new task detail view that can be accessed using a navigation link on our task list.

Isn't it nice how easy it suddenly seems to implement new functionality when using components with proper encapsulation? The great thing about component-oriented development is that your development time for new functionality is decreased with the number of reusable components that you already created.

Once more, we experienced the power of composition using components, and reusing existing components, we were able to easily implement higher components that provide more complex functionality.

In the next chapter, we will look at how to use the charting library Chartist and create some wrapper components that allow us to build reusable charts. Additionally, we will build a dashboard for our task management system, where we will see our chart components in action.

Spaceship Dashboard

9

When I was a child, I loved to play spaceship pilot. I piled up old carton boxes and decorated the interiors to look like a spaceship cockpit. With a marker, I drew a spaceship dashboard on the inside of the boxes, and I remember playing in there for hours.

The thing that's special about the design of cockpits and spaceship dashboard is that they need to provide an overview and control over the whole spaceship, in very limited space. I think the same applies to application dashboards. A dashboard should provide the user with an overview and a sense of the overall status of what's going on.

In this chapter, we will create such a dashboard for our task management application. We will make use of the open source charting library Chartist to create good looking, responsive charts and provide an overview of open tasks and project statuses:

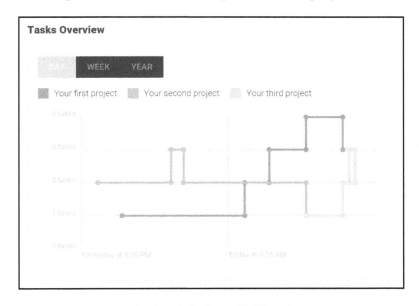

A preview of the tasks chart that we will build in this chapter

On a higher level, we will create the following components in this chapter:

- **Project summary**: This is the project summary that will provide a quick insight into the overall project status. By aggregating the efforts of all tasks in a project, we can provide a nice overall effort status, for which we have created the components in the previous chapter.
- **Project activity chart**: Without any labels or scales, this bar chart will give a quick sense of the activity on projects in the last 24 hours.
- **Project tasks chart**: This chart will provide an overview of the task progress on projects. Using a line chart, we will display the count of open tasks over a certain time period. Using the toggle component that we created in Chapter 2, *Ready, Set, Go!*, we'll provide an easy way for the user to switch the timeframe displayed on the chart.

Introduction to Chartist

In this chapter, we will create some components that will render charts, and we should look for some help in rendering them. Of course, we can follow a similar approach to what we used in Chapter 6, *Keeping up with Activities*, when we drew our activity timeline. However, when it comes to more complex data visualization, it's better to rely on a library to do the heavy lifting.

It shouldn't be a surprise that we'll use a library called Chartist to fill this gap, because I've spent almost two years writing it. As the author of Chartist, I feel very lucky that we've found a perfect spot in this book to make use of it.

I'd like to take the opportunity to briefly introduce you to Chartist, before we dive into the implementation of the components for our dashboard.

Chartist claims to provide simple responsive charts. Luckily, this is still the case after three years of existence. I can tell you that the hardest job of maintaining this library was probably protecting it from feature bloat. There are so many great movements, technologies, and ideas in the open source community, and to resist bloating the scope of the library and always stay focused on the initial claim wasn't easy.

Let me show you a very basic example of how you can create a simple line chart, once you've included the Chartist scripts on your website:

```
const chart = new Chartist.Line('#chart', {
  labels: ['Mon', 'Tue', 'Wed', 'Thu', 'Fri'],
  series: [
    [10, 7, 2, 8, 5]
  ]
});
```

The corresponding HTML markup that is required for this example looks as follows:

```
<body>
<div id="chart" class="ct-golden-section"></div>
</body>
```

The following figure shows you the resulting chart that is rendered by Chartist:

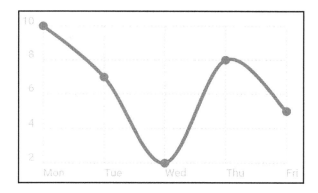

A simple line chart rendered with Chartist

I believe that by saying we'll stick to being simple, we've not promised too much.

Let's look at the second core concern of Chartist, which is to be perfectly responsive. Chartist tries to stick to a very clear separation of concerns wherever possible, which means that it uses CSS for its appearance, SVG for its basic graphical structure, and JavaScript for any behaviors. By following this principle, we've already enabled a lot of responsiveness. We can use CSS media queries to apply different styles to our charts on different media.

While CSS is great for visual styles, there are plenty of elements in the process of rendering charts, which, unfortunately, can't be controlled by CSS. After all, that is the reason why we use a JavaScript library to render charts.

So, how can we control how Chartist renders our charts on different media, if we don't have control over this in CSS? Well, Chartist provides something called **responsive configuration overrides**. Using the browser's matchMedia API, Chartist is able to provide a configuration mechanism that allows you to specify options that you want to use only on certain media (mobile, desktop etc.).

Let's look at a simple example of how we can easily implement responsive behavior using a mobile-first approach:

```
const chart = new Chartist.Line('#chart', {
  labels: ['Mon', 'Tue', 'Wed', 'Thu', 'Fri'],
  series: [
    [10, 7, 2, 8, 5]
  ]
}, {
  showPoint: true,
  showLine: true
}, [
  ['screen and (min-width: 400px)', {
    showPoint: false
  }],
  ['screen and (min-width: 800px)', {
    lineSmooth: false
  }]
]);
```

In this example, the second parameter to the Chartist.Line constructor sets the initial options; we can provide overriding options, annotated with media queries in an array, as the third parameter of the constructor. In this example, we'll override the showPoint option for any media larger than 400 px in width. Media larger than 800 px in width will receive both the showPoint override and the lineSmooth override.

Not only can we specify real media queries to trigger setting changes, but we can also use an overriding mechanism that is very similar to CSS. This way, we can implement various approaches, such as ranged or exclusive media queries, mobile-first, or desktop-first. The responsive options mechanism can be used for all of the options available in Chartist:

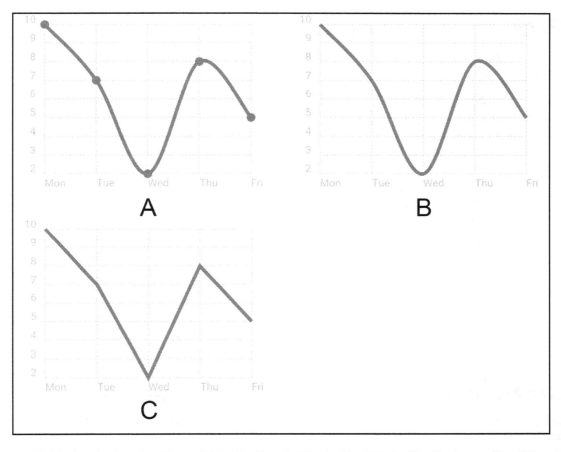

Displaying the previous chart on three different media, left to right, with a media with less than 400 px (A), less than 800 px (B), and more than 800 px (C)

As you can see, implementing complex responsive behavior is a breeze with Chartist. Although our task management application was never meant to be a responsive web application, we can still benefit from this feature, in order to optimize our content.

That's enough about Chartist to get you started. If you would like to know more about my library, I recommend that you check out the project's website at `http://gionkunz.github.io/chartist-js`. On the website, you can also visit the live example page at `http://gionkunz.github.io/chartist-js/examples.html`, where you can hack some charts directly in the browser.

Projects dashboard

In this chapter, we'll create a projects dashboard, which will consist of the following components:

- **Projects dashboard**: This is the main component in the dashboard and represents our whole dashboard view. It's a composition of the rest of the components.
- **Project summary**: This is where we'll display a summary of each project, where we will outline the most important facts. Our project summary component will also include an activity chart component that visualizes project activities.
- **Projects dashboard container**: We also need to create a new container component, to expose our new component tree to the router and connect it to our database.
- **Tasks chart**: This is where we'll provide a visual overview of open tasks over time. All projects will be represented in a line chart that displays the progress of open tasks. We'll also provide some user interaction, so that the user can choose between different timeframes.
- **Activity chart**: This component visualizes activities in a bar chart over a timeframe of 24 hours. This will help our users to quickly identify overall project activities and peaks.

Creating the projects dashboard component

Let's follow our established tradition and start by modelling our data, which we're going to use in our components. We'd like to create a new interface to summarize projects. This includes the project data, tasks, activities, and a short description.

Open our model file, located in `src/app/model.ts`, and add the following interface:

```
...

export interface ProjectSummary {
  project: Project;
  description: string;
  tasks: Task[];
  activities: ProjectActivity[];
}
```

Using this interface, we can aggregate all project relevant data into a single object, which simplifies our development a lot.

Let's move ahead and create our main dashboard component. The projects dashboard component has the responsibility of composing the main dashboard layout, by including our dashboard sub-components. It holds together all of the pieces within our projects dashboard.

Let's create our new projects dashboard component by using the Angular CLI tool:

```
ng generate component --spec false -ve none -cd onpush projects-
dashboard/projects-dashboard
```

Open up the generated component class, located on the path `src/app/projects-dashboard/projects-dashboard/projects-dashboard.component.ts`, and replace the stub code with the following:

```
import {Component, ViewEncapsulation, ChangeDetectionStrategy, Input,
EventEmitter, Output} from '@angular/core';
import {Project, ProjectSummary} from '../model';

@Component({
  selector: 'mac-projects-dashboard',
  templateUrl: './projects-dashboard.component.html',
  styleUrls: ['./projects-dashboard.component.css'],
  changeDetection: ChangeDetectionStrategy.OnPush,
  encapsulation: ViewEncapsulation.None
})
export class ProjectsDashboardComponent {
  @Input() projectSummaries: ProjectSummary[];
  @Output() outActivateProject = new EventEmitter<Project>();

  activateProject(project: Project) {
    this.outActivateProject.emit(project);
  }
}
```

Our dashboard component accepts a `projectSummaries` input, which is a list of project summary objects that conforms to the `ProjectSummary` interface that we just created within our `TypeScript` model file.

A user can activate a project by clicking on a project summary component. Our projects dashboard component uses the output `outActivateProject` to delegate the event to the container, which we'll create later.

Let's take a look at the view of our component, and change the content within the file `src/app/projects-dashboard/projects-dashboard/projects-dashboard.component.html` to the following:

```html
<header class="dashboard-header">
  <h2 class="dashboard-title">Dashboard</h2>
</header>
<div class="dashboard-main">
  <h3 class="dashboard-sub-title">Projects>h3>
 <ul class="dashboard-list">
    <li *ngFor="let projectSummary of projectSummaries"
        class="dashboard-list-item">
      <strong>projectSummary.project.title</strong>
      <p>projectSummary.description</p>
    </li>
  </ul>
</div>
```

For the moment, we only displayed the project title and the description that we'll compute on our project summary objects. In the next section, we will create a new project summary component that will deal with some more complex rendering.

Project summary component

In this section, we'll create a project summary component that will provide some overview information for projects. Within the container component of our projects dashboard component tree, we'll make sure that we aggregate all of the necessary information to summarize projects. Our project summary UI component renders the data provided in the project summary objects, to create nice looking project overview cards.

Let's start building our component using the Angular CLI tool:

```
ng generate component --spec false -ve none -cd onpush projects-
dashboard/project-summary
```

Let's open the component class, located in `src/app/projects-dashboard/project-summary/project-summary.component.ts`, and replace its content with the following code:

```typescript
import {ChangeDetectionStrategy, Component, Input, OnChanges,
SimpleChanges, ViewEncapsulation} from '@angular/core';
import {ProjectSummary, TimeEfforts} from '../../model';

@Component({
```

```
  selector: 'mac-project-summary',
  templateUrl: './project-summary.component.html',
  styleUrls: ['./project-summary.component.css'],
  changeDetection: ChangeDetectionStrategy.OnPush,
  encapsulation: ViewEncapsulation.None
})
export class ProjectSummaryComponent implements OnChanges {
  @Input() projectSummary: ProjectSummary;

  totalEfforts: TimeEfforts;

  ngOnChanges(changes: SimpleChanges) {
    if (changes.projectSummary && this.projectSummary) {
      this.totalEfforts = this.projectSummary.tasks.reduce((totalEfforts,
task) => {
        if (task.efforts) {
          totalEfforts.estimated += task.efforts.estimated || 0;
          totalEfforts.effective += task.efforts.effective || 0;
        }

        return totalEfforts;
      }, {
        estimated: 0,
        effective: 0
      });
    }
  }
}
```

The projectSummary input allows for passing a project summary object into our new UI component. There, we have all of the necessary information for displaying an overview of the project.

If you remember from the previous chapter, Chapter 8, *Time Will Tell*, we've created a nice effort timeline component using SVG. Within our project summary, we would now like to reuse that component. However, we need to compute the total effort from the underlying tasks of our project.

What we need to do is accumulate all task efforts into one overall effort. Using the Array.prototype.reduce function, we can accumulate all task efforts relatively easy. We're depending on the tasks present within our project summary object, which is passed to us with the input projectSummary. Since we'd like to recalculate the total effort when the project information changes, we can use the OnChanges life cycle hook and implement the method ngOnChanges.

Let's create the template of our component, to see how we're going to use the total efforts data to display our efforts timeline component. Open the file on the path `src/app/projects-dashboard/project-summary/project-summary.component.ts`, and amend it with the following content:

```
<div class="summary-title">{{projectSummary.project.title}}</div>
<div class="summary-description">
  {{projectSummary.description}}
</div>
<div class="summary-label">Total Efforts</div>
<mac-efforts-timeline [efforts]="totalEfforts">
</mac-efforts-timeline>
<p>{{totalEfforts | formatEfforts}}</p>
```

After displaying the project title and a description of the project summary, we included our efforts timeline component. We simply pass our computed `totalEfforts` into the `efforts` input, and the efforts timeline component will take care of the rendering. This timeline will now display the total aggregated amount of efforts logged on all tasks of a given project.

In addition to the timeline, we also rendered a formatted efforts text, like the one that we already rendered in the efforts component of the previous chapter. For this, we used the `formatEfforts` pipe.

Now, we still need to integrate our project summary component into the projects dashboard component.

Let's open the template of our projects dashboard, located in `src/app/projects-dashboard/projects-dashboard/projects-dashboard.component.html`, and modify the template to include our project summary component:

```
<header class="dashboard-header">
 <h2 class="dashboard-title">Dashboard</h2>
</header>
<div class="dashboard-main">
  <h3 class="dashboard-sub-title">Projects</h3>
  <ul class="dashboard-list">
    <li *ngFor="let projectSummary of projectSummaries"
        class="dashboard-list-item">
      <mac-project-summary [projectSummary]="projectSummary"
(click)="activateProject(projectSummary.project)">
      </mac-project-summary>
    </li>
  </ul>
</div>
```

We can simply forward the project summary object to our newly created project summary component. Additionally, we've added a click event binding on project summary components, which will trigger our `activateProject` method on the projects dashboard component. This will allow us to implement a programmatic navigation within our container component, which is up next for implementation:

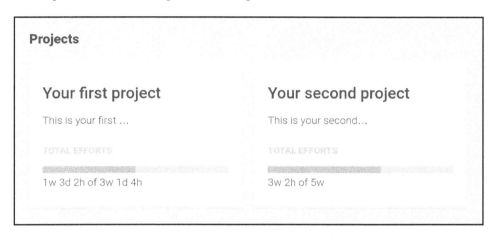

A projects dashboard displaying two project summary components, with the aggregated total effort

Okay; so far, so good. We created two new UI components and reused our efforts timeline component to create an aggregated view of the total task efforts. Now, it's time to integrate our components by creating a new container component and configure the router of our application.

Integrating the projects dashboard

We've created our initial projects dashboard components, and will now work on their integration into our application. We're going to need a new container component, which we'll also expose within the router configuration. We also need to update the navigation component of our application, in order to show a new navigation link to the dashboard view.

Let's start with our new container component and use the Angular CLI tool to create the stubs for it:

```
ng generate component --spec false -ve none -cd onpush container/projects-
dashboard-container
```

Open up the generated component class, located in `src/app/container/projects-dashboard-container/projects-dashboard-container.component.ts`, and replace its content with the following code:

```
import {ChangeDetectionStrategy, Component, ViewEncapsulation} from
'@angular/core';
import {ProjectService} from '../../project/project.service';
import {Observable, combineLatest} from 'rxjs';
import {Project, ProjectSummary} from '../../model';
import {map} from 'rxjs/operators';
import {Router} from '@angular/router';
import {ActivitiesService} from '../../activities/activities.service';
import {TaskService} from '../../tasks/task.service';
import {limitWithEllipsis} from '../../utilities/string-utilities';

@Component({
  selector: 'mac-projects-dashboard-container',
  templateUrl: './projects-dashboard-container.component.html',
  styleUrls: ['./projects-dashboard-container.component.css'],
  encapsulation: ViewEncapsulation.None,
  changeDetection: ChangeDetectionStrategy.OnPush
})
export class ProjectsDashboardContainerComponent {
  projectSummaries: Observable<ProjectSummary[]>;

  constructor(private projectService: ProjectService,
              private taskService: TaskService,
              private activitiesService: ActivitiesService,
              private router: Router) {
    this.projectSummaries = combineLatest(
      this.projectService.getProjects(),
      this.taskService.getTasks(),
      this.activitiesService.getActivities()
    ).pipe(
      map(([projects, tasks, activities]) =>
        projects
          .map(project => ({
            project,
            description: limitWithEllipsis(project.description, 100),
            tasks: tasks.filter(task => task.projectId === project.id),
            activities: activities.filter(activity => activity.projectId
=== project.id)
          }))
      )
    );
  }
```

```
activateProject(project: Project) {
    this.router.navigate(['/projects', project.id]);
  }
}
```

Our newly created container is responsible for gathering all information necessary to create a list of project summary objects. We're using RxJS observables to create a reactive stream of project summary objects. The RxJS utility `combineLatests` allows us to join projects, tasks, and activities into one single stream. Within this joined stream, we are using the `map` operator to create one project summary object for every project obtained from the project service.

We're using our `limitWithEllipsis` helper function to convert the project description into a truncated (if necessary) version, which we're adding directly to our project summary object.

We've also injected the router into our container component, and will use it to do a programmatic navigation to the project view. We've implemented a method, `activateProject`, for this purpose, which we're going to call from our view.

Let's also change the template of our container component where we want to render the projects dashboard UI component and create the necessary bindings to pass our project summary data into the UI component tree. Open the file `src/app/container/projects-dashboard-container/projects-dashboard-container.component.html`, and replace its content with the following code:

```
<mac-projects-dashboard
    [projectSummaries]="projectSummaries | async"
    (outActivateProject)="activateProject($event)">
</mac-projects-dashboard>
```

All we need to do is render our projects dashboard UI component. We're passing our generated project summary objects down into the component input. Since we've implemented this using an observable stream, we need to use the `async` pipe.

When a project gets activated within the projects dashboard UI component, we receive an `outActivateProject` output event, which we can then use to call our `activateProject` method. There, we're using the router to navigate to the given project view.

Alright; now, we have all of the components ready to render our projects dashboard. There are two things left to do. We need to configure our router to activate our newly created container component and create a new navigation item within our app root component.

Let's start with the route configuration. Open up the route configuration file, located in src/app/routes.ts, and apply the following changes:

...

```
import {ProjectsDashboardContainerComponent} from './container/projects-dashboard-container/projects-dashboard-container.component';

export const routes: Route[] = [{
  path: 'dashboard',
  component: ProjectsDashboardContainerComponent
}, {
  path: 'projects/:projectId',
  component: ProjectContainerComponent,
  canActivate: [ProjectContainerGuard],
  children: [{
    path: 'tasks',
    component: TaskListContainerComponent
  }, {
    path: 'tasks/:taskId',
    component: TaskDetailsContainerComponent
  }, {
    path: 'comments',
    component: ProjectCommentsContainerComponent
  }, {
    path: 'activities',
    component: ProjectActivitiesContainerComponent
  }, {
    path: '**',
    redirectTo: 'tasks'
  }]
}, {
  path: '',
  pathMatch: 'full',
  redirectTo: '/dashboard'
}];
```

We've added a new route configuration to activate our projects dashboard container component. In addition, we've changed our default redirect URL to redirect to our dashboard, instead of the first project detail view.

Okay; let's move on and use our new route to create a navigation item within our app root component. Open up the app component template, located in `src/app/app.component.html`, and perform the following changes:

```html
<aside class="side-nav">
  <mac-user-area [user]="user | async"
                 [openTasksCount]="openTasksCount | async">
  </mac-user-area>
  <mac-navigation>
    <mac-navigation-section title="Main">
      <mac-navigation-item title="Dashboard"
                           navId="dashboard"
                           routerLinkActive="active"
                           [routerLink]="['/dashboard']">
      </mac-navigation-item>
    </mac-navigation-section>
    <mac-navigation-section title="Projects">
      <mac-navigation-item *ngFor="let project of projects | async;
trackBy: trackByProjectId"
                           [navId]="project.id"
                           [title]="project.title"
                           routerLinkActive="active"
                           [routerLink]="['/projects', project.id]">
      </mac-navigation-item>
    </mac-navigation-section>
  </mac-navigation>
</aside>
<main class="main">
  <router-outlet></router-outlet>
</main>
```

Awesome! You've just completed all of the steps necessary for integrating our first set of projects dashboard components. You can now preview your changes in the browser. There should be a new navigation item available within the main navigation of the application. Also, when starting the application, you should automatically be redirected to the dashboard view.

You can already play with the efforts aggregation and try to modify a new task effort of a project, to see how the summary will be affected.

In the next section, we will enrich our project summary component with a nice Chartist chart.

Creating your first chart

In this section, we will create our first chart using Chartist, to provide a project activity overview over the past 24 hours. This bar chart will only provide some visual clues about the project activity, and our goal isn't to provide detailed information. For this reason, we will configure it to hide any labels, scales, and grid lines. The only visible part should be the bars of the bar chart.

Processing activity data

Before we start creating the activity chart itself, we need to look at how we should transform and prepare our data for the charts.

Let's look at what data we already have in our system. As far as the activities go, they all have a timestamp stored in the `time` field. However, for our chart, a list of timestamps is not sufficient enough. What we're looking for is a chart that displays one bar for each hour of the past 24 hours. Each one hour bar should represent the count of activities during that time.

The following illustration shows our source data, which is basically a time stream of activity events. On the lower arrow, we can see the data that we need to end up with for our chart:

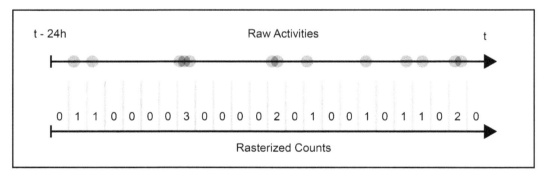

An illustration displaying activities as a time stream, where dots represent activities. By rasterizing the events into one-hour slices, we get something we call rasterized counts, as shown on the bottom arrow.

First of all, we're going to introduce a new interface within our application model. We would like to represent a data value within a list of values, which is getting rasterized.

We use the term rasterization to describe the process of sampling underlying data into slices on a raster. This is very similar to how a digital camera would sample the photons of light rays and accumulate them on a raster which we call pixels.

Since we'd like to not only use a timestamp for rasterization, but also weigh data values differently, depending on situations, we will introduce the following interface to our model, located in `src/app/model.ts`:

```
...

export interface RasterizationData {
  time: number;
  weight: number;
}
```

In the previous figure, we counted all activities within a given hour and added up them up. However, we will need a more specific solution that allows us to incorporate weight while counting. This is especially useful if you want to make certain activities count more than others. By using a property called `weight` on data input to the rasterization process, we can accomplish a weighted count. In fact, we're no longer counting data values within a `timeframe`; we're adding up their weights to get a total weight for a given `timeframe`. This allows us to use negative weights, which will subtract from the total weight. This will be important for the second chart, which we're going to create at a later stage.

Let's implement the function that performs the outlined data transformation. We'll add this function to our time utility module, located in `src/app/utilities/time-utilities.ts`:

```
...

export function rasterize(
  timeData: RasterizationData[],
  timeFrame: number,
  quantity: number,
  now: number = +new Date(),
  fill: number = 0): number[] {

  now = Math.floor(now / timeFrame) * timeFrame;

  return timeData.reduce((rasterized: number[], data: RasterizationData) =>
{
    const index = Math.ceil((now - data.time) / timeFrame);
    if (index < quantity) {
      rasterized[index] = (rasterized[index] || 0) + data.weight;
    }
```

```
    return rasterized;
  }, <number[]>Array.from({length: quantity}).fill(fill)).reverse();
}
```

Let's briefly look at the input parameters of our newly created function:

- `timeData`: This parameter is expected to be an array of rasterization data objects that contains a `time` property set to the timestamp of the event that should be counted. The objects should also contain a `weight` property, which is used to count. Using this property, we can count one event as two, or even count minus values to decrease the count in a rasterized frame.
- `timeFrame`: This parameter specifies the time span of each rasterized frame, in milliseconds. If we want to have 24 rasterized frames, each consisting of one hour, this parameter needs to be set to 3,600,000 (*1 h = 60 min = 3,600 s = 3,600,000 ms*).
- `quantity`: This parameter sets the amount of rasterized frames that should be present in the output array. In the case of 24 frames of one hour, this parameter should be set to 24.
- `now`: This parameter should be set as the point in time when the rasterization process will start. The rasterization will always move backwards in time, so this time marks the end time of our rasterization. The `now` parameter should be a timestamp, in milliseconds.
- `fill`: This is how we can specify how we'd like our rasterized output array to be initialized. In the case of our activity counts, we want this to be set to zero.

The function that we just created is necessary to create the activity chart. The transformation helps us to prepare project activities for the input data of the chart.

Creating an activity chart

It's time to create our first chart component using Chartist! However, before we get into our component, we need to make sure that Chartist is installed within our project. Let's use npm to install Chartist as a dependency:

```
npm install chartist@0.11.0 @types/chartist@0.9.40 --save
```

Chartist is currently written in pure JavaScript. Luckily, the community created a very sophisticated type definition for Chartist, so you can benefit from typed interfaces when using Chartist with TypeScript.

Okay; that's all it takes to get us going with Chartist. Now, let's create our activity chart using the Angular CLI:

```
ng generate component --spec false -ve none -cd onpush projects-
dashboard/activity-chart
```

Let's open the generated template, located on the path `src/app/projects-dashboard/activity-chart/activity-chart.component.html`, and replace its content with the following code:

```
<div #chartContainer></div>
```

As we leave all of the rendering up to Chartist, this is actually everything we need. Chartist needs an element as a container to create the chart in. We set a `chartContainer` local view reference, so that we can reference it from our component and pass it to Chartist.

Let's move on with the chart creation. Open up the component class, located in `src/app/projects-dashboard/activity-chart/activity-chart.component.ts`, and add the following code:

```
import {
  Component, ViewEncapsulation, ViewChild, ElementRef, Input,
ChangeDetectionStrategy
} from '@angular/core';
import * as Chartist from 'chartist';
import {IChartistBarChart} from 'chartist';
import {Activity} from '../../model';

@Component({
  selector: 'mac-activity-chart',
  templateUrl: './activity-chart.component.html',
  styleUrls: ['./activity-chart.component.css'],
  changeDetection: ChangeDetectionStrategy.OnPush,
  encapsulation: ViewEncapsulation.None
})
export class ActivityChartComponent {
  @Input() activities: Activity[];
  @ViewChild('chartContainer') chartContainer: ElementRef;

  chart: IChartistBarChart;
}
```

In addition to the imports from the Angular core module, we're also importing the Chartist namespace object, as well as the interface, `IChartistBarChart`.

Our component takes a list of activities as input, which we're going to transform using our new rasterization function. This transformed data is then used with Chartist to visualize the data. We're using a member, chart, to store the Chartist instance, once created.

Using the ViewChild decorator, we're obtaining the DOM element from our component view, which will be used as a container to create our chart.

Let's continue by adding a method to transform the activity list into something Chartist can work with. Within the same component class file, append the following method:

```
import {
  Component, ViewEncapsulation, ViewChild, ElementRef, Input,
ChangeDetectionStrategy
} from '@angular/core';
import * as Chartist from 'chartist';
import {IChartistBarChart, IChartistData} from 'chartist';

import {rasterize, UNITS} from '../../utilities/time-utilities';
import {Activity, RasterizationData} from '../../model';

@Component({
  selector: 'mac-activity-chart',
  templateUrl: './activity-chart.component.html',
  styleUrls: ['./activity-chart.component.css'],
  changeDetection: ChangeDetectionStrategy.OnPush,
  encapsulation: ViewEncapsulation.None
})
export class ActivityChartComponent {
  @Input() activities: Activity[];
  @ViewChild('chartContainer') chartContainer: ElementRef;

  chart: IChartistBarChart;

  createChartData(): IChartistData {
    const timeData: RasterizationData[] = this.activities.map((activity) =>
{
      return {
        time: activity.time,
        weight: 1
      };
    });

    return {
      series: [
        rasterize(
          timeData,
          UNITS.find((unit) => unit.short === 'h').milliseconds,
```

```
        24,
        +new Date())
      ]
    };
  }
}
```

Within the `createChartData` method, we are first creating a list of rasterization data objects from the list of activities that we provided from our component input. We can use the activity time as a timestamp, and all of our activities currently count the same, so we use a fixed weight of 1.

Now, we would like to extract the count of activities for every hour within the last 24 hours. We can use our `rasterize` function, with the necessary parameters, to transform our activities into exactly that format. The `rasterize` function will always return a list of numbers representing the count of activities within the desired timeframes. Together with the rasterization data, we pass the number of milliseconds for one hour, a total of 24 frames, and the current time as the starting point in time.

Our method returns an object of the type `IChartistData`, which contains the data that we want to visualize with Chartist. The output of our `rasterize` function has exactly the right format for representing a data series in Chartist.

Let's add the remaining code to complete our component class. Code changes are highlighted in bold, while the ellipsis character indicates irrelevant, hidden code:

```
import {
  Component, ViewEncapsulation, ViewChild, ElementRef, Input,
ChangeDetectionStrategy,
  OnChanges, AfterViewInit
} from '@angular/core';
...

...
export class ActivityChartComponent implements OnChanges, AfterViewInit {
  @Input() activities: Activity[];
  @ViewChild('chartContainer') chartContainer: ElementRef;

  chart: IChartistBarChart;

  ngOnChanges() {
    this.createOrUpdateChart();
  }

  ngAfterViewInit() {
```

```
      this.createOrUpdateChart();
  }

  createOrUpdateChart() {
    if (!this.activities || !this.chartContainer) {
      return;
    }

    const data = this.createChartData();

    if (this.chart) {
      this.chart.update(data);
    } else {
      this.createChart(data);
    }
  }

  createChart(data: IChartistData) {
    this.chart = new Chartist.Bar(this.chartContainer.nativeElement, data,
{
      width: '100%',
      height: 60,
      axisY: {
        onlyInteger: true,
        showGrid: false,
        showLabel: false,
        offset: 0
      },
      axisX: {
        showGrid: false,
        showLabel: false,
        offset: 0
      },
      chartPadding: {
        top: 0,
        right: 0,
        bottom: 0,
        left: 0
      }
    });

    this.chart.on('draw', (context) => {
      if (context.type === 'bar' && context.value.y === 0) {
        context.element.attr({
          y2: context.y2 - 1
        });
      }
    });
```

```
    }

    ...
}
```

Let's look into the code in more detail and walk through it step by step.

The `createChart` method creates a new chart instance with the data that is passed to the method. In order to create a new bar chart, we can use the `Chartist.Bar` constructor. As a first parameter, we pass the DOM element of our container view child. Chartist will create our chart in this container element. The second argument is our data, which we get from our method parameter. In the chart options, we'll set everything to achieve a very plain-looking chart, without any detailed information. We disable the grids, hide the labels, and remove any padding.

Additionally, we're using the Chartist draw event to control how zero value bars are drawn. By default, Chartist won't draw a bar when the value for the bar is exactly zero. We can control and change this behavior by implementing our own custom draw event logic.

The `createOrUpdateChart` method checks whether the chart was already created, and only needs to be updated if we really need to create a new chart instance. This simplifies our handling a lot. As we get called from both the `AfterViewInit` and `OnChanges` life cycle hooks, we need to make sure that both the `chartContainer` view child and the `activities` input are ready before we continue.

If the `chart` member is already set to a chart that was previously created, we can use the `update` function on the Chartist instance to update it with the new data. If there's no chart object, we need to create a new chart. We can simply call our `createChart` method for that.

This is great! We've created our first chart component using Chartist! Now, we can go back to our project summary component and integrate the activity chart there, to provide an activity overview. Open up the template of the project summary component, located in the file `src/app/projects-dashboard/project-summary/project-summary.component.html`, and apply the following changes:

```html
<div class="summary-title">{{projectSummary.project.title}}</div>
<div class="summary-description">
  {{projectSummary.description}}
</div>
<div class="summary-label">Total Efforts</div>
<mac-efforts-timeline [efforts]="totalEfforts">
</mac-efforts-timeline>
<p>{{totalEfforts | formatEfforts}}</p>
```

```
<div class="summary-label">Activity last 24 hours</div>
<mac-activity-chart [activities]="projectSummary.activities"></mac-
activity-chart>
```

We added our activity chart component at the bottom of the already existing template. We also created the necessary binding to pass our activities, which we already had available on our project summary object, into the component.

Congratulations! You've successfully integrated the Chartist library into your project, and have used it to visualize project activity on our project summary components.

In the next section, we'll dive a bit deeper into the charting capabilities of Chartist, and will also provide some interactivity using Angular.

Visualizing open tasks

In this section, we will create a line chart component using Chartist, which will display the open task progress of projects over time. To do this, we'll use a line chart with a specific interpolation that provides quantized steps, rather than lines with directly connected points.

We will also provide some interactivity, so that the user will be able to switch the displayed timeframe by using a toggle button. This will allow us to reuse the toggle UI component that we created in Chapter 2, *Ready, Set, Go!*

Preparing task data

First, let's look at the data that we have available in our system, when it comes to project tasks. The `created` attribute is set to the timestamp at the moment when the task was created. If a task is marked as done, however, we currently don't save the timestamp of that moment. In order to produce the chart that we're looking for, we will need to know when a task was completed.

Let's introduce a new property on our task model for this purpose. Open up the `model` file, located in `src/app/model.ts`, and apply the following changes:

```
export interface Task {
  readonly id?: number;
  readonly projectId?: number;
  readonly title: string;
  readonly description?: string;
```

```
  readonly done: boolean;
  readonly order: number;
  readonly created: number;
  readonly completed?: number;
  readonly efforts?: TimeEfforts;
}

...
```

Now we need to make sure to set the `completed` property at the right moment, whenever a task is completed. Let's open the class of our task component, located in `src/app/tasks/task/task.component.ts`, and apply the following changes. Only modify the part in your code that is highlighted in the following code excerpt:

```
...
export class TaskComponent {
  ...

  updateTask(done: boolean) {
    this.outUpdateTask.emit({
      ...this.task,
      done,
      completed: done ? +new Date() : this.task.completed
    });
  }

  ...
}
```

Alright; to complete this exercise, we also want to update our initial data within the in-memory database, to reflect a more accurate scenario. Open the file `src/app/database.ts`, and apply the following changes. Again, only change the parts that are highlighted:

```
import {InMemoryDbService} from 'angular-in-memory-web-api';
import {Activity, Project, Task, User} from './model';

export class Database implements InMemoryDbService {
  createDb() {
    ...

    const hour = 3600000;
    const tasks: Task[] = [
      {id: 1, projectId: 1, title: 'Task 1', done: false, order: 1,
created: +new Date() - hour * 8},
      {id: 2, projectId: 1, title: 'Task 2', done: false, order: 2,
created: +new Date() - hour * 6},
```

```
        {id: 3, projectId: 1, title: 'Task 3', done: true, order: 3, created:
+new Date() - hour * 12,
        completed: +new Date() - hour * 3},
        {id: 4, projectId: 1, title: 'Task 4', done: false, order: 4,
created: +new Date() - hour * 20}
    ];


    ...

  }
}
```

Modeling the problem

First, let's think about the problem of showing open task counts over time. As we're only interested in the number of open tasks at any given time, we can use a model where we put all tasks onto a single timeline, and where we are only concerned with the events of tasks being created or completed. Let's look at the following illustration to get a better understanding of the problem:

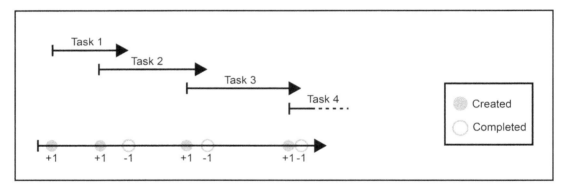

An illustration that shows how we can represent all task timelines on a single timeline, using the created and completed events. The created events count as +1, while the completed events count as -1

The lower arrow is a representation of all tasks of the created and completed events on a timeline. We can now use this information as input to our `rasterize` function, in order to get the data that we need for our chart. As the rasterization data objects that are used as input for the function also support a `weight` property, we can use this to represent the created (+1) or completed (−1) events.

We need to make a slight modification to our `rasterize` function. So far, the `rasterize` function only counts events together in frames. However, for the open task counts, we will look into an accumulation over time. If the task count changes, we need to keep the value until it changes again. In the transformation of activities in the previous section, we didn't use this same logic. There, we only counted events inside frames, but there was no accumulation.

Let's look at the following illustration to see the differences, as compared to the rasterization that we applied when processing activities:

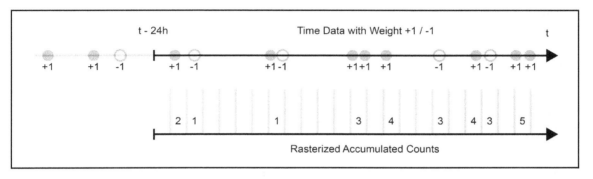

An illustration that shows how we can accumulate the open task count over time

We can count each `weight` property of the rasterization data objects (events) together over time. If there's a change in the accumulated value, we will write the current accumulated value into the rasterized output array.

Let's implement this accumulation feature into our `rasterize` function. Open up the time utility module, on the path `src/app/utilities/time-utilities.ts`, and apply the following changes:

```
export function rasterize(
  timeData: RasterizationData[],
  timeFrame: number,
  quantity: number,
  now: number = +new Date(),
  fill: number = 0,
  accumulate: boolean = false): number[] {

  now = Math.floor(now / timeFrame) * timeFrame;
  let accumulatedValue = 0;

  if (accumulate) {
    timeData = timeData.slice().sort((a, b) => a.time < b.time ? -1 :
```

```
    a.time > b.time ? 1 : 0);
      }

    return timeData.reduce((rasterized: number[], data: RasterizationData) =>
  {
      accumulatedValue += data.weight;
      const index = Math.ceil((now - data.time) / timeFrame);
      if (index < quantity) {
        rasterized[index] = accumulate ? accumulatedValue :
  (rasterized[index] || 0) + data.weight;
      }
      return rasterized;
    }, <number[]>Array.from({length: quantity}).fill(fill)).reverse();
  }
```

Let's walk through the changes that we applied to the `rasterize` function.

First of all, we add a new parameter to our function, with the name `accumulate`. We use ES6 default parameters to set the parameter to `false`, if no value was passed into the function when called.

We define a new `accumulatedValue` variable, which we initialize with zero. This variable is used to keep track of the sum of all `weight` values over time.

The next bit of code is very important. If we want to accumulate the sum of all `weight` values over time, we need to make sure that these values come in sequence. In order to ensure this, we sort the `timeData` list by its items `time` attribute.

In the reduce callback, we increase the `accumulatedValue` variable by the `weight` value of the current `timeData` object.

If the `timeData` object falls into a rasterized frame, we do not increase this frame's count like we did before. In accumulation mode, we set the frames count to the current value in `accumulatedValue`. This will result in all changed accumulated values being reflected in the rasterized output array.

That's all the preparation we need to create our open tasks chart. We were able to refactor our `rasterize` function, which is now able to process time data and produce rasterized data series for various applications. With the use of a negative `weight` property, we can now create data series that increase and decrease, based on open tasks within a project.

Creating an open tasks chart

Let's take a look at the line chart that we're going to create:

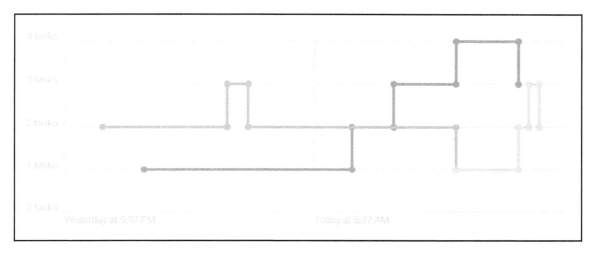

Open tasks visualized with our tasks chart component, using Chartist's step interpolation

We will utilize the refactored `rasterize` function of the previous topic, and will use the new accumulate mode to track open task counts over time.

Let's use the Angular CLI tool to create our new tasks chart component:

```
ng generate component --spec false -ve none -cd onpush projects-
dashboard/tasks-chart
```

Let's edit the component class, on the path `src/app/projects-dashboard/tasks-chart/tasks-chart.component.ts`, and change its content to the following:

```
import {
  AfterViewInit, ChangeDetectionStrategy, Component, ElementRef,
  Input, OnChanges, SimpleChanges, ViewChild, ViewEncapsulation
} from '@angular/core';
import * as Chartist from 'chartist';
import {IChartistData, IChartistLineChart} from 'chartist';
import * as moment from 'moment';

import {rasterize} from '../../utilities/time-utilities';
import {ProjectSummary, RasterizationData} from '../../model';

@Component({
```

```
  selector: 'mac-tasks-chart',
  templateUrl: './tasks-chart.component.html',
  styleUrls: ['./tasks-chart.component.css'],
  changeDetection: ChangeDetectionStrategy.OnPush,
  encapsulation: ViewEncapsulation.None
})
export class TasksChartComponent implements OnChanges, AfterViewInit {
  @Input() projectSummaries: ProjectSummary[];
  @ViewChild('chartContainer') chartContainer: ElementRef;

  chart: IChartistLineChart;

  ngOnChanges(changes: SimpleChanges) {
    this.createOrUpdateChart();
  }

  ngAfterViewInit() {
    this.createOrUpdateChart();
  }

  createOrUpdateChart() {
    if (!this.projectSummaries || !this.chartContainer) {
      return;
    }

    const data = this.createChartData();
    if (this.chart) {
      this.chart.update(data);
    } else {
      this.createChart(data);
    }
  }

  createChartData(): IChartistData {
    const now = +new Date();
    return {
      series: this.projectSummaries.map(projectSummary => {
        const tasks = projectSummary.tasks
          .filter(task => task.projectId === projectSummary.project.id);
        const timeData: RasterizationData[] = tasks.reduce((data, task) =>
{
          data.push({
            time: task.created,
            weight: 1
          });

          if (task.done) {
            data.push({
```

```
            time: task.completed,
            weight: -1
          });
        }
        return data;
      }, []);

      return rasterize(timeData, 600000, 144, now, null, true);
    }),
    labels: Array.from({
      length: 144
    }).map((e, index) => now - index * 600000).reverse()
  };
}

createChart(data: IChartistData) {
  this.chart = new Chartist.Line(this.chartContainer.nativeElement, data,
{
    width: '100%',
    height: 300,
    lineSmooth: Chartist.Interpolation.step({
      fillHoles: true
    }),
    axisY: {
      onlyInteger: true,
      low: 0,
      offset: 70,
      labelInterpolationFnc: value => `${value} tasks`
    },
    axisX: {
      labelInterpolationFnc: (value, index) =>
        index % Math.floor(144 / 2) === 0 ?
          moment(value).calendar() : null,
      labelOffset: {
        y: 10
      }
    }
  }, [
    ['screen and (min-width: 1200px)', {
      axisX: {
        labelInterpolationFnc: (value, index) =>
          index % Math.floor(144 / 4) === 0 ?
            moment(value).calendar() : null
      }
    }], ['screen and (min-width: 1500px)', {
      axisX: {
        labelInterpolationFnc: (value, index) =>
          index % Math.floor(144 / 6) === 0 ?
```

```
                    moment(value).calendar() : null
              }
           }]
        ]);
     }
  }
```

The basic structure of the preceding code should already look familiar to you. We're using the same structure as in our previous chart. However, the line chart that we are going to create now contains much more detailed information. We will render both axis labels and some scales. The *x*-axis of our chart will be a timeline, and we will use the Moment.js library to format the timestamps to a human-readable format.

Let's take a closer look at the `createChartData` and `createChart` methods. There's quite a bit of code here! Let's walk through it, step by step, to gain a better understanding of what's going on.

We use the `projectSummaries` input as a base for our data visualization. We transform the tasks data using our updated `rasterize` function, in order to prepare the data for our line chart.

First, we need to create our transformed series data by mapping the project summary list. The series array should include one data array for each project. Each data array will contain the open project tasks over time.

As the `rasterize` function expects a list of rasterization data objects, we need to first transform the projects task list into this format. We will make use of the weight feature of our `rasterize` function. We can simply create a rasterization data object with a weight of 1 for every event of a created task. For completed tasks, we create a rasterization data object with a weight of −1. This results in the desired input data for our `rasterize` function.

After preparing the data, we can call the `rasterize` function, in order to create a list of open tasks over a certain amount of rasterization frames. We use ten minute timeframes (600,000 ms) and rasterize with 144 frames. This makes a total of 24 hours. So, that's where those two magic numbers come from! However, this code will change a bit when we introduce the interactivity to our chart.

Besides the series data, we also need labels for our chart. We create a new array and initialize this with 144 timestamps, all of which are set to the start of the 144 rasterized frames that we display on the chart.

We now have the series data and the labels ready, and all that's left to do is render our chart. Within the `createChart` method, we're creating our line chart instance using the `Chartist.Line` constructor.

Using the `lineSmooth` configuration, we can specify a special kind of interpolation for our line chart. The step interpolation will not connect each point in our line chart directly, but will rather plot our data in discrete steps, to move from point to point. This is exactly what we're looking for to render the open task counts over time.

Setting the `fillHoles` option to `true` in the step interpolation is very important. Using this setting, we can actually tell Chartist that it should close any gaps in the data (actually null values) and connect the line to the next valid value. Without this setting, we'd see gaps on the chart between the task count changes in our data arrays.

Okay; that's all we need in our component class, for the moment. Let's move on to the rather simple template for our tasks chart component. Open the file, located on the path `src/app/projects-dashboard/tasks-chart/tasks-chart.component.html`, and change its content to the following:

```
<div #chartContainer class="chart-container"></div>
```

Similar to the activity chart component, we only create a simple chart container element, which we already reference in our component class using the view child decorator.

Our tasks chart component is now ready to be integrated into our dashboard. We can achieve this with some small changes to the template of our projects dashboard component. Let's open the file `src/app/projects-dashboard/projects-dashboard/projects-dashboard.component.html`, and apply the following changes:

```
<header class="dashboard-header">
  <h2 class="dashboard-title">Dashboard</h2>
</header>
<div class="dashboard-main">
  <h3 class="dashboard-sub-title">Tasks Overview</h3>
  <div class="dashboard-tasks">
    <mac-tasks-chart [projectSummaries]="projectSummaries">
    </mac-tasks-chart>
  </div>
  <h3 class="dashboard-sub-title">Projects</h3>
  <ul class="dashboard-list">
```

```
        <li *ngFor="let projectSummary of projectSummaries"
            class="dashboard-list-item">
          <mac-project-summary [projectSummary]="projectSummary"
     (click)="activateProject(projectSummary.project)">
          </mac-project-summary>
        </li>
      </ul>
    </div>
```

Good stuff! This is basically all that we need to make our newly created tasks chart appear on our dashboard. You've created a simple line chart to visualize open tasks over time.

Let's further enhance our chart by rendering a chart legend and making the chart interactive for our users.

Creating a chart legend

Currently, there's no way to tell exactly what line on our chart represents what project. We can see one colored line for each project, but we can't associate these colors. What we need is a simple legend that helps our users to associate line chart colors to projects.

Let's look at the required code changes to implement legends on our chart. Open our tasks chart component class, located on the path src/app/projects-dashboard/tasks-chart/tasks-chart.component.ts, and apply the following changes. Irrelevant parts of this change are hidden using the ellipsis character, while effective changes are marked in bold:

```
    ...

    export interface ChartLegendItem {
      title: string;
      class: string;
    }

    @Component({
      selector: 'mac-tasks-chart',
      templateUrl: './tasks-chart.component.html',
      styleUrls: ['./tasks-chart.component.css'],
      changeDetection: ChangeDetectionStrategy.OnPush,
      encapsulation: ViewEncapsulation.None
    })
    export class TasksChartComponent implements OnChanges, AfterViewInit {
      ...
```

```
legend: ChartLegendItem[];

ngOnChanges(changes: SimpleChanges) {
  if (changes.projectSummaries && this.projectSummaries) {
    this.legend = this.projectSummaries.map((projectSummary, index) => ({
      title: projectSummary.project.title,
      class: `series-${index + 1}`
    }));
  }

  this.createOrUpdateChart();
}

  ...
}
```

We've added a local interface in our component module to represent individual legend items. The `title` property is going to be displayed for each item within our legend. The `class` property is used to set an appropriate CSS class, in order to render every legend item with the correct color, to match the colors of lines within our chart.

In the `OnChanges` life cycle hook, we simply map the project summary objects to a list of legend objects. The template string `` `series-${index + 1}` `` will generate the necessary class names to render the right color into our legend.

Using this legend information, we can now go ahead and implement the necessary template changes to render the legend in our tasks chart component. Open the template, located on the path `src/app/projects-dashboard/tasks-chart/tasks-chart.component.html`, and apply the following changes:

```
<ul class="series-list">
  <li *ngFor="let series of legend"
      class="series {{series.class}}">{{series.title}}</li>
</ul>
<div #chartContainer class="chart-container"></div>
```

Well, that was a piece of cake, right? However, the result speaks for itself. We created a nice legend for the chart in just a couple of minutes:

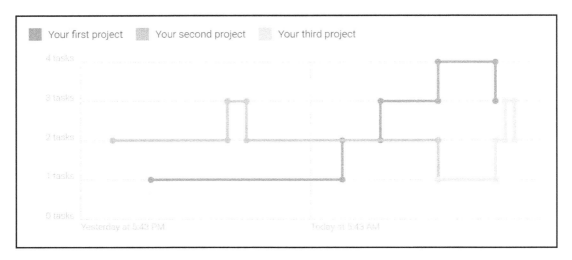

Open tasks chart with our added legend

In the next topic, we're going to add some user interaction to our chart and let our users control the timeframe that we're using to render our data.

Making the tasks chart interactive

Currently, we hardcoded the timeframe of our open task chart to be 144 frames, each 10 minutes long, making a total of 24 hours displayed to the user. However, maybe our users will want to change this view.

In this topic, we will create a simple input control using our toggle component, which will allow our users to change the timeframe settings of the chart.

We will provide the following views as options to choose from:

- **Day**: This view will rasterize into 144 frames, each consisting of 10 minutes, which makes a total of 24 hours
- **Week**: This view will rasterize into 168 frames, each consisting of one hour, which makes a total of seven days
- **Year**: This view will rasterize into 360 frames, each representing a full day

Let's start the implementation by modifying the tasks chart component `TypeScript` file, located on the path `src/app/projects-dashboard/tasks-chart/tasks-chart.component.ts`:

```
...

export interface ChartTimeFrame {
  name: string;
  timeFrame: number;
  amount: number;
}

@Component({
  selector: 'mac-tasks-chart',
  templateUrl: './tasks-chart.component.html',
  styleUrls: ['./tasks-chart.component.css'],
  changeDetection: ChangeDetectionStrategy.OnPush,
  encapsulation: ViewEncapsulation.None
})
export class TasksChartComponent implements OnChanges, AfterViewInit {
  ...

  timeFrames: ChartTimeFrame[] = [{
    name: 'day',
    timeFrame: 600000,
    amount: 144
  }, {
    name: 'week',
    timeFrame: 3600000,
    amount: 168
  }, {
    name: 'year',
    timeFrame: 86400000,
    amount: 360
  }];
  timeFrameNames = this.timeFrames.map((timeFrame) => timeFrame.name);
  selectedTimeFrame = this.timeFrames[0];

  ...

  selectTimeFrame(timeFrameName: string) {
    this.selectedTimeFrame = this.timeFrames.find((timeFrame) =>
timeFrame.name === timeFrameName);
    this.createOrUpdateChart();
  }

  createChartData(): IChartistData {
```

```
          const now = +new Date();
          return {
            series: this.projectSummaries.map(projectSummary => {
              ...

              return rasterize(timeData, this.selectedTimeFrame.timeFrame,
                this.selectedTimeFrame.amount, now, null, true);
            }),
            labels: Array.from({
              length: this.selectedTimeFrame.amount
            }).map((e, index) => now - index *
    this.selectedTimeFrame.timeFrame).reverse()
          };
        }


      ...
    }
```

Let's briefly go over these changes. First, we added another local interface to represent the timeframe choices presented to the user. The ChartTimeFrame interface consists of a name property, which we'll use to present to the user. We also stored the timeFrame and amount properties for each chart timeframe object. These two properties represent the number of milliseconds for each frame and the frame count, respectively.

The new timeFrames member is set to an array of timeframe objects. These are the choices we'll present to the user, and they reflect the settings we discussed at the beginning of this section. The timeFrameNames member contains a list of timeframe names, which is directly derived from the timeFrames list. Finally, we have a selectedTimeFrame member, which simply points to the first available timeframe object to start with.

In the createOrUpdateChart function, we no longer rely on hardcoded values for the task count rasterization, but we refer to the data in the selectedTimeFrame object. By changing this object reference and calling the createOrUpdateChart function again, we can now switch the view on the underlying data dynamically.

Finally, we added a new selectTimeFrame method, which we will call from our component view to switch to a different timeframe.

Let's look at the necessary template changes to enable the switching of timeframes. We're using our toggle UI component that we created at the very beginning of this book:

```
<mac-toggle [buttonList]="timeFrameNames"
            [activeButton]="selectedTimeFrame.name"
            (outActivate)="selectTimeFrame($event)"></mac-toggle>
<ul class="series-list">
```

```
<li *ngFor="let series of legend"
    class="series {{series.class}}">{{series.title}}</li>
</ul>
<div #chartContainer class="chart-container"></div>
```

From the bindings to the `toggle` component, you can already tell that we rely on the `timeFrameNames` member of our component to represent all selectable timeframes. We also bind to the `activeButton` input property of the `toggle` component using the `selectedTimeFrame` property of our tasks chart component. When the user activates a toggle button, we call the `selectTimeFrame` function, where the timeframe is switched and the chart is updated.

This is all that we need to enable switching the timeframe on our chart. The user can now choose between the year, week, and day views.

Excellent work! You've added interactivity to the tasks chart by reusing the `toggle` UI component. Let's take a look at the final result of our work:

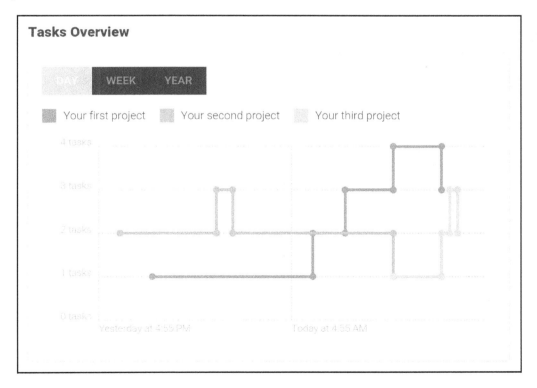

Final tasks chart, which is now rendered within our application dashboard

Summary

In this chapter, we learned about Chartist and how to use it in conjunction with Angular to create good looking and functional charts. We can leverage the power of both worlds to create reusable chart components that are nicely encapsulated.

Just like in most real cases, we always have a lot of data available. However, bringing that data into the right shape is sometimes tricky. In this chapter, we learned how we can transform existing data into a form that is optimized for visual representation.

In the next chapter, we will look at building a plugin system in our application. This will allow us to develop portable functionality that is packaged into plugins. Our plugin system will render new plugins dynamically, and we will use it to develop a simple agile estimation plugin.

Putting Things to the Test 10

Writing tests is crucial for the maintainability of your code. It's a known fact that having a good range of tests, covering most of your functionality, is as important as the functionality itself.

The first thing that comes to mind when thinking about tests is probably code quality assurance. You test the code that you write, so this is definitely ensuring the quality of your code. However, there are many other important aspects of writing tests:

- **Resistance to unexpected changes**: Your tests define what your code is supposed to do. They test whether your code conforms to your specifications. This has several benefits, the most obvious of which is probably a resistance to unexpected changes in the future. If you modify the code in the future, you'll be less likely to break your existing code, because your tests will validate whether the existing functionality still works as specified.
- **Documentation**: Your tests define what your code should do. At the same time, they display the API calls that are required to use the concerned functionality. This is the perfect documentation for any developer. Whenever I want to understand how a library really works, the tests are the first thing I look at.
- **Avoiding unnecessary code**: The practice of writing tests forces you to limit your code to fulfill the requirements of your specification, and nothing more. Any code in your application that is not reached in your automated tests can be considered dead code. If you stick to a merciless refactoring approach, you'll remove such unused code as soon as possible.

So far, we haven't considered testing in our book at all, and, given its importance, you may wonder why I am approaching this now, in the very last chapter of the book. In a real project, we'd definitely create tests much earlier, if not at first. However, I hope you understand that in this book, we postponed this rather important topic until the end for a reason. I really love testing, but, as we're mainly focused on the component architecture of Angular, placing this chapter at the end seemed more logical.

In this chapter, we'll look into how to perform proper unit testing on your components. We'll focus on unit testing; automated, end-to-end testing is beyond the scope of this book. We'll look into how to test user interaction with components, but not at the level it would be done in end-to-end testing.

In this chapter, we will delve into the following topics:

- An introduction to the Jasmine testing framework
- Writing simple tests for components
- Creating Jasmine spies and observing component output properties
- Learning about Angular testing utilities, such as `inject`, `async`, `TestBed`, `ComponentFixture`, `DebugElement`, and more
- Mocking components
- Mocking existing services
- Creating tests for our `Efforts` UI component
- Creating tests for our `TaskListContainer` component

An introduction to Jasmine and Karma

Jasmine is a very simple testing framework that comes with an API; it allows you to write **Behavior-Driven Development** (**BDD**) style tests. BDD is an agile software development process for defining specifications in a written format.

In BDD, we define that an agile user story consists of multiple scenarios. These scenarios closely relate to, or even replace, the acceptance criteria of a story. They define requirements on a higher level, and they are mostly written narratives. Each scenario consists of three parts:

- **Given**: This part is used to describe the initial state of the scenario. The test code is where we perform all of the setup that is needed to execute the test scenario.
- **When**: This part reflects the changes that we perform on the system being tested. Usually, this part consists of some API calls and actions that reflect the behavior of a user of the system.
- **Then**: This part specifies what the system should look like after the given state and the changes applied in the *when* part. In our code, this is the part that is usually at the end of our test function, where we use assertion libraries to verify the state of the system.

Jasmine comes with an API that makes it very easy to write tests that are structured according to the BDD style. Let's look at a very simple example of how we can use Jasmine to write a test for a shopping cart system:

```
describe('Buying items in the shop', () => {
  it('should increase the basket count', () => {
    // Given
    const shop = new Shop();
    // When
    shop.buy('Toothpast');
    shop.buy('Shampoo');
    // Then
    expect(shop.basket.length).toBe(2);
    expect(shop.basket).toContain('Toothpaste');
    expect(shop.basket).toContain('Shampoo');
  });
});
```

Jasmine provides us with a `describe` function, which allows us to group certain scenarios on the same subject. In this example, we used the `describe` function to register a new test suite for tests concerning buying items in a shop.

Using the `it` function, we can register individual scenarios that we'd like to get tested. Within the `describe` callback function, we can register as many scenarios as we like. It's also possible to nest `describe` calls, in order to further group our scenarios.

Inside the callback function of the Jasmine `it` function, we can start writing our test. We can use BDD style comments to structure the code inside our test.

You don't necessarily need to run Jasmine in the browser, but if you do so, you'll get a nice summary report of all of the tests and their states:

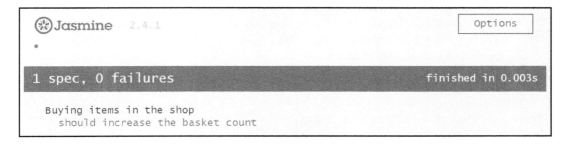

Jasmine provides a nice visual report of all of your test specifications, which also allows you to rerun individual tests and provides you with more options

Jasmine comes with three parts that are relevant to us:

- **Jasmine core**: This contains the test definition APIs, the assertion library, and all of the other core parts of the testing framework
- **Jasmine HTML**: This is the HTML reporter, which will write all test results to the browser document, and will even provide options to rerun individual tests
- **Jasmine boot**: This is the file that bootstraps the Jasmine framework for the browser and performs any setup that is needed with the HTML reporter

Karma and integration to Angular CLI

Jasmine is the default test framework that ships with the Angular CLI tool. The CLI tool installs Jasmine, along with the popular test runner Karma, which allows you to run your tests in the browser of your choice.

By using Karma, we don't need to take care of installing and configuring Jasmine within our project. Karma takes care of that, and it also provides a lot of extras.

A project generated with the Angular CLI comes with two files relevant for running tests with Karma and Jasmine:

- `/karma.conf.js`: This file contains the configuration for the Karma test runner. It's already created for running Angular tests within the browser. By default, it's configured to run tests within a real Chrome browser. However, you can change that to a headless version of Chrome, to a different browser, or even to PhantomJS, which is a really fast and lightweight headless browser.
- `/src/test.ts`: This file is the main entry file for running your tests. It's automatically generated for you when you create a new project using the CLI. This file contains all of the necessary preparations to run Angular tests within your browser using Karma. It also uses dynamic imports, in order to discover any test files (filenames ending with `.spec.ts`) within your project, and passes them to Karma for execution.

The Angular CLI comes with a set of predefined commands, in order to execute the tests within your project. It supports running all tests once, in order to verify your current state. However, sometimes, it's very useful to keep your tests running when working on your application. This supports you in test-driven development approaches, where you'll want to have a constant feedback loop from your tests.

Let's start testing by running two different commands using the Angular CLI tool. Make sure that you're within your project folder, and execute the following command:

```
ng test --watch false
```

The preceding code will start a single test run within your project. Since we have not added any tests yet, you should see an output similar to this one:

```
17 06 2018 00:24:12.000:INFO [karma]: Karma v1.7.1 server started at http://
17 06 2018 00:24:12.002:INFO [launcher]: Launching browser Chrome with unlim
17 06 2018 00:24:12.006:INFO [launcher]: Starting browser Chrome
17 06 2018 00:24:22.656:INFO [Chrome 62.0.3202 (Linux 0.0.0)]: Connected on
Chrome 62.0.3202 (Linux 0.0.0): Executed 0 of 0 ERROR (0.019 secs / 0 secs)
```

A single execution (single run) using the Angular CLI, with no tests present

A single run of your tests is nice when you're about to pull a new release, or if you want to verify the quality of a certain state of your code. Within this chapter, we're going to add a few tests to our existing components, and it will be nice to see our tests evaluated when we're performing our changes. For this purpose, we're starting Karma using its file watch functionality. By running the following Angular CLI command, you can start Karma in watch mode. This will keep your Terminal busy with testing, similar to the `serve` command within the Angular CLI.

Let's start the Angular CLI in test watch mode by running the following command:

```
ng test
```

As you can see, we're fully omitting the `watch` command-line parameter this time. By default, the Angular CLI will run Karma in watch mode when you execute the `test` command.

 If you like to benefit from constant feedback when running your tests, you should always start two Terminal sessions, one executing the Angular CLI server (`ng serve`) and another one running Karma in watch mode (`ng test`).

Writing our first test

Now that we are all set with the testing setup, we can start writing our first test. In this section, we will create a first test for the efforts component that we created in `Chapter 8`, *Time Will Tell*.

As Angular components are just classes, we can already test a lot of their functionality by instantiating the component class and testing its methods. Tests that can be performed like this should always be considered first. Tests that don't involve the rendering logic of your components can run without Angular compiling and bootstrap the component.

The efforts component uses a method to add a certain amount of hours to the effective time worked on a task. Within the template of the efforts component, we're providing three buttons, to add some common amounts of hours. Let's create our first test for the method, `addEffectiveHours`, in our efforts component. For this test, we'd like to start simple and create the component class instance manually. This allows us to test its basic functionality without the need to start the Angular template compiler, change detection and other

When creating a new component with the Angular CLI, a corresponding `spect.ts` file, containing some basic tests, will be created for you. However, we've always created new components using the flag `--spec false`, which prevents this step. Let's create our first spec file manually, by creating a new file on the path `src/app/efforts/efforts/efforts.component.spec.ts`.

Open the created file and add the following content:

```
import {EffortsComponent} from './efforts.component';
import {TimeEfforts} from '../../model';

describe('EffortsComponent', () => {
  it('should add eight hours correctly', () => {
    // Given
    const hour = 3600000;
    const component = new EffortsComponent();
    component.efforts = {
      estimated: 0,
      effective: 0
    };
    component.outEffortsChange.subscribe((efforts: TimeEfforts) => {
      // Then
      expect(efforts.effective).toBe(hour * 8);
    });

    // When
    component.addEffectiveHours(8);
  });
});
```

Karma loads our spec files, and it already loaded Jasmine prior to executing our test. We can therefore safely rely on the global `describe`, `it`, and `expect` functions that are exposed by Jasmine.

As you can see, we don't really need to bootstrap Angular in order to test some of our components' functionality. Simply by testing the component class instance, we can already execute some of our specifications.

To illustrate how we structure our test in a BDD way, we've added some comments, indicating the "given", "when" and "then" sections.

Within the given section, we create a new efforts component instance. We then set the efforts input property of our component to a new efforts object, containing an estimated and effective duration of zero. In the when section, we call the method `addEffectiveHours`, with a parameter of 8 hours.

Now, we'd like to test whether our method call is performing as we expected. Our efforts component is a pure UI component that does not store any of its state. Instead, it delegates any state changes using output properties. In the context of our test, the `outEffortsChange` output is triggered after a call to the method `addEffectiveHours`.

Since event emitters present on component output properties are just observables, we can simply subscribe to the output in order to validate our test. We use the Jasmine helper function, `expect`, in order to assert whether the updated effective efforts property is what we expect it to be after our test.

If you had the Angular CLI test command still running when writing this first test, you should now see a successful test execution on your Terminal output. Otherwise, just start the test runner again, using the command `ng test` on your Terminal:

```
17 06 2018 08:06:25.576:INFO [launcher]: Starting browser Chrome
17 06 2018 08:06:36.364:WARN [karma]: No captured browser, open http://localhost:9
17 06 2018 08:06:36.765:INFO [Chrome 62.0.3202 (Linux 0.0.0)]: Connected on socket
Chrome 62.0.3202 (Linux 0.0.0): Executed 1 of 1 SUCCESS (0.025 secs / 0.005 secs)
```

Terminal and Angular CLI ng test command, showing our first test running successfully

Spying on component output

In testing, a common practice is to spy on function calls during the execution of tests, and then evaluate these calls, checking whether all functions were called correctly.

Jasmine provides us with some nice helpers, in order to use `spy` function calls. We can use the `spyOn` function of Jasmine to replace the original function with a `spy` function. The `spy` function will record any calls, and we can evaluate how many times they were called, and with what parameters.

Let's look at a simple example of how to use the `spyOn` function:

```
class Calculator {
  multiply(a, b) {
    return a * b;
  }
  pythagorean(a, b) {
    return Math.sqrt(this.multiply(a, a) + this.multiply(b, b));
  }
}
```

We will test a simple calculator class that has two methods. The `multiply` method simply multiplies two numbers and returns the result. The `pythagorean` method calculates the hypotenuse of a right-angled triangle with two sides, a and b.

You might remember the formula for the Pythagorean theorem from your early school days:

$$a^2 + b^2 = c^2$$

We will use this formula to produce c from a and b, by getting the square root of the result of a*a + b*b. For the multiplication, we'll use our `multiply` method, instead of using arithmetic operators directly.

Now, we want to test our calculator `pythagorean` method, and, as it uses the `multiply` method to multiply a and b, we can spy on the method to verify our test result in depth:

```
describe('Calculator pythagorean function', () => {
  it('should call multiply function correctly', () => {
    // Given
    const calc = new Calculator();
    spyOn(calc, 'multiply').and.callThrough();
    // When
    const result = calc.pythagorean(6, 8);
    // Then
    expect(result).toBe(10);
    expect(calc.mul).toHaveBeenCalled();
    expect(calc.mul.calls.count()).toBe(2);
    expect(calc.mul.calls.argsFor(0)).toEqual([6, 6]);
    expect(calc.mul.calls.argsFor(1)).toEqual([8, 8]);
```

```
    });
  });
```

The `spyOn` function of Jasmine takes an object as the first parameter and the function name of the object on which we'd like to spy as a second parameter.

This will effectively replace the original `multiply` function in our class instance with a new `spy` function of Jasmine. By default, `spy` functions will only record function calls, and they won't delegate the call to the original function. We can use the `.and.callThrough()` function to specify that we'd like Jasmine to call the original function. This way, our spy function will act as a proxy, and will record any calls at the same time.

In the then section of our test, we can inspect the `spy` function. Using the `toHaveBeenCalled` matcher, we can check whether the spy function was called after all.

Using the `calls` property of the `spy` function, we can inspect in more detail and verify the call count, as well as the arguments that individual calls received.

We can apply the knowledge that we gained about Jasmine spies to our component tests. As we know that all output properties of components contain an event emitter, we can actually spy on them to check whether our component sends output.

Inside components, we call the `emit` method on event emitters, in order to send output to parent component bindings. As this is an asynchronous operation, and we'd also like to test our components without needing to involve parent components, we can simply spy on the `emit` method of our output properties.

It's generally a good practice to avoid asynchronous operations in unit tests, if possible. By using Jasmine spies, we can mock certain function calls that would result in asynchronous operations.

Let's change our first test of the efforts component to use Jasmine spies, rather than relying on observable subscriptions. Open the file `src/app/efforts/efforts/efforts.component.spec.ts`, and perform the following changes:

```
import {EffortsComponent} from './efforts.component';

describe('EffortsComponent', () => {
  it('should add eight hours correctly', () => {
    // Given
    const hour = 3600000;
    const component = new EffortsComponent();
```

```
    component.efforts = {
      estimated: 0,
      effective: 0
    };
    spyOn(component.outEffortsChange, 'emit');

    // When
    component.addEffectiveHours(8);

    // Then
    expect(component.outEffortsChange.emit).toHaveBeenCalledWith({
      estimated: 0,
      effective: hour * 8
    });
  });
});
```

We've created a Jasmine spy that spies on the `outEffortsChange` output property. More precisely, we're spying on any calls to the `emit` method of the underlying event emitter.

Since we're no longer relying on a callback registered with the `subscribe` method on our event emitter output, we now have a much cleaner testing code. The testing code is perfectly structured into the given, when, and then sections of our BDD style test, and no subscription with a callback function needs to be used.

Using the `toHaveBeenCalledWith` assertion helper in Jasmine allows us to carefully evaluate the `spy` function and check whether the recorded calls match what we expected them to be.

Utilities to test components

So far, we have tested our components with plain vanilla JavaScript. The fact that components are in regular classes makes this possible. However, this can only be done for very simple use cases. As soon as we want to test components for things that involve template compilation, user interaction on components, change detection, or dependency injection, we'll need to get a little help from Angular to perform our tests.

Angular comes with a whole bunch of testing tools that can help us out here. In fact, the platform-agnostic way that Angular is built allows us to exchange the regular view adapter with a debug view adapter. This enables us to render components in such a way that we can inspect them in greater detail.

The Angular CLI has already enabled this for us, and if you check the content of the file `src/test.ts`, you can see that there's a special preparation step that enables our testing Angular platform. The following core excerpt shows the relevant content of our default test entry point, which was generated by the Angular CLI tool when we created our project:

```
...
import { getTestBed } from '@angular/core/testing';
import {
  BrowserDynamicTestingModule,
  platformBrowserDynamicTesting
} from '@angular/platform-browser-dynamic/testing';

...

getTestBed().initTestEnvironment(
  BrowserDynamicTestingModule,
  platformBrowserDynamicTesting()
);
...
```

Using the `initTestEnvironment` function of the `@angular/core/testing` module, we can actually initialize a test platform injector, which will then be used in the context of our Angular testing.

From the `@angular/platform-browser-dynamic/testing` module, we can import a special testing platform factory function, as well as the Angular browser testing module.

This code helps us to set up a testing environment that relies on a special platform for testing within a browser. Additional debug information will be present in the runtime when we're using this platform.

Injecting in tests

Injecting Angular dependencies in tests is made easy by two helper functions. The `inject` and `async` functions are available through the `@angular/core/testing` package, and they help us inject dependencies into our tests.

Let's look at this simple example, where we inject the document element using the inject wrapper function. This test is irrelevant for our application, but it illustrates how we can make use of injection in our tests:

```
import {DOCUMENT} from '@angular/common';
import {inject} from '@angular/core/testing';

describe('Application initialized with test providers', () => {
  it('should inject document', inject([DOCUMENT], (document) => {
    expect(document).toBe(window.document);
  }));
});
```

We can simply use inject to wrap our test function. The inject function accepts an array as the first parameter, which should include a list of injectable types. The second parameter is our actual test function, which will now receive the injected document.

The async function, on the other hand, helps us with a different concern. What if our tests actually involve asynchronous operations? Well, a standard asynchronous Jasmine test would look as follows:

```
describe('Async test', () => {
  it('should be completed by calling done', (done) => {
    setTimeout(() => {
      expect(true).toBe(true);
      done();
    }, 2000);
  });
});
```

Jasmine provides us with a nice way to specify asynchronous tests. We can simply use the first parameter of our test functions, which resolves to a callback function and is called done, by convention. By calling this callback function, we can tell Jasmine that our asynchronous operations are done, and we would like to finish the test.

Using callbacks to indicate whether our asynchronous test is finished is a valid option. However, this can make our test quite complicated, if many asynchronous operations are involved. It's sometimes even impossible to monitor all of the asynchronous operations that are happening under the hood, which also makes it impossible for us to determine the end of our test.

This is where the `async` helper function comes into play. Angular uses a library called Zone.js to monitor any asynchronous operations in the browser. Simply put, Zone.js hooks into any asynchronous operations and monitors when they are initiated, as well as when they are finished. With this information, Angular knows exactly how many pending asynchronous operations there are.

If we're using the `async` helper, we can tell Angular to automatically finish our test when all of the asynchronous operations in our test are done. The helper uses Zone.js to create a new zone, and also to determine whether all microtasks executed within this zone are finished.

Let's look at how we can combine injection with an asynchronous operation in our test:

```
import {describe, expect, it, inject, async} from '@angular/core/testing';
import {DOCUMENT} from '@angular/platform-browser';

describe('Application initialized with test providers', () => {
  it('should inject document', async(inject([DOCUMENT], (document) => {
    setTimeout(() => {
      expect(document).toBe(window.document);
    }, 2000);
  })));
});
```

By combining `inject` with `async` (wrapping), we can now test asynchronous operations in our test, without any hassle. The `async` helper will make our test wait until all asynchronous operations have completed. We don't need to rely on a callback, and we have the guarantee that even internal asynchronous operations will complete before our test finishes.

Zone.js is designed to work with all asynchronous operations in the browser. It patches all core DOM APIs, and makes sure that every operation goes through a zone. Angular also relies on Zone.js to initiate change detection. It waits for zones (any asynchronous operations within the browser) to terminate, in order to execute change detection. This is pretty smart, since the only possible moment for your application state to change is right after asynchronous operations are terminated.

Using TestBed for running Angular tests

Angular comes with another very important testing utility. So far, we have only tested the component class of our components. However, as soon as we need to test components and their behaviors in our application, a few more things will be involved:

- **Testing the view of components**: It's sometimes required that we test the rendered view of components. With all of the bindings in our view, dynamic instantiation using template directives and content projection, it can be hard to write deterministic tests.
- **Testing change detection**: As soon as we update our model in our component class, we will want to test the updates that are performed via change detection. This involves the whole change detection behavior of our components.
- **User interaction**: Our component templates probably contain a set of event bindings, which trigger some behaviors in user interaction. We'll need a way to test the state after user interactions.
- **Overriding and mocking**: In a testing scenario, it's sometimes required to mock certain areas in our components, in order to create a proper isolation for our test. In unit testing, we should only be concerned with the specific behavior that we want to test.

The `TestBed` class, which is available through the `@angular/core/testing` package, helps us with the previously listed concerns. It's our main tool for testing components.

Let's look at a very simple example of how we can use the `TestBed` class to test the view rendering of a simple dummy component:

```
import {Component} from '@angular/core';
import {TestBed, async} from '@angular/core/testing';

@Component({
  selector: 'mac-dummy',
  template: 'dummy'
})
class DummyComponent {}

describe('DummyComponent', () => {
  beforeEach(async(() => {
    TestBed.configureTestingModule({
      declarations: [DummyComponent],
    }).compileComponents();
  }));
```

```
it('should render its view correctly', async(() => {
  const fixture = TestBed.createComponent(DummyComponent);
  expect(fixture.nativeElement.textContent).toBe('dummy');
}));
});
```

The `beforeEach` function is a Jasmine helper that allows us to execute something before each and every test within a given test suite. Within the `beforeEach` callback, we're using the `TestBed` class imported from `@angular/core/testing`, in order to prepare our testing environment.

The `configureTestingModule` method on the `Testbed` class allows us to configure a dynamic Angular module that defines the whole context for our test. The configuration object that we're passing to the method is exactly the same as the one that we pass to the `@NgModule` decorator factory, when defining Angular modules. It supports `import`, `providers`, `declarations`, and all other properties of Angular modules. This allows us to create a very specific and isolated testing environment, where we can test only the things we really need to.

Also, note that we're using the Angular `async` helper to wrap our `beforeEach` callback function. This is necessary, since the `compileComponents` method call is an asynchronous operation that compiles all components present within our dynamic testing module. This will ensure that when we enter our test methods, the compilation performed within the `beforeEach` callback is finished, and we can start our testing.

> When testing components, you need to make sure that you're including all of the necessary dependencies within the dynamic module created by the `configureTestingModule` call. This includes any sub-components present within the component, under tests, pipes, services, and any other dependencies of your component.

Component fixture

In our test, we use the `createComponent` method of the `Testbed` class to create a new component instance of our dummy component. As a result of that method call, we'll receive a component fixture object that will help us to further perform testing on our component.

The component fixture is a wrapper around our component being tested, which allows us to further inspect and manipulate our test case. We can now use the `nativeElement` property of the fixture to access the root DOM element of the created component, and to assert on the text content of that element, to verify whether the component has rendered correctly.

Let's look at the `ComponentFixture` type, and the available properties and methods, in more detail:

Member	Description
detectChanges()	This executes change detection on the root component that was created in the context of the fixture. The template bindings will not automatically be evaluated after creating a component using the `Testbed` class. It's our own responsibility to trigger change detection. Even after we change the state of our components, we need to trigger change detection again. This manual change detection may sound cumbersome, but it's important to have full control of any operation performed during a test. We always want a test to be fully deterministic.
destroy()	This method destroys the underlying component and performs any cleanup that is required. This can be used to test the `OnDestroy` component's life cycle.
componentInstance	This property points to the component class instance, and it is our main interaction point if we want to interact with the component.
nativeElement	This is a reference to the native DOM element at the root of the created component. This property can be used to directly inspect the rendered DOM of our component.
elementRef	This is the `ElementRef` wrapper around the root element of the created component.
debugElement	This property points to an instance of `DebugElement` that was created in the component view rendering pipeline when using the testing browser platform. The debug element provides us with some nice utilities to inspect the rendered element tree and test user interaction. We'll take a closer look at this later, in another section.

Mocking child components

We've now looked at a very simple dummy component, and how to test it using the Angular `TestBed`, in conjunction with the `inject` and `async` helper functions.

This is great, but it doesn't really reflect the complexity that we face when we need to test real components. Real components have a lot more dependencies than our dummy component. We rely on child directives, and probably injected services, to obtain data.

Of course, the Angular `TestBed` also provides us with the tools that we need to test more complex components, while keeping the necessary isolation in a unit test.

First, let's look at an example, where we'd like to test a parent component that uses a child component to render a list of numbers. In this test, we'd only like to test the parent component, and we're not interested in how the child component renders the list. We want to remove the behavior of the child component from our test by providing a mock component for the child component during the test, allowing us to easily verify that the data is received by the child component:

```
@Component({
  selector: 'mac-child',
  template: '<ul><li *ngFor="let n of numbers">Item: {{ n }}</li></ul>'
})
class ChildComponent {
  @Input() numbers;
}

@Component({
  selector: 'mac-parent',
  template: '<mac-child [numbers]="numbers"></mac-child>'
})
class ParentComponent {
  numbers = [1, 2, 3];
}
```

This is our starting point. We have two components, and we'll only be interested in testing the parent component. However, the child component is required by the parent component, and it implies a very specific way to render the numbers that are passed by the parent. We would only like to test whether our numbers were passed successfully to the child component. We don't want to involve the rendering logic of the child component in our test. This is very important, because changing only the child component could break our parent component test, which is what we want to avoid.

Now, we want to create a mock of our child component, in the context of our test:

```
@Component({
  selector: 'mac-child',
  template: '{{ numbers.toString() }}'
})
class MockChildComponent {
  @Input() numbers;
}
```

In our mock child component, it's important that we use the same selector property as the real component. Otherwise, the mocking will not work. In the template, we use a very simple output of the numbers input, which enables an easy inspection. The toString method on an array will just render all elements, separated by commas.

It's also important that we provide the same input properties as the original component. Otherwise, we won't imitate the real component correctly.

Now, we can go ahead and prepare for our test. By simply adding our mock child component to the declarations of our dynamic test module, we can make sure that our parent component uses our mock component, instead of the real child component:

```
describe('ParentComponent', () => {
  beforeEach(async(() => {
    TestBed.configureTestingModule({
      declarations: [
        ParentComponent,
        MockChildComponent
      ],
    }).compileComponents();
  }));

  it('should pass numbers to child correctly', async(() => {
    const fixture = TestBed.createComponent(ParentComponent);
    fixture.detectChanges();
    expect(fixture.nativeElement.textContent).toBe('1,2,3');
  }));
});
```

As a result, we decouple the parent component from the child component, in the context of our test. We need this level of separation in order to create a proper isolation of our unit test. As our mock child component simply renders the string representation of the passed array, we can easily test the text content of our fixture.

The definition of a unit test is to test a single unit and isolate the unit from any dependencies. If we want to stick to this paradigm, we need to create a mock for every dependent component. This can easily get us into a situation where we need to maintain more complexity, for the sake of our tests. The key lies in finding the right balance. You should mock dependencies that have a great impact on the subject, and ignore dependencies that have a low impact on the functionality that you'd like to test.

Mocking services

Let's look at a different use case, where we have a component that injects a service in order to obtain data. As we only want to test our component, and not the service it relies on, we somehow need to sneak in a mock service instead of the real service. Since we can define our dynamic test module for our needs, we can simply use the `providers` property on our module definition to introduce mock services.

First, we should declare our base component and a service that it relies on. In this example, the numbers component injects a numbers service, where it obtains an array with numbers:

```
@Injectable()
class NumbersService {
  numbers = [1, 2, 3, 4, 5, 6];
}

@Component({
  selector: 'mac-numbers',
  template: '{{ numbers.toString() }}'
})
class NumbersComponent {
  numbers: number[];

  constructor(numbersService: NumbersService) {
    this.numbers = numbersService.numbers;
  }
}
```

Now, we need to create a mock service that provides the data required in our test and isolates our component from the original service:

```
@Injectable()
class MockNumbersService {
  numbers = [1, 2, 3];
}
```

In this simplified example, we just provide a different set of numbers. However, in a real mocking case, we could exclude a lot of steps that are unnecessary and could potentially create side effects. Using a mock service also ensures that our test, which is focused on the numbers component, will not break because of a change in the real numbers service.

Now, let's look at the test case and see how we can use `TestBed` to provide our mock service, instead of the real one:

```
describe('NumbersComponent', () => {
  beforeEach(async(() => {
    TestBed.configureTestingModule({
      declarations: [NumbersComponent],
      providers: [{
        provide: NumbersService,
        useClass: MockNumbersService
      }]
    }).compileComponents();
  }));

  it('should render numbers correctly', async(() => {
    const fixture = TestBed.createComponent(NumbersComponent);
    fixture.detectChanges();
    expect(fixture.nativeElement.textContent).toBe('1,2,3');
  }));
});
```

Using the `providers` property in the dynamic test module definition, we can provide dependencies to the component under test. This allows us to substitute dependencies that are used in the component. We can simply create a provider that provides our substitute mock numbers service when the numbers service is requested within the dependency injection.

Sometimes, we don't have full control of our dependencies; for example, when we're obtaining a predefined set of providers by an imported module. The `TestBed` helps us in such situations by providing additional override methods. Let's look at the preceding example again; this time, we're using an override mechanism to sneak in our mock service:

```
describe('NumbersComponent', () => {
  beforeEach(async(() => {
    TestBed.configureTestingModule({
      declarations: [NumbersComponent],
      providers: [NumbersService]
    });
    TestBed.overrideProvider(NumbersService, {useValue: new
MockNumbersService()});
    TestBed.compileComponents();
```

```
  }));

  it('should render numbers correctly', async(() => {
    const fixture = TestBed.createComponent(NumbersComponent);
    fixture.detectChanges();
    expect(fixture.nativeElement.textContent).toBe('1,2,3');
  }));
});
```

Using the `overrideProvider` method allows us to override the previously specified real service with our mock service. This is an important tool when you're testing large applications that rely on imported Angular modules, which won't be under your full control.

The `Testbed` class of Angular allows us to perform tests in a very simple, isolated, and flexible fashion. It plays a major role when writing unit tests for components. If you'd like to read more about the available methods in the `Testbed` class, you can visit the official documentation website at `https://angular.io/api/core/testing/TestBed`.

Now, it's time to use our new knowledge about the `Testbed` utility class and start to test our application components in action!

Testing components in action

In the previous topic, we learned about the `Testbed` utility class, and how to use it to test components in an isolated testing environment. We learned about the `inject` and `async` helpers, as well as how to mock components and services.

Now, let's use this knowledge to work on our tests for the efforts component. If you take a look at the template of our efforts component, you'll remember that we rely on two child components:

- **Duration:** The two duration components within the template are used to enter both the duration values for estimated as well as effective efforts spent on tasks. It's a good idea to mock out that component when you want to perform tests on the efforts component. The duration component itself relies on the rather complex editor component.

- **Efforts Timeline**: As it is a purely graphical component to represent our task efforts, we don't really want it to participate in our test of the efforts component. However, since this component does not really interfere with our efforts behavior, we don't necessarily need to mock it. Let's use the real component in this specific instance.

Alright; let's continue writing tests for our efforts component. So far, we've only tested the component class methods of our efforts component. We would now like to continue by mocking the duration component and using the Angular `TestBed` to create a new component instance.

If you don't have it running already, it would be a good time to start the test framework using the Angular CLI tool. Use the command `ng test` in your command line while inside of the project folder.

Open the test file, located on the path `src/app/efforts/efforts/efforts.component.spec.ts`, and perform the following changes:

```
import {Component, EventEmitter, Input, Output} from '@angular/core';
import {TestBed, async, ComponentFixture} from '@angular/core/testing';
import {EffortsComponent} from './efforts.component';
import {EffortsTimelineComponent} from '../efforts-timeline/efforts-
timeline.component';

@Component({
  selector: 'mac-duration',
  template: '{{ duration }}'
})
class MockDurationComponent {
  @Input() duration: number;
  @Output() outDurationChange = new EventEmitter<number>();
}

describe('EffortsComponent', () => {
  let fixture: ComponentFixture<EffortsComponent>;

  beforeEach(async(() => {
    TestBed.configureTestingModule({
      declarations: [
        EffortsComponent,
        MockDurationComponent,
        EffortsTimelineComponent
      ],
    }).compileComponents();
```

```
    fixture = TestBed.createComponent(EffortsComponent);
  }));

    ...
});
```

Our newly introduced mock duration component might look a bit tenuous, but this is actually all that we need for our current tests of the efforts component. The duration component should just accept a `duration` input and expose an `ourDurationChange` output. This is the interface that is expected within the template of our efforts component. Since we don't want to rely on any of the duration component internals, including the use of the editor component, the template of our mock duration component simply renders the duration input. This way, we can easily verify whether the correct duration is rendered within our mock component.

Now, let's create our first test, using the component instance and fixture created with the `Testbed`. Apply the following changes to the effort test file:

```
    ...

describe('EffortsComponent', () => {
   ...

  it('should render initial efforts correctly', () => {
    // Given
    const component = fixture.componentInstance;
    component.efforts = {
      estimated: 1,
      effective: 2
    };

    // When
    fixture.detectChanges();

    // Then
expect(fixture.nativeElement.textContent).toBe('Estimated:1Effective:2+1h+4
h+1d');
  });

   ...

});
```

In our tests, we'd like to test whether the effort component initializes the duration child components (respectively, our mock duration component) with the right content.

Using the component fixture that is provided by the `Testbed` utility class, we can start to interact with the created component. Using the `componentInstance` member of the component fixture, we can set the required input properties of our efforts component.

As we're responsible for handling change detection in our tests manually, we use the `detectChanges` method on our fixture to update the component view. This will initiate the change detection life cycle on our component and perform the necessary view updates.

After the view updates of both duration components, we can run our assertions to validate the updated DOM by getting the text content of the `nativeElement` property on our fixture.

Using the text content property of our whole component fixture might be good, in some circumstances. However, sometimes, this does not provide the necessary granularity for a good assertion. In some scenarios, when we have more DOM elements involved, it won't be sufficient to directly assert on the root component's `textContent` property. It would probably include a lot of noise, which we're not interested in for our assertion. We should always try to narrow our assertion to the fewest details possible.

Within our newly created test, we need to assert with the string `Estimated:1Effective:2+1h+4h+1d`, in order to validate the correct rendering of our components. However, this also includes the labels of our add buttons, which is not exactly what we want to test here. Remember, we always want to narrow our test down to exactly one single unit and avoid any dependencies on things outside of our specific test case.

Let's try to enhance our test and assert on more specific parts of our component view. As we have access to the native DOM element on our fixture, we can simply use the DOM API to select child elements, in order to narrow our assertion:

```
expect(fixture.nativeElement.querySelector('mac-
duration').textContent.trim()).toBe('1');
```

This would successfully select the DOM element of our first mock duration component, and we can only check the text content inside the duration component.

Although this would be a feasible approach, Angular provides us with a much better approach to solve this problem.

Provided by the component fixture, we have access to the debug element tree that is created by the test browser platform, in the context of our test. Debug elements allow us to do an advanced inspection of the element tree that was created by Angular while rendering our components. It also contains an advanced querying API, which allows us to search for certain elements in the component tree.

Let's rewrite our test to use the advanced capabilities provided by the debug element, and assert on both the estimated and effective duration components views individually:

```
...
import {By} from '@angular/platform-browser';
...

describe('EffortsComponent', () => {
  ...

  it('should render initial efforts correctly', () => {
    // Given
    const component = fixture.componentInstance;
    component.efforts = {
      estimated: 1,
      effective: 2
    };
    const [estimatedDurationElement, effectiveDurationElement] =
fixture.debugElement
      .queryAll(By.directive(MockDurationComponent));

    // When
    fixture.detectChanges();

    // Then
    expect(estimatedDurationElement.nativeElement.textContent).toBe('1');
    expect(effectiveDurationElement.nativeElement.textContent).toBe('2');
  });

  ...

});
```

The query and queryAll methods that are available on every debug element object allow us to query the Angular view tree like we would query a DOM tree, using querySelector and querySelectorAll. The difference here is that we can use a predicate helper to query for matching elements. Using the By helper class, we can create these predicates, which will then be used to query the debug element tree.

There are currently three different predicates available, using the `By` helper:

Member	Description
`By.all()`	This is the predicate that will result in querying for all of the child `DebugElement` objects of the current `DebugElement` object.
`By.css(selector)`	This is the predicate that will result in querying for `DebugElement` using the specified CSS selector.
`By.directive(type)`	This is the predicate that will result in querying for the `DebugElement` that contains the specified directive.

Going back to our test, we can now use the query method on the fixture debug element, in order to query for our duration components. As we've exchanged the real duration component with our mock duration component, we need to query for the latter. We use a predicate, `By.directive(MockDurationComponent)`, which will successfully query for the debug element object that represents the host elements of our two mock duration components.

The `query` method of the debug element object will always return a new debug element object of the first found element, if there was a match. It will return `null` if the queried element was not found.

The `queryAll` method of a debug element will return an array of many debug elements, which will contain all elements that match the predicate. If there are no matching elements, this method will return an empty array.

Testing component interaction

Although UI interaction testing is probably part of end-to-end testing, we'll look at how to test basic user interaction with your components. In this topic, we'll test the efforts component when the user clicks on one of the buttons to add effective effort hours.

Let's add a new test to our existing efforts component test file, located on the path `src/app/efforts/efforts/efforts.component.spec.ts`:

```
it('should add one day of effective efforts on button click', () => {
  // Given
  const day = 3600000 * 8;
  const component = fixture.componentInstance;
  component.efforts = {
    estimated: 0,
    effective: 0
```

```
  };
  const addDayButton = fixture.debugElement
    .queryAll(By.css('button'))[2];
  spyOn(component.outEffortsChange, 'emit');

  // When
  addDayButton.triggerEventHandler('click', null);

  // Then
  expect(component.outEffortsChange.emit).toHaveBeenCalledWith({
    estimated: 0,
    effective: day
  });
});
```

We want to set a Jasmine spy up on the `outEffortsChange.emit` function for our test. This way, we can later check whether our efforts component successfully emits the event when we click on the button to add a day of effective efforts.

In the given section, we're preparing everything for our test. We initialize the `efforts` input of our component with a new object. We also query for the debug element of the button within the efforts component view that adds one day to the effective effort. We use the `queryAll` method to get a list of all three buttons, and select the third by accessing the array element with the index 2. The `css` predicate factory allows us to pass a CSS selector to query for debug elements.

In the when section of our test, we can simulate a `click` event on the `addDayButton` debug element by using the method `tiggerEventHandler`. Using this method, you can trigger an event that you'd like to be emitted on the underlying element. Angular event listeners that listen for that event will be triggered synchronously.

Within the then section of our BDD style test, we can simply evaluate the Jasmine spy that we've created on the `outEffortsChange` output property of our component.

Testing user interaction on components is made very easy by using the debug element. We can also decouple our tests from the underlying DOM event architecture by using the `triggerEventHandler` helper method.

> The `triggerEventHandler` method operates on the virtual element tree of Angular, rather than the actual DOM tree. Due to this, we can also use this method to trigger event handlers that are attached to component output properties.

Summary

In this last chapter of the book, we learned how to write concise unit tests for our components. We followed a BDD style approach of writing tests, and we also covered the basics of the JavaScript testing framework, Jasmine.

We learned about the debugging tools that are available in Angular, and how to set up an environment for testing. Using the Angular `Testbed` utility class, we were able to perform tests in a very flexible but precise way. We also learned about the debug view tree and the component fixture. These allowed us to perform clever inspections and apply practical queries to the rendered views, in order to assert expected results.

We used the `inject` and `async` helpers to inject dependencies, and to run asynchronous tests at the same time. We built mock components, in order to isolate our tests from the rest of our application.

Other Books You May Enjoy

If you enjoyed this book, you may be interested in these other books by Packt:

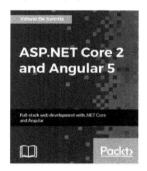

ASP.NET Core 2 and Angular 5
Valerio De Sanctis

ISBN: 9781788293600

- Use ASP.NET Core to its full extent to create a versatile backend layer based on RESTful APIs
- Consume backend APIs with the brand new Angular 5 HttpClient and use RxJS Observers to feed the frontend UI asynchronously
- Implement an authentication and authorization layer using ASP.NET Identity to support user login with integrated and third-party OAuth 2 providers
- Configure a web application in order to accept user-defined data and persist it into the database using server-side APIs
- Secure your application against threats and vulnerabilities in a time efficient way
- Connect different aspects of the ASP. NET Core framework ecosystem and make them interact with each other for a Full-Stack web development experience

Angular 6 for Enterprise-Ready Web Applications
Doguhan Uluca

ISBN: 9781786462909

- Create full-stack web applications using Angular and RESTful APIs
- Master Angular fundamentals, RxJS, CLI tools, unit testing, GitHub, and Docker
- Design and architect responsive, secure and scalable apps to deploy on AWS
- Adopt a minimalist, value-first approach to delivering your app with Kanban
- Get introduced to automated testing with continuous integration on CircleCI
- Optimize Nginx and Node.js web servers with load testing tools

Leave a review - let other readers know what you think

Please share your thoughts on this book with others by leaving a review on the site that you bought it from. If you purchased the book from Amazon, please leave us an honest review on this book's Amazon page. This is vital so that other potential readers can see and use your unbiased opinion to make purchasing decisions, we can understand what our customers think about our products, and our authors can see your feedback on the title that they have worked with Packt to create. It will only take a few minutes of your time, but is valuable to other potential customers, our authors, and Packt. Thank you!

Index

M

main navigation
  building 128
  composition, with content projection 129
model
  introducing, for comments 161, 162
Mozilla Developer Network documentation
  reference 30

N

navigation component 131
navigation components
  creating 131, 132, 133, 134, 135
navigation item component 131
navigation section component 131
NgModule
  about 26
  benefits 24, 25, 26
Node.js
  about 37
  reference 37
npm 37

O

object-oriented programming (OOP) 9
open tasks chart
  creating 341, 344, 345
open tasks
  problem, modeling 338, 339
  task data, preparing 336
  visualizing 336

P

pipe
  used, for integrating tags 250, 251, 252
Precision Graphics Markup Language (PGML) 210
project activity chart 314
project comments
  tag selection, integrating in 265, 266, 267, 268
project component
  creating 114, 115
  integrating 121, 122
project navigation

providing 136, 137
project service 110, 111, 112, 113, 114
project summary 314, 318
project summary component
  building 320, 321, 322
project tasks chart 314
projects dashboard component
  creating 318, 319
projects dashboard container 318
projects dashboard
  about 318
  integrating 323, 325, 326
projects
  about 110
  composing, router used 187, 189
  guarding 199, 200, 201
Protractor 39
pure components 96, 98, 99

R

reactive programming
  with RxJS 77, 78, 79
router configuration 181, 183
router
  used, for composing projects 187, 189
routes
  for application 184, 185
routing
  implementing, for application 184, 185
  with container components 181
RxJS
  reactive programming 78, 79

S

Scalable Vector Graphics (SVG)
  about 210, 211, 212
  styling 213, 214
services
  creating, for logging activities 204, 206, 207
  mocking 371, 372, 373
shadow DOM 20
spaceship dashboard 313
SVG components
  building 215, 216, 217

Synchronized Multimedia Integration Language
    (SMIL) 216
syntactic sugar 27

T

tabbed interface component
  creating 123, 124, 125, 126, 127
tag input directive
  creating 254, 255, 256, 258
tag input
  supporting 253
tag management 244
tag model 245
tag selection
  integrating, in project comments 265, 266, 267,
    268
  integrating, within editor component 262, 264,
    265
tags select component
  creating 259, 260, 261, 262
tags service
  creating 246, 247
tags
  enabling, for tasks 294, 296
  integrating, pipe used 250, 251, 252
  rendering 247, 248, 249
task chart
  interactive making 348, 350
task data service 63, 64, 65, 66, 68
task details
  about 286, 287, 288, 290
  navigating to 291, 292, 293
task list container
  updating 115, 116, 117, 118, 119, 120
task list
  creating 50, 51
  purifying 102, 103, 104, 106
task management application
  features 42
  vision 42
task model
  enabling, for ordering 270
task service

data, loading 84, 85, 87, 88
tasks chart 318
tasks
  adding 55, 57, 58
  filtering 68, 69, 70, 72, 73, 74
  managing 41
  tags, enabling for 294, 296
template elements 19
template strings 30, 31
TestBed
  used, for running Angular tests 366
testing components
  working 373, 374, 375, 376, 377
tests
  Angular dependencies, injecting 363, 365
  writing 357, 358, 359
TypeScript
  about 31, 32, 38
  history 32
  immutability 95
  reference 32

U

UI framework 16, 18
user area component
  about 154, 155, 156, 157
  integrating 158, 159
user interaction
  testing, with component 378
user service 153
users
  dealing with 151, 152

V

Vector Markup Language (VML) 210

W

web standards 19
Webpack 39

Z

Zone.js 365

www.ingramcontent.com/pod-product-compliance
Lightning Source LLC
Chambersburg PA
CBHW080607060326
40690CB00021B/4617